Medical Law

CORE TEXT SERIES

Medical Law

JONATHAN HERRING

Fellow in Law
Exeter College, University of Oxford

Series Editor
NICOLA PADFIELD

Fitzwilliam College, Cambridge

OXFORD
UNIVERSITY PRESS

OXFORD
UNIVERSITY PRESS

Great Clarendon Street, Oxford OX2 6DP

Oxford University Press is a department of the University of Oxford.
It furthers the University's objective of excellence in research, scholarship,
and education by publishing worldwide in

Oxford New York

Auckland Cape Town Dar es Salaam Hong Kong Karachi
Kuala Lumpur Madrid Melbourne Mexico City Nairobi
New Delhi Shanghai Taipei Toronto

With offices in

Argentina Austria Brazil Chile Czech Republic France Greece
Guatemala Hungary Italy Japan Poland Portugal Singapore
South Korea Switzerland Thailand Turkey Ukraine Vietnam

Oxford is a registered trade mark of Oxford University Press
in the UK and in certain other countries

Published in the United States
by Oxford University Press Inc., New York

British Library Cataloguing-in-Publication Data

Data available

Library of Congress Cataloging in Publication Data

Data available

Typeset by Newgen Imaging Systems (P) Ltd., Chennai, India
Printed in Great Britain
on acid-free paper by
Clays Ltd, St Ives Plc

ISBN 978-0-19-959253-1

10 9 8 7 6 5 4 3 2 1

Preface

This book is designed to provide the reader with an accessible and stimulating account of medical law and ethics. There are few areas of law which are as fast moving as this. Rarely a day passes when there is not a story in the newspapers which is of relevance to medical law and ethics. Also, there are few areas which arouse such intense passions as the ones discussed in this book. As students of medical law, however, it is important to take a cool, hard look at the issues. The excitement of the debate can mean that some students are unable to provide an accurate summary of the law. This book, therefore, contains plenty of case summaries, so that you can demonstrate to the examiner your knowledge of the case law. There are also clear statements of the key statutory principles so that you can discuss these in exams.

I hope that having read through the chapters in this book you will want to read more about some of the topics. There is plenty of further reading that you can look into. I have deliberately not sought to present a particular view. Quite the opposite, in most chapters I have presented the key arguments in the debates in the form of different 'Speakers' arguing over a case. You will need to think through the issues for yourself. Better still, discuss them with your friends. There is nothing better for clarifying your own views than talking them through with others.

In the writing of this book I was grateful for the support and help of many colleagues and friends, including Sandra Fredman, Charles Foster, Imogen Goold, and George P. Smith. An especial thank you to Philip Moore for his excellent proof reading. Above all I thank my wife Kirsten Johnson and my children, Laurel, Joanna, and Darcy for their love and patience.

Jonathan Herring

Contents

Detailed contents

Table of cases

Cases reported in case summaries are listed in bold.

Table of statutes

Extracted statutes are listed in bold.

Table of secondary legislation

Extracted legislation is listed in bold.

Table of international instruments

Extracted instruments are listed in bold.

Key ethical and legal principles

SUMMARY

In this chapter, we will start with some of the grand ethical approaches that can be taken to medical issues. By 'grand theories' I mean theories of general application that can be used to deal with any kind of ethical issue. Then we shall look at some of the more specific ethical principles that are said to govern the issues. We shall then consider some of the key legal principles, before considering how law and ethics interact in this area. Finally, we shall examine some of the key overarching issues for medical lawyers and ethicists.

Introduction

1.1 Before getting down to the nitty gritty of particular issues in medical law, this chapter will start by looking at some of the basic legal and ethical principles involved when considering issues to do with medicine. You are no doubt aware of the fierce debates over issues such as euthanasia which have been going on for decades. We seem to be no nearer a consensus on those issues today than we were centuries ago. But there are issues still of considerable significance which receive little attention in the media. Do we own our bodies? Can medical confidences ever be broken? Do patients owe responsibilities or just have rights? So there is a lot more to medical law and ethics than abortion and euthanasia. We will start by looking at some of the general approaches to ethical issues that have been proposed.

Grand theories

1.2 Here we are considering some of the grand theories that can be used to deal with medical issues. We shall focus on just three:

- Consequentialism
- Deontology
- Ethics of care

Consequentialism

1.3 A 'consequentialist' approach, as its name suggests, focuses on the consequences of an action. In deciding whether an act is good or not the actor should consider the consequences: the act is good if the consequences are good, but wrong if they are bad. This approach therefore rejects deontology, which we shall discuss shortly, which suggests that certain acts (e.g. killing an innocent person) are prohibited whatever the consequences.

1.4 Consequentialism has the appeal of being common sense: it is how we usually make decisions. When deciding which party you will go to you consider which will give you the most pleasure; or when deciding what to order at a restaurant you ask yourself which will taste best. However, there are some difficulties with consequentialism which need unpacking.

The definition of a good consequence

1.5 What counts as a good consequence? I suggested a moment ago when looking at the menu in a restaurant that you would choose what food would taste best. But that might be disputed: what about the healthiness of the alternatives? Or the fact that there might be ethical concerns about the origins of some options? Are such factors to be considered in determining what a good consequence is?

1.6 A popular form of consequentialism is utilitarianism, which originates in the writing of Jeremy Bentham (1748–1832). Utilitarianism argues that our focus should be on whether actions produce pleasure or happiness. But we should not only consider the happiness of the actor, but also the happiness of all those affected. So the question simply becomes: which act will most increase the sum of human happiness? Other consequentialists would take a broader view and include not just happiness, but other factors such as health and friendship in the calculation of what is good. They argue that most people do not just seek happiness in life, but recognize the values of other goods, too (see Hope 2005).

Remote goods

1.7 Going back to the issue of what to choose on the menu. If the diner, trying to be a good consequentialist, is considering what goods will be produced, how many people should he or she take into account? Should he or she take into account the pleasure or otherwise that the waiter or chef or the suppliers of the restaurant or other diners, if an item is in short supply? Once you take into account *all* the possible consequences of a decision, shopping and dining could become intolerable. It could well be time for breakfast by the time you considered every factor! In the medical context, the question for a consequentialist is: is it just a matter of deciding what is best for the patient, or are the interests of the patients' family, other patients of the National Health Service (NHS), or NHS staff all to be considered, too?

Rule consequentialism

1.8 In light of some of the difficulties mentioned, some commentators support 'rule consequentialism' (e.g. Brandt 1992). That is, one can adopt a general rule in a category of cases, which will generally promote the people's welfare. Hence, we can support the rule that you must not walk on the grass, even if a particular individual who crosses the grass won't damage it; if everyone does, the grass will become worn. Such an argument is sometimes used in relation to euthanasia: if it is made lawful it may be beneficial to some patients, but many others would be pressurized into agreeing to be killed. Overall well-being will therefore be promoted if we had a law that prohibited euthanasia, even though for some individuals the rule will not be beneficial.

Unpalatable results

1.9 Consequentialism could justify a doctor killing a nurse and using her organs to save four patients in need of a transplant. On a straightforward utilitarian approach, it could be argued that more good will come from the death of the nurse than harm: one person killed to save four lives. Yet, most people when faced with that example find that unacceptable. It may be that this result could be avoided by a consequentialist by pointing to the social harms that might follow if people could be killed at random in order to save the lives of those who need organs, but it would not be a straightforward argument.

Difficulties with practical application

1.10 As already indicated, consequentialism can be difficult to apply in practice. We do not know the consequences of our actions in some cases. Even if we did, it can be hard to compare the goods that different people might receive. In difficult cases, there is little to guide us in deciding what makes a good consequence.

Motivations

1.11 A consequentialist approach does not deal with motivations. This can make it hard to explain why a doctor who is performing an intimate examination in an appropriate manner, but is gaining sexual pleasure is not doing anything wrong. Just by looking at his actions and their consequences we are required by consequentialism to determine they are good, unless the patient discovers his motivations.

> **R v. Tabassum [2000] EWCA 90** The appellant was convicted of three counts of indecent assault. He had no medical training but he persuaded three women to let him examine their breasts, after stating that he was undertaking an examination into breast cancer. He touched their breasts. The evidence was that he touched them in the same way that a person undertaking a proper breast examination would have done. However, the women gave evidence that they only consented because they thought he was medically qualified.
>
> It was held that the appellant was properly convicted. The victims had been deceived into the quality of the act, if not the nature. The victims had consented to the touching itself, but as part of a medical treatment/research. As they had not consented to the acts, the appellant was guilty.

1.12 Despite all of these concerns, utilitarians have a significant role to play in medical ethics. It forms a central part of many professionals' thinking. After all, it would be hard to imagine not thinking, 'Now, what treatment will produce the best results for this patient.' So, consequentialism must have some role to play in medical ethics. The real question is whether other values have a role to restrict its application.

Deontology

1.13 Deontology does not focus on the results of an action, but argues that certain acts are right in and of themselves. In a way, they rest on certain 'Thou shalt not…' rules. Hence, a deontologist might take the view that one must never lie, even if telling the truth causes hurt. For them, the ends do *not* justify the means. Immanuel Kant's writings have been especially influential for many deontologists and in particular his maxim that a person must never be used as a means to an end of producing good for someone else. Applying this maxim would, for example, make it quite clear that in the hypothetical case discussed above, the nurse could not be killed to save the four patients. To do so would be using her as the means to achieve a good for someone else.

1.14 The difficulty for deontologists is in deciding what these cardinal rules are. For some, these might be found in religious texts, but there are plenty of deontologists who do not base their views on religion. For them, deontological principles can be found in the natural order of life or as widely accepted principles. The difficulty can be for deontologists who disagree over which principles apply; there can be no easy resolution to their disagreements. Consequentialists can debate long into the night about how they weigh up the consequences, but deontologists have no ready common ground to decide which principles to apply.

1.15 Many people seek to mix deontology and consequentialism. So we have principles that generally apply, but in a case where very serious wrongdoing will result we will depart from the principle. So we might say people should not torture, but we might be willing to accept that if thousands of lives would be saved, then may be we will depart from our principle. This is not a strict deontological approach because it accepts that there may be extreme consequences in which it is appropriate to depart from the principle. Nor is it a consequentialist approach because an act which would produce slightly good consequences but which breached the principle would not be justified.

An ethic of care

1.16 This approach to dealing with ethical issues has found particular support among feminist writers, although certainly not all its supporters are feminists and, indeed, many feminists would not support it. At its heart is a rejection of 'abstraction' in ethics. That is the use of general rules or approaches to resolve ethical dilemmas. Rather, we must consider the particular individuals in the context of their relationships. What might be appropriate to those involved in one dilemma, might not be appropriate to another group of people in the same dilemma. So, typical of an ethic of care approach is a response which starts, 'Well, it all depends on the context of the particular case...'

1.17 Carol Gilligan posed the following scenario, taken from the work of the American psychologist, Lawrence Kohlberg, to a number of children:

> In Europe, a woman was near death from a special kind of cancer. There was one drug that the doctors thought might save her. It was a form of radium that a druggist in the same town had recently discovered. The drug was expensive to make but the druggist was charging ten times what the drug cost him to make. He paid $200 for the radium and charged $2,000 for a small dose of the drug. The sick woman's husband, Heinz, went to everyone he knew to borrow the money, but he could only get together about $1,000 (which was half of what it cost). Heinz told the druggist that his wife was dying and asked him to sell it to him cheaper or let him pay later. The druggist said, 'No, I discovered the drug and I am going to make money from it.' Heinz got desperate and broke into the man's store to steal the drug for his wife. Should the husband have done that?

Gilligan found that although some provided a ready 'Yes' or 'No' answer, others—especially girls—provided answers which showed they thought that the answer depended on other imponderables; or they sought to find a solution to the dilemmas, with, for example, Heinz entering into further discussions with the druggist or asking others for help.

1.18 Core to an ethic of care is an emphasis on promoting caring relationships, rather than promoting individual rights (Mahowald 2006). Rather than seeing us as autonomous people who are able to exercise our rights, the law should start with an assumption that we are ignorant, vulnerable, and interdependent. So our ethical and legal approaches should be structured to support caring relationships, rather than to promote freedom. That is why we cannot use abstract principles because what works in one set of relationships may not work in another.

1.19 Ethics of care also emphasizes the importance of responsibilities within caring relationships. The focus is on what is the proper obligation within the context of the relationships. In doing this, it highlights one of the themes in some deontological writing, that of obligation, but it does so in the context of relationships.

1.20 Critics of an ethic of care tend to highlight various difficulties. The obvious one is that it does not provide clear guidance for lawyers and doctors on what to do in a difficult ethical dilemma. Supporters of an ethic of care would reply that this is the point: each case needs to be dealt with by considering the particular relationships involved. In its nature, this means that a general rule cannot be used. This creates a particular problem for lawyers who seek to use an ethic of care.

Law has traditionally been based on providing clear guidance and regulation. An approach involving an ethic of care would seek to give the parties involved room to negotiate an approach that would be suitable to their situation.

Applying the theories

1.21 Let us consider a hypothetical case and how using these general approaches might lead to a different approach:

> Alfred, aged 20, has a severe mental illness. He is unable to make decisions for himself. His sister, Susan, has a kidney disorder and needs a kidney transplant. Alfred is the only person available to donate an organ.

Speaker 1 (utilitarian)

1.22 The key question here must be what will produce the best outcome. Here, if Alfred donates the kidney, Susan's life will be saved, while Alfred will suffer the pain of the operation. That indicates that the best outcome will be produced if the donation goes ahead. It really is that simple.

Speaker 2 (deontologist)

1.23 There is a key principle here: you must never use one person as a means to benefit another person. That principle goes back to the writing of Immanuel Kant. Here, Alfred is being used solely as a means of benefit to Susan. Once we start allowing people lacking capacity to benefit others, where will we stop? Those lacking capacity will be seen simply as resources to be used for the benefit of others. To treat people in that way is to deny their humanity. We should treat those lacking capacity in the way that promotes *their* best interests, not the interests of others.

Speaker 3 (ethic of care)

1.24 We need to know much more about the context of this case. What is the relationship between Alfred and Susan. What has Susan done for Alfred in the past? What is she likely to do in the future? Could this donation be seen as a fair part of the give and take of an ongoing relationship between Alfred and Susan? If their relationship has not been close, it is hard to see how this could be part of a caring relationship. Rather, it looks exploitative. If, however, they are in a close, caring relationship the boundary between what is in Alfred's best interests and what is in Susan's becomes much more complex. It could then be that the donation will be an appropriate part of an ongoing relationship.

Key ethical principles

1.25 Tom Beauchamp and James Childress (2003) have written a book on medical ethics which has proved hugely influential. It is a highly respected approach to medical ethics and is widely used within the medical profession. They argue that anyone considering how to look at a particular ethical dilemma should consider four principles:

- Autonomy
- Non-malfeasance
- Beneficence
- Justice

Beauchamp and Childress argue that considering an issue with these principles in mind will bring out all of the key issues. What they are advocating is, therefore, a way of approaching ethical dilemmas, rather than providing a particular solution to them. Both a supporter and opponent of euthanasia could approach the issue using these principles and reach different answers. This, however, is the source of its appeal. It provides an approach which can be used by ethicists examining ethical issues from a wide range of viewpoints. Let us consider each of these principles separately.

Autonomy

1.26 Autonomy has become a key principle in medical law. Indeed, in his book, Charles Foster (2009) claims that medical law and ethics has become 'boring' because autonomy has become the sole principle in use. That may be a bit of an exaggeration, but there is no doubt that it has become a central principle. At the heart of the notion of autonomy is that each person should be allowed to make their choices as to how they live their lives. Indeed, it is central to our notion of humanity that we should be free to make decisions for ourselves. Children and those lacking capacity have decisions made on their behalf, but adults do not normally expect others to be able to force them to do something. Of course, there are exceptions to this principle: the criminal law prohibits conduct which causes harm to others, but generally you are free to live your life as you wish. If you want to spend your time bird-watching, reading law books, or eating Pot

Noodle, you are free to do so, however foolish or undesirable some people might find such activities.

1.27 So what is the relevance of this for medical ethics? In the past, medical paternalism ruled. That meant that patients were expected to follow the instructions of their doctors and to be compliant. The doctor was the expert: on visiting the doctor you were examined, answered questions, and then accepted the prescribed treatment. Now, however, the principle of autonomy gives the patient the right to have a say about treatment. But, and this is an important point, the right to refuse treatment is protected more strongly than the right to demand treatment. So, if a patient with capacity refuses to consent to treatment, it would be unlawful to provide that treatment. However, if a patient demands a particular treatment, the doctor is entitled to refuse to give it, if the doctor decides it is not appropriate. Contrast these two cases:

> ***Re B (Adult: Refusal of Treatment)*** **[2002] EWHC 429 (Fam)** Ms B, aged 41, suffered a serious injury to her spinal column and suffered complete paralysis from the neck down. She was kept alive by a ventilator. She requested the removal of the ventilator. Butler Sloss P confirmed that she had an absolute right to refuse treatment and that following the withdrawal of her consent it was unlawful to keep her on the ventilator. This was even though the judge urged Ms B to reconsider her position and found that she had much to offer society.

> ***R (Burke) v. GMC*** **[2005] 3 FCR 169** Leslie Burke suffered from a serious degenerative condition. He was concerned that at some point in the future, doctors would decide to withdraw food and hydration from him and sought a declaration that he would get the treatment he needed. The Court of Appeal refused. Although autonomy gave him the right to refuse treatment, he did not have the right to demand that doctors give him treatment, which the doctors had decided would be inappropriate. The doctors would take into account his wishes to continue to receive hydration and nutrition, but they would not be compelled to give it to him.

So, in effect, the law offers a strong protection for the right to refuse treatment, but not to consent to treatment. Why is that? First, it said that an acknowledgement that having treatment forced on you against your wishes is a greater interference to your autonomy than not being able to have the treatment you want. Contrast, for example, having a nose ring put on you without your consent and being told you cannot have the nose ring you wanted: the former would be a greater sense of infringement of rights than the latter. Second, it acknowledges that there is a balance to be struck between the autonomy of the patient and the doctor. Had Mr Burke won his case and a doctor been forced to provide treatment of which he disapproved, this would have interfered with the doctor's autonomy. However, in a case of refusal of treatment, there is no autonomy interests (or only very limited ones) of other parties that are involved.

1.28 Just to emphasize further the point being made: in the previous paragraph, we have been discussing patients who have capacity. If a patient does not have capacity but does have wishes based, for example, on a delusion, these will not be protected in an orthodox view of autonomy because they do not represent the genuine wishes of the patient. There is considerable debate about when a patient lacks capacity and what weight, if any, should be attached to the wishes of a patient who lacks capacity. We shall discuss these in Chapter 4.

The principle of non-malfeasance

1.29 The principle of non-malfeasance establishes a core principle: a medical professional should not harm a patient (Gillon 1994). This is a time-honoured principle for medics and is founded on the Hippocratic Oath (a declaration of key principles for doctors that dates back to the fifth century BC): 'I will use treatment to help the sick according to my ability and judgement, but I will never use it to injure or wrong them'. This is also known as the principle *primum non nocere*, 'First, do no harm.' At first sight, this seems such an obvious principle that it should be uncontroversial.

1.30 But it is more complex than it at first appears. First, there is a case of 'using' one patient to help another.

> **Re Y [1997] 2 FCR 172** An adult with serious mental disorders (Y) lacked the capacity to make decisions. Her sister needed bone marrow from her in order to provide life-saving treatment. The court held that the donation of bone marrow would be a benefit to Y because if the sister died, that would affect Y's mother's state of mind, and she played a major role in the care of Y.

We will discuss this case later in Chapter 4, but for now it is enough to say that it highlights how the principle of 'harm' can be flexible. It shows how creative reasoning can find a benefit in treatment which might appear to cause only harm.

1.31 Second, there may be cases where a patient wishes to be harmed. A parent may wish to donate their kidney to save the life of their child, or even to donate it to a stranger. In such a case, is the principle of non-malfeasance infringed? It might be argued not. It could be said that in deciding whether or not a patient is harmed, we allow the patient to decide what is or is not harm. The difficulty in taking this line is that the principle of non-malfeasance almost collapses into the principle of autonomy. A different response is that the principle of non-malfeasance must then be balanced against the principle of autonomy. However, that raises the issue of how we can balance these competing principles.

1.32 The BMA (2004) reports this case:

Surgeon's refusal to meet a patient's request

Mr P had two sons, aged 33 and 29. Both sons had Alport's syndrome, an inherited condition that causes kidney failure. Mr P successfully donated a kidney to his younger son. His older son, R, received a cadaveric kidney, but the transplant failed. As it had been a poor match, R developed antibodies that made him incompatible with 96 per cent of the population. Finding a suitable kidney was therefore extremely unlikely, unless his parents were suitable donors. Mrs P was told that she was not suitable. Mr P wanted to donate his second kidney to R.

Mr P argued it would be better for him to be on dialysis than his son. He was retired and prepared for the lifestyle change that dialysis would bring. Despite finding support from some doctors, Mr P's request was turned down by three transplant teams. Some of the deliberations of the third were filmed and shown on television.

Members of the transplant team had mixed views about Mr P's request. Some understood and felt they would want to do the same for their own children. Although some believed that the benefits were one sided, others agreed that there could be emotional benefits for Mr and Mrs P if the transplant was a success for R. There were also concerns about the impact on the family (the younger brother was opposed to the operation) and about how R in particular would feel about the effects on his father's length and quality of life. The resource implications of ending up with two people on dialysis rather than one if the transplant was not successful were also discussed.

The decision rested with the transplant surgeon. Although he knew that Mr P understood the nature and implications of his request, and that he could see ethical and rational justifications for the operation taking place, he knew that ultimately he would feel unable to perform the operation. Mr P was therefore turned down.

As a last resort, Mrs P was tested again to see if she might be a match. Although she had been rejected several times in the past, she was found to be a match.

It seems in this case that the doctors placed great weight on the principle of non-malfeasance. They have a duty not to harm a patient and that trumped any obligation to help other patients.

The principle of beneficence

1.33 The principle of beneficence is the flip side of the principle of non-malfeasance: it requires medical professionals to do good for their patients. Again, it finds an echo in the Hippocratic Oath where a physician promises to 'follow that system of regime which, according to my ability and judgement, I consider for the benefit of my patients'. This reflects the straightforward idea that in deciding what treatment to give a patient, the medical professional should decide which will benefit the patient most. It is most evident in cases where a court has to decide what treatment should be given to a child or a person lacking capacity.

> **NHS Trust v. A (A Child) [2007] EWHCA 1696 (Fam)** The NHS Trust sought a declaration that it would be lawful to carry out a bone marrow transplant on a seven-month-old child (A). A had a severe genetic defect in her immune system. Without the treatment, A would die, probably by the age of one. Experts held that with the treatment, there was a 50% chance of a lasting cure. There was a 10% chance of dying during the treatment; a 30% chance the treatment would not be successful; and a 10% chance it would succeed, but would cause her a significant impairment. The treatment would be painful and unpleasant. A's parents believed that she had already suffered enough and did not want to put her through further medical procedures. They were also distressed to learn that the procedure would render A infertile. The parents therefore refused to consent.
>
> Held: The key question for the court was what was in A's best interests. It was held that it was better to be alive and infertile, than dead. The fertility was not a big issue. In essence, the question came down to 50% of a full life with the procedure. The opportunity this offered, as compared to certain death, meant that it was in her best interests to receive the treatment.

1.34 Nowadays, the principle is problematic because it has resonances of paternalism. As mentioned when we discussed the principle of autonomy, the patient is the one who has the right to decide what treatment doctors should provide and the medical professional should respect that choice. So it may be that the role of the doctor is to recommend the best treatment, but it can only be given where the patient consents. The beneficence principle clearly has an important role to play in the treatment of patients who lack capacity, where, as we shall see in Chapter 4, the key legal principle is that decisions should be made based on what is in the patient's best interests.

1.35 There is a further difficulty. We live in a time of health care rationing. Indeed, we always have and always will. Decisions have to be made about what treatments can and cannot be provided. That means that sometimes the best treatment cannot be given to a patient because the state cannot afford it. The necessity for rationing, at least in a National Health Service, gives the principle of beneficence a slightly hollow ring. However, it should be remembered that the number of cases where a person is denied treatment for rationing purposes is small. In day-to-day dealings, the principle of beneficence is what guides medical professionals.

Justice

1.36 The final of the four principles is justice. Patients should be treated by health care professionals in a way which is fair, equitable, and reasonable. Few would disagree with that. The difficulty comes in applying that principle. The notion of justice becomes most prominent in relation to rationing. When decisions are made about whose treatment it is and when treatment cannot be afforded, it is important that patients are treated in a way which is fair, just, and equitable.

Balancing the principles

1.37 As we have already indicated, the principles as stated in the abstract have received widespread support. The difficulty is in dealing with cases where they conflict. Consider this hypothetical case:

> Bruce, a 35-year-old, has been offered a part in a play of a character who has no ear. The job is a major break for him and he is determined to make a success of it. He asks Dr Akfar to remove his ear. Dr Akfar seeks advice on the ethical approach to take.

This is a case where the principles conflict. The principle of autonomy requires us to respect Bruce's decision about his body, and which treatment he wishes to receive. On the other hand, we have Dr Akfar's autonomy to consider, too. If he is strongly opposed to providing the treatment, it would interfere with his autonomy to remove the ear. The principle of non-malfeasance comes into play. Removal of the ear may be seen as harm and therefore to infringe this principle. However, how is harm to be defined? Can we include emotions, too? In which case, it might be argued that the pleasure Bruce will get from the removal of the ear will outweigh any physical pain. Or should the view be taken that it is for the patient to determine whether or not the removal of the ear is harmful? The principle of beneficence may come into this, too. If Bruce will suffer psychologically if the ear is not removed, would it not benefit him to have it removed, in which case that may be the best treatment for him? Finally, justice might be relevant, too: is it a just allocation of resources to fund the removal of the ear if there are more important procedures which should attract funding? As this example shows, the difficulty with the Beauchamp and Childress approach is that although it helpfully throws up the key issues, it does not provide the answers. Indeed, Beauchamp and Childress make it clear that highlighting the key issues is all they are trying to do with their approach.

Intersecting medical ethics and law

1.38 How should medical law and ethics relate? The first point to make is that we should not assume that ethics and law necessarily match. What is unethical should not necessarily be unlawful and, indeed, what is ethical should not necessarily be lawful. Let's explore that a bit more. First, something might be unethical, but still lawful. An obvious example would be a doctor who is rude to a patient. That might be unethical, but it would not be unlawful. This reflects a much broader point in relation to law and ethics, which is that the law should not render unlawful all immoral behaviour, or else we would all be in prison! The law is left to enforce those moral obligations which involve a serious harm to the victim or where non-legal sanctions cannot adequately deal with the breach. Hence, where conduct is unlawful, we need to ask whether the breach is sufficiently serious to justify the use of the law.

1.39 Second, there are some issues over which the ethical position is controversial. Different people take different views (Messer 2002). In such a case, the law needs to provide some kind of response. Typically, this will be to leave space to allow individuals to act as they see fit. The issue of abortion may be a good example. The law regulates abortion to some extent, as we shall see in Chapter 7, but, at least in relation to early abortions, in effect the decision is the woman's. However, in more controversial late abortions, there is greater restriction on when an abortion may be permitted. This may reflect the fact that in relation to later abortions, many feel that abortion should not be permitted on any ground. Of course, others will disagree and think the law should not even regulate later abortions. The law on abortion also respects the views of medical professionals who oppose abortion by granting them rights which protect conscientious objection to abortion. So, in this area of such controversy, the law seeks to take a fairly neutral course, allowing individuals to decide for themselves, while granting professionals the ability not to be involved.

1.40 Another option for the law can be to discourage but not outlaw the activity. An example of this is surrogacy, where couples are permitted to enter surrogacy contracts, but these are not enforceable, and must not be commercial. This may reflect an approach which in effect says, 'We don't like surrogacy, we are not going to encourage it, but we are not going to outlaw it.'

1.41 There is a further factor to be taken into account here and that is that while ethicists seek to determine the correct answer to dilemmas, law has a different function. It must provide guidance for those wanting to know what the law is and must provide a means by which a court can determine whether or not a person has broken the law. Both these points need further discussion. One role for the law is to inform people what is and is not lawful. Indeed, it is a fundamental aspect of the rule of law that the law should be clear and easy to follow. This is significant because, while the ethical solution to a problem may involve a complex consideration of various issues and may indeed take a lengthy discussion to explain, law does not have that luxury: it needs to distil its directions down to a few easily followed guidelines. This may mean that the legal response lacks some of the sophistication or finesse of the deepest ethical analysis of the field.

1.42 As suggested, law must be able to be used in the court room. It must provide a test of legality that is readily susceptible to determination in a court. For example, some ethicists place much weight on the motivation behind the actor's behaviour: were they motivated by kindness or malice? That may be of great ethical significance, but it is problematic for lawyers. It is not easy for a court to assess what the motivations of an individual were. So some issues which might not be susceptible of proof may be of significance for ethicists, but need to be downplayed in so far as the legal response goes.

CONCLUSION

As we have seen in this chapter, there are a range of perspectives from which one can examine medical law and ethics. Indeed, disagreements over the general approach to take manifest themselves in the fierce disputes over issues such as euthanasia or abortion. Many of the arguments in the chapter that follow can be regarded as reflecting a difference between taking a deontological or consequentialist approach.

FURTHER READING

Beauchamp, T., and Childress, J. (2003) *Principles of Biomedical Ethics* (Oxford: Oxford University Press).

Bentham, J. (1789, repr. 1961) *An Introduction to the Principles of Morals and Legislation* (Garden City, NJ: Doubleday).

Brandt, T. (1992) *Morality, Utilitarianism, and Rights* (Cambridge: Cambridge University Press).

Foster, C. (2009) *Choosing Life, Choosing Death* (Oxford: Hart).

Fulford, K., Dickenson, D., and Murray, T. (eds) (2002) *Health Care Ethics and Human Values: An Introductory Text with Readings and Case Studies* (Oxford: Blackwell).

Gillon, R. (1993) 'Medical Ethics: Four Principles Plus Attention to Scope', *British Medical Journal* 309: 184–8.

Glannon, W. (2005) *Biomedical Ethics* (Oxford: Oxford University Press).

Gostin, L. (2008) *Public Health Law: Power, Duty, Restraint* (Berkeley, CA: University of California Press).

Herring, J. (2010) *Medical Law and Ethics*, 3rd edn (Oxford: Oxford University Press).

Hope, T. (2005) *A Very Short Introduction to Medical Ethics* (Oxford: Oxford University Press).

Hursthouse, R. (1999) *On Virtue Ethics* (Oxford: Oxford University Press).

Jonsen, A. (2003) *The Birth of Bioethics* (Oxford: Oxford University Press).

Mahowald, M. (2006) *Bioethics and Women* (Oxford: Oxford University Press).

Messer, N. (2002) *Theological Issues in Bioethics* (London: Darton Longman and Todd).

Miola, J. (2007) *Medical Ethics and Medical Law* (Oxford: Hart).

Pattinson, S. (2009) *Medical Law and Ethics* (London: Sweet and Maxwell).

Sheldon, S., and Thomson, M. (eds) (1998) *Feminist Perspectives on Healthcare Law* (London: Cavendish Publishing).

Tong, R. (1997) *Feminist Approaches to Bioethics: Theoretical Reflections and Practical Applications* (Boulder, CO: Westview Press).

Veitch, K. (2007) *The Jurisdiction of Medical Law* (Aldershot: Ashgate).

SELF-TEST QUESTIONS

1 David asks a doctor to cut off his arm because he feels it does not belong to him. What ethical principle should guide the doctor's response?

2 Are there any circumstances in which it is permissible to treat a patient without their consent?

3 Alfred needs a kidney, without which he will die. Brian is his cousin and is the person whose kidney could be used. Brian is unsure whether to donate or not. Should the doctor just sedate him and remove the kidney?

4 Susan has donated her kidney to her youngest daughter. Her eldest daughter has now fallen ill and needs a kidney, too. Susan is ready to donate her remaining organ, even though she will need to spend the rest of her life on kidney dialysis. Should the doctors respect Susan's wishes? What if Susan wished to donate a heart, which would obviously result in her death?

2

Rationing and delivery of health care

SUMMARY

This chapter will look at the structure of the National Health Service (NHS) and the way health care is delivered in this country. It will focus first on the controversial issue of rationing. It will explain how rationing decisions are made and the cases where litigation has been brought to challenge rationing decisions. It will also examine the ethical principles behind rationing. It will then look at how health care is delivered in England and the structure of the NHS.

An introduction to rationing

2.1 Rationing of medical treatment has been taking place for a long time. However, it is only in recent years that the issue has been brought out into the open. In the past, it was generally assumed that this was done by individual doctors, in essence deciding that it was not worth the patient receiving any further treatment because they were so ill. Financial pressures on the NHS and a greater acknowledgement of the rights of patients has meant that this kind of 'under-the-carpet' rationing has been consigned to history. Now decisions on rationing are more openly discussed and there is a far greater degree of transparency than in the past. That, of course, is not to say that the issue is any the less controversial!

Must we ration?

2.2 The idea of refusing a patient the treatment that they need is not palatable. And to some, for example Light (1997), it has been too quickly assumed by many commentators that we should ration health care. If the NHS cannot afford the treatment the patients need, we should increase taxation so that it can! That is a good point, but it is unlikely to resolve the issue. There is a whole range of treatment that we could provide on the NHS that people could claim: health supplements, cosmetic surgery, hair transplant, etc. As technologies develop an ever-increasing number of remedies become available. These in turn lead to higher expectations among the general public about what they can expect from medicine. Further, it means that people are living longer. This all means that there is a seemingly inexhaustible demand for medical resources. We do need somewhere to draw the line around what will be provided on the NHS. That is probably an inescapable question. What it is right to emphasize is that we must always be looking at what treatments are denied as a result of where the line is drawn and consider whether taxation should be increased to move the line so that more treatments are provided (Newdick 2005).

Who rations?

2.3 One of the difficulties in considering rationing is that it occurs at different levels and in different ways. There are essentially four levels:

- Central Government: the government determines the levels of taxation and how the money generated is divided between different government departments (e.g. health, defence, education). Of course, a decision to cut back on the allocation to health may well mean that a patient will not receive a treatment they otherwise would have.

- NICE: National Institute for Clinical Excellence (NICE) is a body which determines which treatments are recommended for use on the NHS. This body will be discussed later but it plays an important role in determining whether treatments are cost-effective.

- PCTs: Primary Care Trusts (PCTs) must allocate their budget between different calls for health care resources. These will be determined by local priorities. However, they must ensure they follow NICE guidelines. This means that they have only limited discretion in allocating spending. Still, it may be that a PCT in one part of the country decides to spend more money on a particular area of medicine than other PCTs.

- Individual doctors: at the end of the day, doctors still play a major role in rationing. While in some cases there may be clear guidance from PCTs on what treatments are recommended, doctors often decide whether or not a particular treatment is appropriate for a patient. It is unknown how much rationing is disguised by a doctor determining that a particular treatment is 'not appropriate' for a particular patient.

The law on rationing

2.4 The National Health Service Act 2006, s. 1 sets out the key legal foundations for the NHS as follows:

1 National Health Service Act 2006

(1) The Secretary of State must continue the promotion in England of a comprehensive health service designed to secure improvement—

(a) in the physical and mental health of the people of England, and

(b) in the prevention, diagnosis and treatment of illness.

(2) The Secretary of State must for that purpose provide or secure the provision of services in accordance with this Act.

(3) The services so provided must be free of charge except in so far as the making and recovery of charges is expressly provided for by or under any enactment, whenever passed.

It is notable that this provision is very vague. Even more so, bearing in mind sections 2 and 3:

2 Secretary of State's general power

(1) The Secretary of State may—

(a) provide such services as he considers appropriate for the purpose of discharging any duty imposed on him by this Act, and

(b) do anything else which is calculated to facilitate, or is conducive or incidental to, the discharge of such a duty.

3 Secretary of State's duty as to provision of certain services

(1) The Secretary of State must provide throughout England, to such extent as he considers necessary to meet all reasonable requirements—

(a) hospital accommodation,

(b) other accommodation for the purpose of any service provided under this Act,

(c) medical, dental, ophthalmic, nursing and ambulance services,

(d) such other services or facilities for the care of pregnant women, women who are breastfeeding and young children as he considers are appropriate as part of the health service,

(e) such other services or facilities for the prevention of illness, the care of persons suffering from illness and the after-care of persons who have suffered from illness as he considers are appropriate as part of the health service,

(f) such other services or facilities as are required for the diagnosis and treatment of illness.

2.5 These provisions rely on the phrase 'to such extent as he considers necessary'. This grants the Secretary of State broad discretions in deciding how to meet the health needs of the nation. It would be very hard to argue that the Secretary of State was acting in breach of these provisions (*R* v. *Secretary of State for Social Services ex p Hincks* (1980) 1 BMLR 93).

European Union law

2.6 Claims for medical treatment can be made under European Union law. These are exemplified by the following case:

R (Watts) v. *Bedford PCT* **[2004] EWCA 166** Mrs Watts was suffering pain in her hips due to osteoarthritis. She was placed on an NHS waiting list and told the procedure was likely to take a year. She arranged to have the procedure performed in France. She relied on the so-called Form E11 procedure which gave a right to a citizen to be treated in another EU Member State at the expense of their own government if such treatment was not available from their own government. The PCT refused to pay, arguing that the one year wait was within normal waiting times and she would not suffer undue delay. The Court of Appeal focused on Article 49 of the EU Treaty (note: this is now Article 56 TFEU) which gave a right to obtain services and Article 22 which provided the right to treatment. Article 49 it was held did not apply to medical treatment, but Article 22 did. However, it only applied where the treatment was available in the time 'normally necessary for obtaining the treatment' in their home country, bearing in mind their health and probable course of the disease. The case went to the European Court of Justice (ECJ) where it was confirmed that a UK citizen could only require the NHS to fund treatment if the NHS had authorized it. The NHS had to consider the clinical needs of the patient and their medical history and the likely course of the illness. Budgetary considerations could not be relied upon as a reason for refusing to pay.

This certainly opens the door to patients who are told to wait for treatment to decide that they will seek agreement that the NHS will pay for treatment overseas. Christopher Newdick (2005) is concerned that this procedure will be taken up by the articulate and the wealthy, but not those with less experience in asserting their rights or who are too ill to travel.

Judicial review

2.7 By far the most common way of challenging rationing decisions in courts is by way of judicial review. Judicial review proceedings can be brought against a public authority which has made a decision affecting the complainant. There are three bases on which the decision could be challenged:

- Illegality
- Unreasonableness
- Procedural improprietary

We will say a little more about these before looking at the approach taken by the courts in rationing cases.

2.8 Illegality involves a claim that the PCT did not have the legal power to make the decision. Alternatively, it can be a claim that factors that should not have been taken into account were used in making the decision. A claim of unreasonableness has a special meaning in judicial review. It requires proof that the decision-maker acted in a way in which no reasonable decision-maker might act (*Associated Provincial Picture Houses* v. *Wednesbury Corporation* [1948] 1 KB 223). This is a difficult test to satisfy. Regularly courts in judicial review will indicate that the decision made was not the one the judges would have made, but it cannot be said that the decision was one no reasonable decision-maker could have made. This means that except in the most blatantly inappropriate rationing decisions, it is unlikely that the court will conclude that an unreasonable decision has been made. The final category of procedural impropriety is the most likely to be used. Here the focus is on whether the decision-making process was fair and open.

2.9 There have been a number of rationing cases which have already appeared before the courts and there are a number of principles which have emerged:

- The courts have accepted that rationing decisions need to be made and these might result in a particular patient not receiving treatment (*R* v. *North and East Devon HA ex p Coughlan* [2001] QB 213; *AC* v. *Berkshire West PCT* [2010] EWHC 1162 (Admin)).

- A policy which stated that a particular treatment would never be funded is unlikely to be lawful (*R* v. *NW Lancashire HA ex p A, G and D*). That is because it will fail to consider each case individually and so cannot be procedurally fair.

- Patients should be informed of the basis of the decision and given an explanation why they are being denied any treatment (*R (Ross)* v. *West Sussex Primary Care Trust* [2008] EWHC 2252 (Admin)).

- The decision-makers must take into account relevant factors and especially any guidance from NICE or NHS circulars (*R* v. *Derbyshire HA ex p Fisher* [1997] Med LR 327).

- The decision-maker should take into account any factors that make the patient's case exceptional: *R (Rogers)* v. *Swindon Primary Care Trust* [2006] EWCA Civ 329; *AC* v. *Berkshire West PCT* [2010] EWHC 1162 (Admin).

- If the decision-maker has created a legitimate expectation that a certain form of treatment will be funded (e.g. by the public announcements it has made), then it may be unlawful not to offer it.

- Where the treatment which is denied is life-saving treatment, then the decision will be subject to particularly strict scrutiny (*R (Ross)* v. *West Sussex Primary Care Trust* [2008] EWHC 2252 (Admin)).

2.10 The following cases give good examples of the approach the courts have been taking to the case law:

***R* v. *Cambridge HA ex p B* [1995] 2 All ER 129** B, aged 10, suffered from Leukemia. The medical team dealing with her case estimated that she had between six and eight weeks to live and decided that no further treatment should be offered. Her father discovered some doctors in the United States who would have offered further treatment. The Health Authority decided that the alternative treatment was experimental and too expensive. A judicial review of the resources was sought. Laws J at first instance emphasized the right to life under Article 2 of the ECHR [European Convention on Human Rights]. He held that there had to be a compelling reason that was required before refusing life-saving treatment. Simply referring to limited resources was insufficient. However, the Court of Appeal overturned his ruling. It stressed that the court was not in the position of assessing the wisdom of resourcing decisions. The court could look at the single patient before it, but not properly weigh up the competing claims of all the other patients that a local authority had to consider.

***R (Rogers)* v. *Swindon NHS PCT* [2006] EWCA 392** Ms Rogers had breast cancer and asked her PCT to fund Herceptin, a cancer drug, which was yet to be licensed. The early trials had suggested that the drug was effective for the kind of cancer Ms Rogers had. The policy adopted by the PCT was that Herceptin was only to be used in exceptional personal or clinical circumstances. Having considered her case, it determined there were none. However, the Court of Appeal found their decision unlawful. They accepted that it was permissible for a health authority to have an 'only in exceptional circumstances' policy. However, that was so only if the decision-maker genuinely believed there could be exceptional circumstances. In effect, the court decided that although the health authority said they would fund the treatment in exceptional circumstances, in fact they operated a policy of never funding it. The health authority had not developed a system for determining what would count as being exceptional. Another issue was that the health authority had not referred to cost being a relevant factor that the authority would take into account. It could not therefore rely on funding issues to deny her treatment.

***R (Otley)* v. *Barking and Dagenham NHS PCT* [2007] EWHC 1927 (Admin)** Ms Otley sought a judicial review of the decision of her PCT not to fund an anti-cancer drug. Other treatments had not proved successful. Her consultant recommended Avastin, a drug not then approved for use in the NHS. She privately funded five cycles of treatment, with significant success. The oncologist applied for further treatments from the NHS. The Trust's panel concluded that the use of the drug would not significantly prolong Ms Otley's life and would not be cost-effective. When the decision was appealed the panel asked for a detailed report on the drug, which recommended that in exceptional cases Avastin should be used. One of the panel queried the proportions used of the drugs.

The Court of Appeal held that the panel had acted irrationally and unlawfully. The querying of the proportion was an irrelevant query as it had been shown that the combination of drugs had been effective for Ms Otley. The panel had failed properly to consider the fact that there was a chance that the treatment could provide Ms Otley successful treatment, not just giving her a few months more life, but a significantly longer time. The PCT had not sought to rely on a lack of resources and so the question was simply whether the drugs appeared to offer a reasonable benefit, which they did.

R (Ross) v. West Sussex Primary Care Trust [2008] EWHC 2252 (Admin)
Mr Ross sought a judicial review of the refusal of the NHS Trust to fund his treatment for cancer. The standard drugs had initially worked well, but they could no longer be used due to another medical condition that he developed. His consultant had therefore recommended a new drug which was not normally available on the NHS. The panel considering the recommendation accepted that without the new drug Mr Ross's life expectancy was limited. However, it found that the treatment was not clinically efficacious, nor cost-effective. Further, they concluded that Mr Ross's case was not exceptional. Mr Ross appealed and produced a report from an expert that held that within the terms of the Trust's criteria his case was exceptional.

The Court of Appeal found the PCT's policy unlawful as it said that funding for such a drug could be permitted in exceptional cases, but then held that exceptional cases arose where a patient was not a 'representative group of patients'. This automatically ruled a patient as not exceptional if there was another patient like him. Further, the panel had misunderstood some of the evidence. That contradicted the normal meaning of the word 'exceptional'. Where a case was exceptional and involved end-of-life issues, the PCT should be less restrictive when considering cost-effectiveness issues. The Trust had acted irrationally in refusing to fund Mr Ross's treatment.

AC v. Berkshire West PCT [2010] EWHC 1162 (Admin) A PCT refused to fund breast augmentation for C. C suffered from gender identity disorder and was living as a woman. The Trust funded only 'core' surgical procedures for gender identity disorder patients, which include genital surgery, but not breast augmentation surgery. C referred to another patient (X) who had been born a woman, but who had a congenital absence of breast tissue and had received funding because she had a history of psychological illness related to the issue.

It was held that courts in rationing cases had to acknowledge that NHS budgets were under severe pressure from increasingly expensive new drugs and procedures, and the rising longevity of the population. Trusts had to have policies for which treatment would be routinely funded. It was proper for a Trust to have a general policy, but to allow exceptions in exceptional circumstances. In this case, it had been shown that X's case was exceptional in that she suffered from a psychological disorder. C's distress was less severe. There was no discrimination against a transsexual patient, because the same test had been applied to both X and C, namely considering the extent of their distress.

Analysis of the courts' approach

2.11   The courts appear to be treading a fine line. On the one hand, they are refusing to enter the actual merits of rationing decisions. So far, they have not been willing to decide whether the authority is right to give treatments to patients in category X, but not those in category Y. So in *AC* v. *Berkshire West PCT* [2010] EWHC 1162 (Admin), Bean J was not willing to overrule a PCT's decision that gender reassignment surgery was a low priority. The point is that typically in these cases the court will hear from the anguished patient who is denied treatment, but not from the other equally anguished patients who would lose out if the applicant won their case for funding. On the other hand, they have been willing to test carefully how closely health authorities follow their published guidelines (Syrett 2007).

2.12   There is much wisdom in this tack. First, the courts are not in a good position to assess whether the rationing decision is appropriate. To do this properly, the court would need to look at all the categories of expenditure facing the authority and hear evidence on the seriousness and nature of all the alterative conditions. That would last forever! And involve the cash-strapped NHS Trust in even more expenditure in explaining its decisions to a court. And there is no reason why the court is likely to be better at making such decisions than health care authorities. More significantly, health care authorities are politically accountable for their decisions in a way that courts are not.

2.13   One way of understanding the approach taken by the courts is that the courts are seeking to enhance the political accountability of the health care Trusts for their decisions (Syrett 2008). The grounds for their decisions must be made public and be followed. This means that if what they are doing is unacceptable, political pressure can be applied to change political accountability. That may be the best way of controlling rationing decisions. Consider, for example, the difficulty that the health authority got into in the case of *R (Rogers)* v. *Swindon*

NHS PCT [2006] EWCA 392 after failing to state that economic considerations were a factor in deciding whether a patient got treatment. The case will compel health authorities to be more open about the fact that economics do play a part in deciding whether a patient receives treatment and in what ways it is relevant. That will mean that PCTs will be more open to scrutiny from the public and the government. If the policies adopted by PCTs are unacceptable, it is better that they are changed as a result of political pressure rather than judicial censure.

Ethical approaches to rationing

2.14 How can we decide who should get treatment? At its starkest, a health Trust may have to decide whether to fund treatment for one category of patients or another. How can such decisions be made?

2.15 It is important before entering that debate to distinguish between clinical and rationing decisions. There will be cases where it is decided that a particular treatment is not effective. For example, if it was shown that counselling treatments were more effective at treating moderate depression than medication, a PCT may decide not to provide medication for depression. That would not be a rationing decision, but rather a clinical one. The reason for the decision is not cost but efficacy of treatment. Of course, often it is not so straightforward and rather is a mixture of these factors. If it was shown that counselling treatment was nearly as effective as medication, but it is significantly cheaper, a cash-strapped PCT might prefer the counselling. Such a decision would be a combination of clinical and rationing factors.

2.16 In discussing the ethical approaches to rationing, one has come to dominate the answer: the Quality Adjusted Life Year (QALY) approach. This has become a widely supported approach. It involves a consideration of three factors:

    1 How many years will the treatment benefit the patient?

    2 What will be the quality of any improvement gained from the treatment?

    3 How expensive is the treatment?

In essence, the approach seeks to find out whether a drug offers good value for money. Those treatments which create a significant improvement for the patient over many years will create significant QALY, while a treatment which only provided a minor benefit and/or for a short time would score lowly. So, a treatment that offered a year of significantly improved benefit would be preferred over a treatment which provided two years of only a marginal benefit. Usually, a zero score is used for no improvement in life quality, whereas a one would be given for a treatment which restored a patient from near death to full health.

2.17 One of the major benefits of QALY is that it provides a way of comparing the cost-effectiveness of radically different treatments: is treating depression more effective than treating an ingrown toenail? At first, seeking to choose between them seems impossible, but a QALY approach offers some way of doing that. It can assess how much improvement in quality of life a treatment offers and for how long. As we shall see, NICE has relied on QALYs as a way of determining whether or not to recommend treatment. There needs to be a very good reason before it will approve treatments costing over £30,000 per QALY.

2.18 At its heart, QALY is simply common sense: we prefer treatments which, given their cost, provide a good improvement in life for a reasonably long time. However, there are difficulties with its use:

- How do we assess improvement in quality of life? Is it possible to put a figure on how much an improvement in quality of life is when dealing with depression or back pain? Or, more dramatically, being in a wheelchair or going blind? It might be argued that these things cannot readily be compared.

- One difficulty in particular is that different people will respond differently to different losses. Losing a finger may or may not impact upon you significantly, depending on whether, for example, playing a musical instrument is important to you.

- QALYs involve discrimination. Two groups in particular might claim this: older people and those with disabilities. In relation to older people, it is much harder to establish many QALYs as opposed to a younger person. Indeed, if a younger and older person both suffer from the same condition, the younger person will establish more QALYs much more easily than the older person. In relation to a disabled person, it is arguable that they will not be able to establish as great an improvement as an able-bodied person in their quality of life, if that is already badly affected by their disability.

- The QALYs approach can provide unpalatable results, particularly if it is used in an unthinking way. Take a person suffering from serious mental illness, who has little awareness of their condition. It might be argued that providing them with basic care or treatment is not really improving their quality of life. There is another issue here, too. It might produce questionable results. Schlander (2008) suggests that under a QALY approach, treatment for erectile dysfunction would be far more cost-effective than treatment for multiple sclerosis. But is that an acceptable conclusion? Of course, it may be argued that such a conclusion demonstrates that the QALY calculation has not been done properly. But not necessarily, because medicines for common conditions (such as erectile dysfunction) are usually much cheaper than for rarer conditions (such as multiple sclerosis).

- There is an issue over whether in considering QALYs, we should take into account the number of people affected. Let us say that it will cost the same to give one person 10 QALYs as it will to give ten people 1 QALY. Are we to treat these as both equally cost-effective? Mathematically the benefit may be the same, but otherwise it might be arguable either way. For the one person we are looking at a very significant life-changing benefit, whereas for the ten the improvement is less significant. Or is it better to benefit the many rather than the few?

- Should rationing only consider the interest of the patient receiving the treatment or can their relatives and carers be taken into account. An example will be considered here of a treatment for incontinence for a patient who is suffering from dementia. Let us say that the treatment will be of little benefit to the patient, who is barely aware of the condition. But it will be of huge benefit to his carer. Can the improvement in quality of life of the carer be a factor to take into account?

2.19 One particularly controversial issue concerns whether or not we should take into account the fault of the patient in deciding to ration treatment. Should we, for example, spend less on smoking-related illnesses on the basis that the patient has brought these conditions upon himself? Or even more crudely, if having to choose between two patients, one of whom caused their own condition and the other who is blameless, is it not more appropriate to select the blameless? While such an approach would have some support among the tabloid press, it is a dangerous road to go down. We do not really know the extent to which people are responsible for their illnesses. Smoking relates not just to personal choice but to a broad range of socio-economic circumstances. Further, there is a danger that prejudice can affect how this principle is applied. Someone might readily criticize the obese for their illness, but not criticize the workaholic banker who suffers a heart attack or participant in extreme sports who injures them-selves. NICE draws a helpful distinction between taking a person's lifestyle choices as a reason for denying treatment because a patient is at fault, which it thinks is inappropriate, and where the lifestyle choices indicate that a particular treatment will not be effective (e.g. because the patient will continue to smoke), which it thinks can be a relevant factor.

We will now turn to consider some of the issues concerning the structure of the NHS generally.

The NHS Constitution

2.20   The government has produced a constitution for the NHS which sets out its seven core principles. These are:

1.   The NHS provides a comprehensive service, available to all irrespective of gender, race, disability, age, sexual orientation, religion or belief.

2.   Access to NHS services is based on clinical need, not an individual's ability to pay.

3.   The NHS aspires to the highest standards of excellence and professionalism.

4.   NHS services must reflect the needs and preferences of patients, their families and their carers.

5.   The NHS works across organisational boundaries and in partnership with other organisations in the interest of patients, local communities and the wider population.

6.   The NHS is committed to providing best value for taxpayers' money and the most effective, fair and sustainable use of finite resources.

7.   The NHS is accountable to the public, communities and patients that it serves.

2.21   The NHS Constitution explains:

The NHS belongs to the people. It is there to improve our health and well-being, sup-porting us to keep mentally and physically well, to get better when we are ill and, when we cannot fully recover, to stay as well as we can to the end of our lives. It works at the limits of science—bringing the highest levels of human knowledge and skill to save lives and improve health. It touches our lives at times of basic human need, when care and compassion are what matter most. (NHS 2010: 2)

2.22 The NHS Constitution informs patients of the NHS of the rights they are entitled to. It tells readers that they have the right to

- receive NHS services free of charge, apart from certain limited exceptions sanctioned by Parliament;

- access NHS services. You will not be refused access on unreasonable grounds;

- expect your local NHS to assess the health requirements of the local community and to commission and put in place the services to meet those needs as considered necessary;

- in certain circumstances, to go to other European Economic Area countries or Switzerland for treatment which would be available to you through your NHS commissioner;

- not to be unlawfully discriminated against in the provision of NHS services including on grounds of gender, race, religion or belief, sexual orientation, disability (including learning disability or mental illness) or age;

- be treated with a professional standard of care, by appropriately qualified and experienced staff, in a properly approved or registered organisation that meets required levels of safety and quality;

- expect NHS organisations to monitor, and make efforts to improve, the quality of healthcare they commission or provide;

- drugs and treatments that have been recommended by NICE for use in the NHS, if your doctor says they are clinically appropriate for you;

- expect local decisions on funding of other drugs and treatments to be made rationally following a proper consideration of the evidence. If the local NHS decides not to fund a drug or treatment you and your doctor feel would be right for you, they will explain that decision to you;

- receive the vaccinations that the Joint Committee on Vaccination and Immunisation recommends that you should receive under an NHS-provided national immunisation programme;

- dignity and respect, in accordance with your human rights;

- accept or refuse treatment that is offered to you, and not to be given any physical examination or treatment unless you have given valid consent. If you do not have the capacity to do so, consent must be obtained from a person legally able to act on your behalf, or the treatment must be in your best interests;

- be given information about your proposed treatment in advance, including any significant risks and any alternative treatments which may be available, and the risks involved in doing nothing;

- privacy and confidentiality and to expect the NHS to keep your confidential information safe and secure;

- access to your own health records. These will always be used to manage your treatment in your best interest;

- choose your GP practice, and to be accepted by that practice unless there are reasonable grounds to refuse, in which case you will be informed of those reasons;

- express a preference for using a particular doctor within your GP practice, and for the practice to try to comply;

- make choices about your NHS care and access to information to support these choices. The options available to you will develop over time and depend on your individual needs. Details are set out in the *Handbook* to the NHS Constitution;

- be involved in discussions and decisions about your healthcare, and to be given information to enable you to do this;

- be involved, directly or through representatives, in the planning of healthcare services, the development and consideration of proposals for changes in the way those services are provided, and in decisions to be made affecting the operation of those services;

- have any complaint you make about NHS services dealt with efficiently and to have it properly investigated;

- know the outcome of any investigation into your complaint;

- take your complaint to the independent Health Service Ombudsman, if you are not satisfied with the way your complaint has been dealt with by the NHS;

- make a claim for judicial review if you think you have been directly affected by an unlawful act or decision of an NHS body; and

- compensation where you have been harmed by negligent treatment.

2.23 The exact legal nature of these rights is unclear. Some would be capable of legal enforcement, but others are too vague to be accepted as legal rights. They may be taken into account by courts when considering claims a patient may bring against the NHS. The Health Act 2009, s. 2 requires NHS bodies to have regard to the NHS Constitution. That is rather vague, but it could be used in a judicial review case of a decision by an NHS body.

2.24 The Constitution not only lists patients' rights, but it also lists their responsibilities:

- You should recognise that you can make a significant contribution to your own, and your family's, good health and well-being, and take some personal responsibility for it.

- You should register with a GP practice—the main point of access to NHS care.

- You should treat NHS staff and other patients with respect and recognise that causing a nuisance or disturbance on NHS premises could result in prosecution.

- You should provide accurate information about your health, condition and status.

- You should keep appointments, or cancel within reasonable time. Receiving treatment within the maximum waiting times may be compromised unless you do.

- You should follow the course of treatment which you have agreed, and talk to your clinician if you find this difficult.

- You should participate in important public health programmes such as vaccination.

- You should ensure that those closest to you are aware of your wishes about organ donation.

- You should give feedback—both positive and negative—about the treatment and care you have received, including any adverse reactions you may have had. (NHS 2010: 9)

These appear to be largely unenforceable, save insofar as they reflect normal principles of the criminal law. It will be interesting to see whether in time these become more clearly defined and whether there will be a way that they become enforceable.

The structure of the NHS

2.25 The structure of the NHS is labyrinthine. Its complexity makes it enormously difficult to describe. The task is made even harder by the continuous structural change that has bedevilled the NHS, with organizations being created, merged, and destroyed at an astonishing rate. It is basically possible to examine the structure as consisting of four levels:

1 Policy-making and centralized planning: this task is carried out primarily by the Department of Health.

2 Supervision, inspection, and regulation: this task is now often carried out by 'arm's length institutions'. These institutions are created by and are responsible to the Department of Health but are independent of it.

3 Service commissioners: these bodies decide which health services are 'purchased' and from whom. This is carried out by, for example, PCTs. They have the responsibility for assessing the health needs of people in their area and ensuring that their needs are appropriately met.

4 Health care providers: those on the front line who directly provide the health care to patients and include, for example, doctors and nurses.

We will now look at some of the key bodies within the NHS.

The Care Quality Commission

2.26 The Care Quality Commission oversees what might broadly be called 'quality control' within the NHS and, indeed, the provision of health and social care generally. It is independent of government. It issues regulations and guidance on particular areas. These may be backed up by inspections or looser forms of enforcement. The National Health Service Act 2008 gives the Commission a wide range of powers to carry out its task. Its primary role is to ensure the provision of health services of a consistently high standard.

Strategic Health Authorities

2.27 Strategic Health Authorities (SHAs) are responsible for ensuring that the health service needs of the people in their area are met. There are ten SHAs in

England. Their main responsibilities are

- developing plans for improving health services in their local area;
- making sure local health services are of a high quality and are performing well;
- increasing the capacity of local health services—so that they can provide more services; and
- making sure national priorities—for example, programmes for improving cancer services—are integrated into local health service plans.

Primary Care Trusts (PCTs)

2.28 PCTs play the major role in the direct provision of health care and this is reflected in the fact that they receive 80 per cent of the NHS budget. They are responsible for finding out what the health needs of their particular area are, deciding which needs should be met and how. They will commission health care providers (hospitals, GPs, etc.) to meet those needs as appropriate. There are 152 PCTs in England.

Special health authorities

2.29 Special health authorities are national bodies and focus on a particular need. The NHS Blood and Transplant Authority is the best known example. It oversees organ transplants and blood donation across England.

Local authorities

2.30 The provision of social services (as opposed to health care) is the responsibility of the local authority. They can either provide the services themselves or purchase them from other providers. The distinction between social services and health care is a problematic one, as we shall see. Social services cover assistance in living independently and will cover the provision of 'meals on wheels', assistance in washing, and sheltered accommodation, for example. These are not regarded as health care.

NHS Trusts

2.31 NHS Trusts are responsible for the provision of health services in their area. NHS Trusts were created by the NHS and Community Care Act 1990.

Although Trusts are accountable to the Secretary of State and must comply with directions on matters such as staffing, they are intended to have a wider degree of freedom than they did in the earlier history of the NHS.

2.32 Foundation Trusts were first created through the Health and Social Care (Community Health and Standards) Act 2003. They are run by a board of governors made up of local managers, staff, and members of the public. Foundation Trusts have far more financial and organizational freedom than other NHS Trusts. This freedom is supposed to mean that they can best meet the particular needs of people in their area. Such Trusts are, of course, still within the NHS and are subject to performance inspections. The intention was that by 2008, all NHS hospitals would have attained Foundation Trust status. However, by 2010 only 129 hospitals had been able to satisfy the criteria.

General practitioners

2.33 GPs are doctors who look after the health of those who are listed with them. As well as providing general health advice and prescribing medicines, they can also carry out simple surgical operations and give vaccinations. GPs will often work with a team of health care professionals, including nurses, midwives, and physiotherapists. If the GP is not able to deal with a patient's problem, she or he will refer the patient to a hospital for tests or treatment, which may involve a meeting with a specialist consultant. In the summer of 2010, the government instigated reforms in the NHS that would give GPs a much bigger role in commissioning services from NHS Trusts.

Having considered some of the key bodies involved in the NHS we shall consider some of the major issues facing NHS provision.

The health/social care divide

2.34 One of the precepts of the NHS is that it should be free at the point of delivery. That principle is found in the NHS constitution. Services must be free of charge unless there is an express statutory provision saying that patients may be charged for them. There is, for example, provision to require payment for wigs, drugs, and optical and dental appliances. This makes the definition of what is a service that can be expected of the NHS crucial, because if a service does not fall under the purview of the NHS, it may be subject to charging. The reinforcement of the distinction between health and social care in recent years has meant that services previously offered free under the NHS are now classified as personal care and need to be paid for. This has become a key and complex distinction.

2.35 The point is powerfully made that those who are unable to provide their own personal care are in that position because they are suffering some kind of health problem (Pattinson 2009). Their problems are therefore symptoms, at least, of their ill health. Indeed, without the personal care, they are likely to develop further health problems. So, whether the inability to care is seen as an aspect of health promotion or dealing with the consequence of ill health, the distinction is hard to justify. Indeed, it is hard to avoid the perception that the division has more to do with attempts to cut costs to the state, while holding on to the claim that health services are provided free at the point of delivery, than being one based on a sound policy.

The provider/purchaser distinction

2.36 An important distinction is drawn between the commissioning of services and the provision of services. The concept was introduced under the Conservative government of the 1990s with the creation of the 'internal market'. The idea behind it is that, by giving a PCT the power to decide from whom to purchase the health services needed, the health care providers will strive to offer an excellent service to ensure that they are selected. In short, it creates a form of competition between health care providers seeking to provide better services than each other. This, it was hoped, would drive up the standards within the NHS. The Labour governments of 1997–2010 sought to distance itself from the notion of competition and instead preferred to use the concept of partnership, the idea being that health service commissioners and health service providers work together in partnership to meet the needs of the people in a particular area. The current Coalition government that came into power in 2010 has indicated that it wishes to see GPs play a bigger role in commissioning services. Even with 'partnership' there is still the threat that if a health service provider is not providing services of the required standard then the health service commissioners will look elsewhere. The use of partnership rather than competition is more about changing the atmosphere of relationships between providers and commissioners than changing the central idea that providers should keep striving to offer a high level of service.

Decentralization

2.37 One of the key themes in the current NHS is to devolve power to local PCTs and frontline staff. The argument is that frontline staff are in the best position to know what patients in their area of the country need and how best to meet those needs. The independence given to PCTs is seen as key to enabling local NHS bodies to meet needs in their area. An important part of the move to decentralization is the use of Foundation Trust hospitals, which have significantly greater freedom over their budgets than the NHS Trust hospitals.

Targets

2.38 One of the main ways that governments in recent years have sought to improve the services provided by the NHS has been through the use of targets. A huge range of issues from reducing suicide rates to waiting times has been subject to targets. Great pressure is placed upon NHS bodies to meet these. One of the new roles of the Care Quality Commission will be to ensure that NHS bodies comply with the National Service Frameworks, which set out standards expected of the NHS. Where standards are met, the government naturally seeks to claim credit for a very tangible benefit of the extra funding it has put into the NHS.

2.39 Targets provide a very concrete measure of improvement. Without them politicians may fear that the money given to the NHS will go into a 'black hole', and there will be no measure of improvement to which politicians can point and say, 'that outcome has resulted from the improvements we have made'. Of course, where, for example, patients have received treatment more quickly because of waiting-list targets, the patient benefits. However, the concern is that targets will skew priorities and that Trusts will be seeking to meet the targets, rather than actually meeting the health needs of those in their area (Audit Commission 2003).

Choice

2.40 'Choice' has become one of the 'buzz words' of the modern NHS. It reflects what might be seen as a shift from seeing the patient as the 'recipient' of care, to treating her or him as a consumer who chooses what services she or he wants. Supporters argue that increased choice will lead to increased satisfaction as individuals get the treatment they really want, and improved quality of services as health care providers vie to be the providers of choice for patients.

2.41 At first, giving patients choice may appear to be an inevitable good, but this is not beyond dispute. Providing a choice will cost money and that raises the question about its cost-effectiveness. Also, offering a choice means we must accept that on occasion the wrong choice will be made. It might also be argued that it is a little misleading to talk about choice when, given rationing within the NHS, the choices of an individual patient must be weighed against the interests of the general public. Can we really allow patients to choose treatments under the NHS which are not cost-effective? Will not that amount to a waste of precious NHS resources? Surely we cannot let one patient's choice mean another is denied treatment they need? There are also concerns that choice empowers the educated middle class, who are in a better position to make 'choices' and to insist that their wishes are met; and conversely disadvantages weaker members of society, who are not in a position to make a choice, or do not have the voice to insist upon it. Exercising choice may require having the means to travel to a hospital far from one's home, and this may not be possible for those with low incomes. Indeed, if a majority of people in an area with a struggling hospital choose to go elsewhere for treatment, this may lead to the closing of the hospital and the restriction of choice for those less able to travel.

2.42 In *R (Booker)* v. *NHS Oldham* [2010] EWHC 2593 (Admin), the extent to which patients could be required to pay for NHS services was considered.

> **R (Booker) v. NHS Oldham [2010] EWHC 2593 (Admin)** Ms Booker had been rendered tetraplegic, following a car accident. When Ms Booker had been awarded damages the insurance company had been required to privately fund her care. The PCT then withdrew its provision for nursing care. While the PCT accepted that it could not refuse to fund a person's care because they were capable of funding their care privately, they argued that this case was different because she had been awarded damages by the court specifically to fund her care.
>
> It was held that the decision to withdraw care was unlawful and irrational. There was a basic principle of tort law that a claimant could spend their damages as they wished. They were not obliged to spend it on the loss for which it was ordered. There was therefore no difference between Ms Booker and a patient who was wealthy enough to fund her own care. It was a central principle that the NHS was not a means tested service and that care was provided based on needs, not their financial position.

CONCLUSION

This chapter has considered the harsh reality that the NHS cannot afford to meet the health care needs of every citizen. This means difficult decisions have to be made about who gets what treatment. As we have seen, this involves a tricky balance between ensuring that value for money is obtained, while making sure that there is no discrimination in the provision of health care resources. The courts have tended to steer clear of the debates, requiring health care Trusts to make public their policies and ensure that they follow them, rather than striking down policies as unfair. The chapter has also looked at the complex structure of the NHS and the balance between the need to ensure equal provision of health care for everyone, while giving power to local Trusts to set priorities.

FURTHER READING

Audit Commission (2003) *Achieving the NHS Plan* (London: Department of Health (DoH)).

Claxton, K., and Culyer, A. (2006) 'Wickedness or Folly? The Ethics of NICE's Decisions', *Journal of Medical Ethics* 32: 375–7.

Claxton, K., and Culyer, A. (2007) 'Rights, Responsibilities and NICE: A Rejoinder to Harris', *Journal of Medical Ethics* 33: 462–4.

Cookson, R., and Dolan, P. (2000) 'Principles of Justice in Health Care Rationing', *Journal of Medical Ethics* 26: 323–9.

Denier, Y. (2008) 'Mind the Gap! Three Approaches to Scarcity in Health Care', *Medicine, Health Care and Philosophy* 11: 73–87.

Harrington, J. (2009) 'Visions of Utopia: Markets, Medicine and the National Health Service', *Legal Studies* 29: 376–99.

Harris, J. (2005) 'It's Not NICE to Discriminate', *Journal of Medical Ethics* 31: 373–5.

Harris, J. (2006) 'NICE is Not Cost Effective', *Journal of Medical Ethics* 32: 378–80.

King, J. (2007) 'The Justifiability of Resource Allocation', *Modern Law Review* 70: 197–224.

Light, D. (1997) 'The Real Ethics of Rationing', *British Medical Journal* 315: 112–15.

McLachlan, H. (2005) 'Justice and the NHS: A Comment on Culyer', *Journal of Medical Ethics* 31: 379–82.

Meadowcroft, J. (2008) 'Patients, Politics and Power: Government, Failure and the Politicisation of UK Health Care', *Journal of Medicine and Philosophy* 33: 427–44.

National Health Service (NHS) (2010) *The NHS Constitution* (London: NHS).

Newdick, C. (2005) *Who Should We Treat?* (Oxford: Oxford University Press).

Pattinson, S. (2009) *Medical Law and Ethics* (London: Sweet and Maxwell).

Rhodes, R., Battin, M., and Silvers, A. (2005) *Medicine and Social Justice* (Oxford: Oxford University Press).

Schlander, M. (2008) 'The Use of Cost Effectiveness by the National Institute for Health and National Institute for Clinical Excellence (NICE): (Not Yet an) Exemplar of a Deliberative Process', *Journal of Medical Ethics* 34: 534–9.

Smith II, G. (2008) *Distributive Justice and the New Medicine* (London: Edward Elgar).

Sunstein, C. (2004) 'Lives, Life-years, and Willingness to Pay', *Columbia Law Review* 104: 205–52.

Syrett, K. (2002) 'NICE Work: Rationing, Review and the "Legitimacy Problem" in the New NHS', *Medical Law Review* 10: 1–27.

Syrett, K. (2006) 'Deconstructing Deliberation in the Appraisal of Medical Technologies: NICEly Does It?', *Modern Law Review* 69: 869–94.

Syrett, K. (2007) *Law, Legitimacy and the Rationing of Healthcare: A Contextual and Comparative Perspective* (Cambridge: Cambridge University Press).

Syrett, K. (2008) 'NICE and Judicial Review: Enforcing "Accountability for Reasonableness" through the Courts?', *Medical Law Review* 16: 127–40.

SELF-TEST QUESTIONS

1 Do the courts do enough to protect patients' rights when hearing rationing cases?

2 Alf is denied cancer treatment because his NHS Trust only offers the drug to exceptional cases? Alf has asked the Trust how they decide whether a case is exceptional. They simply explain it is assessed on a case-by-case basis. Assess Alf's chances of bringing a successful claim against the Trust.

3 Is choice for patients a good thing in health care provision?

3

Medical negligence

SUMMARY

This chapter will consider the circumstances in which a patient can sue their doctor or other medical professional after a mistake has caused them a loss. It sets out when the medical professional owes a patient a duty of care, how the court determines whether that duty of care has been breached, and the rules on when the breach will be found to cause the loss. The chapter will consider whether the current law is appropriate and alternatives to the law will be considered.

Introduction

3.1 Unfortunately, sometimes when you go to the doctor things go wrong. Sometimes they go terribly wrong. Indeed, it has been estimated that there were over a million 'incidents' reported in the NPSA (National Patient Safety Agency 2009). Often these incidents do not cause any lasting harm. The wrong pill is given, but its side effects are minimal. There is a misdiagnosis made, but it is spotted at the next appointment. However, when a lasting injury is caused, it is not surprising that patients turn to the law to seek redress. That will be the focus of this chapter.

Legal wrongs

3.2 Where there has been medical malpractice there are three main legal consequences which could follow:

- A criminal prosecution: this could range from gross negligence manslaughter, a sexual offence, or a charge of battery. In fact, it is rare for doctors to face criminal charges unless they are clearly very blameworthy.

- A civil action: this will normally be brought in tort and damages can be awarded as a result.

- Disciplinary proceedings brought by the NHS or the relevant professional body (e.g. the General Medical Council (GMC)): the primary aim of these will be to determine the correct response to the professional's actions: do they need retraining or even removing from the profession. They do not normally lead to money being paid to a patient, but may lead to a formal recognition that a wrong was done and perhaps an apology.

Criminal law

3.3 Criminal proceedings following medical malpractice are rare and so these will be discussed briefly. It need hardly be said that just because a defendant is a doctor this does not provide him with a defence. For example, a male doctor who has sexual intercourse with a patient without his or her consent will be committing the offence of rape.

3.4 There are two issues which require further discussion. The first is the offence of gross negligence manslaughter, which is discussed in more detail in Chapter 9. What is significant for this chapter is that this offence is committed even though the defendant does not intend to cause the patient serious harm. Most criminal offences require proof that the defendant intended to cause harm or was reckless as to causing harm to the victim. This offence can, however, be committed by a defendant who is grossly negligent in their job and thereby causes death. There has been some debate over whether it is fair to make doctors liable for this offence (see Brazier and Allen 2007; and Quick 2006). Their job requires them to deal regularly with life or death issues, often at speed. Their careers are dedicated to saving lives and therefore they are distinct from those who kill others who might be convicted of gross negligence, while driving too fast or danger-ously firing weapons in public places.

3.5 The second issue is where doctors are alleged to have touched patients without their consent, these commonly involve sexual assaults. These cases often turn on whether or not there was consent given by the victim. The courts have held that a patient will not be found to have consented if he or she is deceived as to the identity of the person doing the touching or the nature of the acts. While there are some cases that are straightforward, there can be cases where this is not so obvious:

> *R v. Richardson* **(1998) 43 BMLR 21** A dentist had been barred from practicing dentistry by her professional body. Nevertheless, she carried on performing dentistry. She was charged with an assault occasioning actual bodily harm (Offences Against the Person Act 1861, s. 47). It was not suggested that she had provided bad treatment to her patients but that her patients did not consent to the treatment because had they known that she had been disqualified they would not have consented. The Court of Appeal overturned the conviction. The patients had consented after being deceived by the defendant, but the deception did not relate to her identity nor to the nature of the acts. The deception did not, therefore, negate their consent.

> *R v. Tabassum* **[2000] Lloyd's Rep Med 404** A defendant purported to be expert in breast examination and persuaded a number of women to allow him to exam-ine their breasts. He was convicted of a sexual assault. His conviction was upheld. Although he touched them in the places for and in the way done in a proper breast examination, he was deceiving as to the nature of the acts. The women thought he was touching them for medical purposes, but in fact he was touching them with a sexual motivation.

The law of the tort of negligence

3.6 If A wishes to sue B (a medical professional) in the tort of negligence she must show

- B owed A a duty of care;
- B breached the duty of care; and
- B's breach of duty caused A a loss.

Each of these factors requires careful consideration.

The duty of care

3.7 The law on a duty of care in cases of clinical negligence is based on the general law of tort. You have probably already studied it when considering tort law (see Hedley 2011). In brief, you owe a duty of care to anyone you may foreseeably injure. In other areas of the law the issue becomes complex, but for medical lawyers it is rarely an issue. A medical professional will obviously owe a duty of care to a patient they are looking after. However, just occasionally the issue arises.

3.8 In *Goodwill* v. *BPAS* [1996] 2 All ER 161, it was held that a doctor giving contraceptive advice to a patient owed her a duty of care, but did not owe a duty of care to anyone the patient then had sex with. In *West Bromwich Albion* v. *Wl-Safty* [2006] EWCA Civ 1299, a doctor treating a football player owed the player a duty of care, but not the club. In both these cases it could not be said that the doctor had assumed responsibility for losses caused to third parties. It would have been different in *Goodwill* if the patient was married and she made it clear that the contraception would be for the benefit of the couple; or in *West Bromwich Albion* if the club had specifically sought the advice of the doctor.

Breach of the duty

3.9 The next issue, breach of the duty, is far more controversial. Normally in the law of negligence, a breach of duty arises if the defendant falls below the standards expected of a reasonable person. However, it is more complex than that in medical cases. For them the *Bolam* test is used, named after the leading case of *Bolam* v. *Friern HMC* [1957] 2 All ER 267. There it was held by McNair J:

> A doctor is not guilty of negligence if he has acted in accordance with a practice accepted as proper by a responsible body of medical men skilled in that particular art. (at p. 269)

Although *Bolam* was itself a first instance case, it has been approved on several occasions by the House of Lords, most recently in *Bolitho* v. *City and Hackney HA* [1997] 4 All ER 771. The significance of the *Bolam* test is that a doctor will have a defence to a clinical negligence claim if he or she can show that there is a responsible body of medical opinion which would have found the way the doctor acted acceptable. So, even though other doctors, perhaps even most doctors, would not approve of the way the doctor acted, he will not be negligent if he can find a responsible body of medical opinion. This can make it very difficult for the claimant. It will not be enough to produce a few expert witnesses who are critical of what the doctor did. The claimant must be confident that the defendant will not be able to find an expert who represents a body of opinion which would find what the doctor did as acceptable.

3.10 In *Bolitho* v. *City and Hackney Health Authority* [1998] AC 232, the House of Lords approved the *Bolam* approach, but indicated that some had interpreted it too broadly. Their Lordships emphasized that the approach taken by the defendant had to be approved by a *responsible* body of medical opinion and had to rest on a *logical basis*. The judge would be entitled to conclude that the view that the doctor acted reasonably was not reasonable, responsible, or respectable, even if there were experts who suggested it was. That indicates that it will not be enough for a defendant just to find a respected doctor to support him, the judge will consider carefully whether the view that the defendant acted in a responsible way is reasonable and logical.

> **Bolitho v. Hackney HA [1997] 4 All ER 771** A child was admitted to hospital suffering from respiratory difficulties. A nurse summoned the doctor in charge of the case. The doctor did not attend. Later, the child collapsed and suffered cardiac arrest. He suffered severe brain damage. Expert evidence suggested that had a doctor attended he would have arranged for intubation to ensure an airway. This would have avoided cardiac arrest. The judge, rejecting the claim, found that the doctor had breached the duty in failing to attend, but that had she attended she would not have arranged for the intubation.
>
> The House of Lords held that where the claim led to an omission, the court had to determine whether the failure to attend was negligent and that also if the doctor had attended it would have been negligent to arrange the procedures which would have avoided the harm. In this case, the judge had found that the failure to attend was negligent but the doctor would not have intubated. The key question was, therefore, whether it would have been negligent not to intubate. Expert evidence had suggested that a responsible body of opinion would not have intubated. Therefore, the claim had failed because the *Bolam* test was not satisfied. When applying the *Bolam* test and deciding a professional was not negligent, the court had to be satisfied that the body of opinion supporting the professional was a responsible body and that the opinion had a logical basis. That meant that it had been shown that the proponents of the opinion had directed their minds to the risks and benefits of acting in the way promoted and had reached a defensible conclusion. Only rarely would it be found that a responsible professional opinion was incapable of withstanding logical analysis. In

this case it could not be said that the professional opinion was irresponsible or lacking in logical foundation.

3.11 The best way to appreciate the use of the *Bolam* test is to consider some of its applications:

> **Marriott v. West Midlands HA [1999] LL Rep Med 453** A patient had suffered a fall. The GP prescribed painkillers, but did not suggest a full neurological examination. A neurological examination was recommended by many experts because of the risk of blood clotting following the fall. One expert said that what the doctor had done was acceptable because the risk of developing blood clots was small. The Court of Appeal held that the expert's view was illogical, although there was a small risk of a blood clot, if that did occur there was a risk of death. They regarded the view that a neurological examination was not necessary as illogical.

> **Brown v. Scarborough and North East Yorkshire NHS Trust [2009] EWHC 3103 (QB)** A surgeon performed a hysterectomy and made a 20 cm incision. Normally, only a 15 cm incision was made for that procedure. The surgeon claimed that the 20 cm incision was appropriate because there might have been complications that he could better deal with if he made a longer incision. It was held that the surgeon's view was not a logical one and was negligent. It did not take into account the fact that the longer incision carried serious risks of harm and that in this patient's case there were no indications that complications were likely. Although the court accepted evidence that incisions of 20 cm were regularly made, these were in cases where there were risks of complications which justified the risk of a longer incision.

> **Morris v. University Hospitals Birmingham NHS Trust (Birmingham County Court, 27 January 2009)** A radiologist had failed to detect a rare abnormality of the lachrymal gland on a CT scan. It was held that this kind of abnormality was very rare and the evidence was that many radiologists would have failed to have detected it. Negligence, therefore, was not proved using the *Bolam* test.

3.12 It should not be thought that it will be common for a judge to conclude that an expert's view on what conduct is acceptable will be found to be irresponsible or illogical. It clearly does happen, as the cases mentioned above show. But it will be 'rare' (*Birch* v. *University College London Hospital NHS Trust* [2008] EWHC 2237 (QB)). Nor should it be thought that a judge will take an expert's word for it that his or her view represents a respectable body of opinion.

> **Burne v. A [2006] EWCA Civ 24** X, a child, had a medical condition which required that he was fitted with a ventriculo-peritoneal shunt. One day, X was vomiting, coughing up phlegm, and complaining of a headache. X's mother phoned her GP (Dr Burne).

Over the telephone, he made a diagnosis of upper respiratory infection. In fact, the shunt had become blocked and this caused B to have a heart attack and suffer brain damage. There were two expert witnesses. The first argued that the vomiting of phlegm in this case had not suggested that the doctor should do more than he had done. The second argued that what the doctor had been told over the phone required a visit from a doctor and admission to hospital. Both experts agreed that the doctor's use of open questions was appropriate. The judge disagreed and held that the doctor was at fault in not asking at least two or three specific questions, which would have revealed whether the shunt was blocked. He found the doctor to be negligent.

On appeal, the Court of Appeal confirmed that the judge was entitled to form his own view on the evidence and that he was not bound by the view of the experts. The judge placed weight on the fact that the patient in this case was a child with a history of illness. While the judge was entitled to decide not to follow either expert, he should have put the issues to the experts and asked them to explain their positions, before disagreeing with them. The case was remitted for a further hearing.

3.13 One point to emphasize is that when deciding whether a medical professional was negligent or not the defendant must be judged in the position they found themselves in. That means that they will be judged by the state of knowledge at the time. So, if at the time when the doctor acted that was a proper way of carrying out the procedure, he or she will not be found negligent even though it is subsequently decided that there is a preferable way of performing the procedure. It also means that if a doctor is acting in an emergency, it will be taken into account in deciding whether or not they were acting negligently.

3.14 The medical professional is only expected to demonstrate the level of skill of a person in their profession. So a GP would not be expected to demonstrate the same diagnostic skill as a specialist in a particular condition. That said, no concession is made for a professional who is inexperienced or exhausted. If you put yourself forward as a professional of a certain standing you must live up to the standards expected, regardless of your personal circumstances. You cannot justify your negligence on the basis that you were exhausted after a long shift, or were distracted because your partner had left you.

Debates over *Bolam*

3.15 The debates over whether the *Bolam* test is appropriate will be presented as two speakers presenting different views.

Speaker 1 (opposing Bolam*)*

3.16 We must oppose the *Bolam* test. In effect, it means that if a defendant can find a doctor friend who says that the way the defendant acted was appropriate, he can escape liability (Teff 1998). This encourages nepotism. Worse, it means that it is doctors rather than the law who decide what is negligent. The law should set the standards of acceptable medical practice and if the doctors fall below that it should not be any defence that other doctors would be just as bad. It should be the same as with driving: if a driver drives dangerously he or she is negligent, even if there were plenty of other equally dangerous drivers around.

3.17 The test is particularly harsh for claimants. How can one know whether there is a group of doctors somewhere who might find what the defendant did acceptable? Even if one obtains the advice of several eminent doctors that what the defendant did was negligent, this is no guarantee of success. Given the huge costs involved, it is unfair to structure the test for negligence in such a way that it is almost impossible to know if one has a successful claim or not.

Speaker 2 (supporting Bolam*)*

3.18 First, Speaker 1 seems to have exaggerated the nature of the *Bolam* test. It is not enough just to find a doctor friend who will support you. *Bolitho* has made it clear that the body of opinion supporting the defendant must be responsible and reasonable (see Woolf 2001).

3.19 The *Bolam* test is the only realistic approach to take. If a judge is faced with two eminent schools of medical practice, he cannot be expected to decide which is right and which is negligent. Judges can be expected to do that of everyday practices such as driving, but in relation to something as complex as medicine that is unrealistic. In any event, if there are two responsible bodies of medical opinion, is it not entirely sensible for the law to say that it is not negligent to follow either. Turning *Bolam* on its head, it would be very harsh to say to a doctor who had followed a responsible body of medical opinion: 'You are negligent because I, the judge, prefer another doctor's view.'

3.20 In fact, there is a lot to be said for encouraging diverse medical practice. If doctors are encouraged to try out novel techniques and alternative practices, this will work for the good of all patients. If all doctors must follow a single approved line in medical practice, then medicine will not be able to develop and respond to new technologies (see Teff 1998).

Causation

3.21 It would be an error to think that the case is won once it is shown that the doctor is negligent. It must also be shown that the negligence caused loss. The key question is the 'but for' test:

> Would the claimant have suffered the loss if the defendant had not acted negligently?

3.22 A good example of this was *Barnett* v. *Chelsea and Kensington HMC* [1968] 1 All ER 1068. There, a man attended casualty complaining of stomach pains. The doctor refused to see the patient and the patient died shortly afterwards. While it was accepted that the doctor was negligent in refusing to see the patient, even if the doctor had seen the patient it was unlikely that the doctor would have been able to save his life. The negligence did not, therefore, cause the death.

The burden of proof

3.23 The claimant must demonstrate that on the balance of probabilities that negligence caused the injury.

> ***Wilsher* v. *Essex AHA* [1988] 1 All ER 871** A baby suffered blindness. It was unclear whether it was caused by the premature birth or by the negligent care given by the medical team. The claimant failed because he could not show on the balance of probabilities that the harm was caused by the negligence.

This decision appeared to set out a straightforward approach, but it has been called into question in *Bailey* v. *Ministry of Defence* [2008] EWCA 883, where it was held that it would be enough if the claimant can show that the negligence was a material cause, even where it was not the only cause, of the injury. So it seems that the position is that *Wilsher* applies in cases where it is not shown that the negligence played a role at all. Where it can be shown that it was at least a cause then the claimant will have established causation.

> ***Bailey* v. *Ministry of Defence* [2008] EWCA Civ 883** Ms Bailey was a patient in a hospital managed by the Ministry of Defence. She had an unsuccessful procedure to remove a gallstone. There was a lack of care and she was not diagnosed as suffering from pancreatitis. She later breathed in vomit, leading to a cardiac arrest and brain damage. The judge found that the cause of the breathing in of the vomit was her

weakness, but that the negligent lack of post-operative care was a material contribution to her weakness. The judge held that it was therefore open to find the Ministry of Defence liable. The Ministry of Defence appealed, claiming that it would need to be shown that but for their negligence the brain damage would not have happened.

The Court of Appeal held that the lack of care from the hospital was a material contribution to the brain injury and that was sufficient to form the basis of a claim in tort. It was enough that the contribution had been shown on the balance of probabilities to be more than a negligible contribution to the cause of the injury. The defence would succeed if they could show that on the balance of probabilities the injuries would have occurred in any event as a result of the non-tortious causes.

3.24 It can get even more complex. In *Bolitho* v. *City and Hackney HA* [1997] 4 All ER 771, a registrar was negligent in failing to attend to a patient with breathing difficulties. One argument was that even if she had attended the boy she may well have decided not to offer treatment and therefore it had not been shown that the negligence of the registrar had caused the loss. This was rejected on the basis that had she not offered treatment that would have been negligent and so causation was established.

Loss of a chance

3.25 The most difficult cases in this area of the law are those where the defendant has suffered the 'loss of a chance'. In such a case, the claimant is suggesting that the defendant's negligence deprived them of a chance to recover. To deal with such cases, the courts have developed some complex rules, governed by these leading cases:

Hotson v. E Berkshire AHA [1987] AC 750 A boy aged 13 was taken to hospital after he had fallen out of a tree and injured his hip. His injury was not properly diagnosed and so he was not offered the treatment that he should have been. The treatment would have had a 25 per cent chance of success. In other words, the treatment probably would not have improved the boy's condition, but it might have. The judge at first instance awarded him 25 per cent of the damages he would have received if the authority had caused the entire injury. However, the House of Lord held that the decision was misguided. The claimant could only claim the damages if the treatment was more likely than not to succeed. In other words, if the treatment had a greater than 50 per cent chance of success then the law assumes the treatment would have worked and he can get the damages for the illness. If the treatment had less than a 50 per cent chance of success he gets nothing.

> **Gregg v. Scott [2005] UKHL 2** Mr Gregg was worried about a lump under his arm and consulted Dr Scott. Dr Scott negligently failed to spot that the lump was a sign of cancer and told Gregg it was benign. Having heard expert evidence, the judge concluded that had Scott correctly diagnosed the cancer, treatment would have been available which would have provided a 42 per cent chance of success. As this was a less than 50 per cent chance of success, it was more likely than not that the treatment would not have provided a cure and therefore he could not obtain any damages. The majority of the House of Lords upheld this finding. The essential point was that it had not been shown on the balance of probabilities that the misdiagnosis caused the loss.

3.26 The issue has been addressed recently in the High Court of Australia, which took a similar approach to that taken in England.

> **Tabet v. Gett [2010] HCA 12** Reema Tabet was admitted to hospital suffering from headaches and nausea. Dr Gett saw her. Three days later a CT scan revealed a brain tumour. She claimed that the failure to order a brain scan earlier meant that she lost a 15 per cent chance of a better outcome.
>
> The Australian High Court accepted that Australian law had not recognized the loss of a chance claim unless there was establishment of an actual physical injury. In a tort case, unlike a contract case, the gist of the action is damage, rather than breach of promise. There were concerns that if a loss of a chance claim was recognized, this might encourage defensive medicine and have an adverse impact on the Medicare system.

3.27 These cases take an 'all-or-nothing' approach. If the 'lost chance of treatment' had a more than 50 per cent chance of success, it is assumed the treatment would have provided a cure and full damages are available. However, if it had less than a 50 per cent chance of success, then it is assumed that the treatment would have failed and so no damages are available.

3.28 Baroness Hale in *Chester* v. *Afshar* [2004] UKHL 41 rejected the argument that in a case where a chance of treatment was lost, the claimant should recover the percentage of their loss. So, where a defendant lost a 25 per cent chance of recovery from a condition which caused £100,000 of harm, they should recover £25,000. Baroness Hale pointed out that while such an approach had its attractions, there were also primary difficulties in it. First, that the damages would never in fact represent the real loss. Either the treatment would not have worked, in which case they were receiving too much, or the treatment would have succeeded, in which case they were receiving too little. As the emphasis of the law of tort was to compensate for loss or injury there was a major flaw in the percentage approach. The second argument is that to change the approach of the law would greatly increase the costs to the NHS. Many patients who currently obtained no damages would be entitled to claim a percentage of their loss.

Debates over the loss of a chance cases

Speaker 1 (opposing the current law)

3.29 The current approach of the courts is unacceptable. Consider two patients, both of whom suffer from the same condition and whose doctors fail to diagnose it in time. Had they been diagnosed properly, patient A would have had a 51 per cent chance of being cured, and had patient B been diagnosed on time he would have had a 49 per cent chance of being cured. A gets the full level of damages and B gets nothing. That would appear all the more unjust if, as is quite possible, B would have been cured of the condition, whereas in fact had A received the treatment it would have had no effect.

3.30 The major error in these cases is to fail to focus on the fact that the doctor has acted negligently. It may well be in A's and B's cases that he has made the same mistake. B's interests have suffered a major setback. He has lost a good chance of a cure. No one would choose to lose the chance of a cure. The failure of the law to recognize that as a loss fails to accord with popular understanding of a loss. Indeed, the fact that people with serious illnesses will pay large sums of money for a chance of a cure, even if it is less than 50 per cent, suggests people do regard the chance of a treatment as being of economic value.

3.31 It is notable that in *Chester* v. *Afshar*, the House of Lords made the important point that a doctor who fails to inform a patient of a risk associated with a treatment should not be able to breach his duty and then escape payment of damages. Otherwise, that will mean that the law is failing to protect patients' rights and failing to uphold doctors' obligations. However, the failure to recognize the loss in *Gregg* made exactly that failure (see Green 2006).

3.32 The answer is obvious and it is that recognized by the minority in *Gregg* v. *Scott*, which is to accept the notion of a loss of chance and to give patients a percentage of the damages. Although it might be said that this will give either too much or too little, in fact it will represent exactly the loss the patient suffered: the chance of a treatment. After all, we can never know what would actually have happened if the correct diagnosis or treatment had been offered. The awarding of a percentage of loss is the best we can do.

Speaker 2 (supporting the current law)

3.33 There is no doubt that the current law can produce some apparently anomalous results, especially with patients whose chances of successful treatment are close to 50 per cent. However, the approach taken by the court accords with the key principles of tort law and has much in practice to recommend it.

3.34 Tort law is based on the principle of compensation for loss and not punishment of wrongdoing. If a medical professional is very negligent, but fortunately that does not cause a loss, it is not the job of tort law to recognize this in damages. There may be issues of professional regulation that arise and not tort law. In a case (such as *Gregg* v. *Scott*) where a doctor fails to make a diagnosis and that deprives the patient of a 42 per cent chance of a successful treatment, we cannot know what would have happened had the treatment been provided. However, the most likely result from the evidence available is that the treatment would not have been successful. It is therefore not unreasonable for the law to take that approach. We must remember as lawyers that we never know with 100 per cent certainty the facts of a case. We have to make a deduction from the evidence available and produce the best legal response available. It's not perfect, but it's the best we can do.

3.35 There are important practical points that must be made, too. First, as Baroness Hale in *Gregg* v. *Scott* made clear, the difficulty with the proposed approach is that it will work against the interests of some patients. If a patient has an 80 per cent chance of a successful treatment, but that chance is lost through negligence, under the proposal they would receive 80 per cent of their damages. However, if only 80 per cent of the damages are available for the payment of his or her care or loss of wages, there will be 20 per cent uncompensated for, even though it is very likely that they were caused by the negligence. Indeed, if we take up the loss of a chance approach, nearly every claim will be have to be reduced as it is rarely 100 per cent certain that a loss was caused by the negligence. Trials will become increasingly complex and last longer, as will negotiations, as the sides battle out the precise percentage likelihood that the negligence caused the loss.

3.36 Second, there must be concerns about the burden of changes in the law to the NHS. Already it pays out vast sums to patients in compensation for negligence, any change in the law's approach that might increase that should not be supported.

Damages

3.37 Once it is found that the defendant's negligence caused the defendant a loss, the court will assess the level of damages that are payable. There is a substantial body of law on calculating damages in negligence cases. Indeed, whole books are taken up on the subject. Medical law courses normally don't require a detailed knowledge of the law, so only a summary will be provided here.

3.38 The key elements of an award of damages in a clinical negligence claim are the following:

- A figure for the loss of the body part or body function: the cases have developed standard sums for certain injuries.
- Damages for pain and suffering caused by the negligence.
- Loss of earnings as a result of the injury: in the case of high earners, this is the largest head of damages.
- Loss of amenity: damages for the loss of being able to engage in activities which the claimant previous enjoyed doing.
- Expenses suffered as a result of the injuries: normally, a patient will receive any medical treatment they need free on the NHS. However, there may be other expenses, including private medical costs that can be recovered.

3.39 Finding the correct level of damages is highly problematic. For one thing, there are some injuries that it is hard to put a sum of money on. What figure correctly represents the loss of an eye, for example? We are often talking about things that cannot be measured in monetary terms. For another, the courts often have to calculate the losses into the future. This will involve guesswork. There have been cases where damages have been awarded on the basis that the patient will need many years of care, but they have unexpectedly died shortly afterwards. One solution to the uncertainties of the future is to award structured settlements where future costs are paid in annual instalments, and can be varied if the claimant's condition worsens or improves. The difficulty is that this means that for both parties the dispute can be hanging over them for years to come.

3.40 One way of restricting damages is to claim that they are too remote. This requires an extent to which the particular kind of damage was foreseeable. The issue was raised in this case:

***R v. Croydon Health Authority* (1997) 40 BMLR 40** The respondent trained as a nurse for those with mental disorders. She applied for a job as a community nurse. Before being employed she was required to undertake a medical examination, which included a chest X-ray. The X-ray revealed a primary pulmonary hypertension, which has a risk of sudden death in pregnancy. The radiologist did not report this either to the respondent or to the potential employer. The respondent started employment, but became pregnant and suffered from hypertension. Fortunately, the baby was born in good health. However, the respondent suffered from depression. The health authority accepted liability for the problems she suffered during the pregnancy and for pain and suffering during the pregnancy. However, it denied being responsible for the loss of earnings due to the birth and subsequent illness or the costs of the child.

It was held that the respondent had given birth to a healthy baby and so the costs of the child could not be recovered. The damages for the pregnancy per se and the cost of bringing up the child were too remote from the scope of the radiologist's duty. Damages were limited to the harm caused by the hypertension and the complications it caused during the pregnancy.

Reduction of award

3.41 There are two ways that an award might be reduced. First, if the patient was contributorily negligent. This would be rare in the context of clinical negligence (Herring and Foster 2009). It might arise if a patient failed to disclose a relevant fact to the doctor and the doctor failed to ask about it. In such a case, it might be found that both the patient and the doctor were negligent and in such a case the patient's damages will be reduced by the proportion to which the patient was to blame. Such a claim could also be made if the patient had suffered an injury as a result of a doctor's negligence but the extent of the injury was increased due to the patient's own negligence (for example, in returning to work too early).

3.42 Second, damages may be reduced if the patient has not mitigated their loss. There is a general duty in tort law on claimants to take reasonable steps to reduce or limit the harm they suffer. An obvious example would be a patient who is harmed by a botched operation. If they then failed to agree to any medical treatment and this then caused their condition to worsen, they would not be entitled to the further losses caused by the failure to receive that treatment.

The problems with the current system

3.43 There are few people who find the current law on medical negligence adequate. Even its supporters accept it is the best of a bad lot of alternatives. The current system costs vast sums of money. In 2009, the NHS Litigation Authority spent nearly £40 million on legal costs dealing with negligence litigation. That is before we start looking at the sums awarded. It is not only expensive in terms of costs, it involves medical professionals in time and stress, when it might be better that they are spending time treating patients. The threat of litigation inhibits doctors from being open about mistakes and learning from them. It also creates stress for patients, which may impede their recovery.

3.44 Such concerns have led to the NHS Redress Act 2006. The Act has not yet come into force. It is designed to deal with claims involving less than £20,000. In effect, the Act requires the setting up of a scheme, separate from the courts, to deal with small claims. The aim is that a tribunal will hear any minor complaints and deal with them by requiring an apology or explanation or the payment of money. It is not proposed that this should replace court actions, but that it should be an alternative to them. It remains to be seen how successful such a scheme would be. Some have proposed a more radical alternative: a 'no fault' scheme.

No-fault schemes for medical negligence

3.45 A no-fault system would mean that a patient who suffered an injury after a medical mishap would be entitled to damages, whether or not they could show that the doctor was to blame. This change would be particularly significant in cases where, although a patient was in a significantly worse state following an operation, it could not be shown exactly why this was or whether the doctor was negligent in the *Bolam* sense. While this would undoubtedly increase the amounts that would need to be paid out, it would decrease the legal costs, as supporter's claim there would be fewer issues a court would need to address.

3.46 England's Chief Medical Officer in the report *Making Amends*, discussed the possibility of a no-fault scheme but dismissed claims that it could cost up to £28 billion. In short, whatever arguments there were in favour of it, it was unaffordable. But that argument should not be seen to mean that the proposal is dead in the water. First, it should be noted that New Zealand operates a no-fault scheme for medical mishaps. While not without its difficulties, it shows that it is perfectly possible for a country to develop a no-fault system. Second, it should be recalled that where there is a medical mishap and there is an injury causing losses, the losses fall somewhere. If there is not a no-fault scheme then the loss falls on the individual or their family. So, we should be discussing, where should the losses caused by medical mishaps fall? The state may not be able to afford the cost, but can the individual victims?

3.47 A rather different concern about a no-fault system of compensation is that it might deprive the law of a way of holding to account a doctor who acts negligently. As Merry and McCall Smith (2001) argue, there is a role for the law in allocating blame for those who fall below expected standards. It may well be that the current system does not do that very well, but at least it tries to recognize that there is blame, which a no-fault system is in danger of overlooking.

3.48 An even more radical solution would be to abolish compensation claims against the NHS altogether and use the money saved to increase benefits for those with disabilities and their carers. Rather than using the pot of money to benefit significantly just a small section of the disabled population, it could be spread more equally among all those with a disability. A child with an horrific disability has need for state support whether that injury was the result of a genetically inherited condition or medical negligence or a mishap.

Regulation by professional bodies and the NHS

3.49 It is important to view the law on clinical negligence alongside the law on professional regulation. The job of clinical negligence law is to compensate patients who are harmed as a result of inappropriate medical conduct. The job of professional regulation is to deal with professional misconduct by way of punishment or retraining. Of course, it may be that a doctor who negligently harms a patient will face proceedings under clinical negligence and also face disciplinary proceedings by a professional body such as the General Medical Council. However, it is quite possible only to face professional regulatory procedures. It may be that the patient who was harmed does not wish to bring legal proceedings. It may be that although the doctor behaved badly, no harm was in fact done and so no damages would be payable. Nevertheless, it might be appropriate for the doctor to be dealt with under rules of professional regulation.

3.50 The law on professional regulation has been changed by the Health and Social Care Act 2008, which creates the Office of the Health Professional Adjudicator (OHPA), which will take over the role of the GMC in professional regulation. The GMC is the doctors' own professional body and traditionally they regulate their fellow professionals. So, the law is currently in a state of flux as the OHPA takes over from the GMC. The doctor could be erased from the medical register, so they cannot practice as a doctor, or they could be restricted in what areas they can practice, or they can be required to be retrained. Other punishments might be a warning or requiring that they be supervised for a certain period of time.

CONCLUSION

This chapter has considered the difficult issue of how to respond to cases where a medical professional has acted wrongly. There is widespread agreement that the current law does not work well. There is so much about medicine that we don't know that it makes it extremely difficult to prove what caused a particular loss. Even if the causation can be shown, there is little agreement of what counts as acceptable medical treatment. The difficulties over the law have produced an expensive and slow system of clinical negligence. Perhaps the best argument in favour of the current system is that the alternatives seem hardly preferable.

FURTHER READING

Bartlett, P. (1997) 'Doctors as Fiduciaries: Equitable Regulation of the Doctor–Patient Relationship', *Medical Law Review* 5: 193–224.

Brazier, M., and Allen, N. (2007) 'Criminalising Medical Malpractice', in C. Erin and S. Ost (eds), *The Criminal Justice System and Health Care* (Oxford: Oxford University Press), pp. 49–96.

Brazier, M., and Miola, J. (2000) 'Bye-Bye Bolam: A Medical Litigation Revolution', *Medical Law Review* 8: 85–114.

Douglas, T. (2009) 'Medical Compensation: Beyond "No Fault"', *Medical Law Review* 17: 30–51.

Green, S. (2006) 'Coherence of Medical Negligence Cases: A Game of Doctors and Purses', *Medical Law Review* 14: 1–21.

Hedley, S. (2011) *Tort Law* (Oxford: Oxford University Press).

Herring, J., and Foster, C. (2009) 'Blaming the Patient: Contributory Negligence in Medical Malpractice Litigation', *Journal of Professional Negligence* 25: 76–90.

Khoury, L. (2006) *Uncertain Causation in Medical Liability* (Oxford: Hart).

Merry, A., and McCall Smith, A. (2001) *Errors, Medicare and the Law* (Cambridge: Cambridge University Press).

Miola, J. (2007) *Medical Ethics and Medical Law* (Oxford: Hart), ch. 4.

National Patient Safety Agency (NPSA) (2009) *Patient Safety Incident Reports in the NHS, 2009* (London: NPSA).

Quick, O. (2006) 'Outing Medical Errors: Questions of Trust and Responsibility', *Medical Law Review* 14: 22–43.

Samanta, A., Mello, M., Foster, C., Tingle, J., and Samanta, J. (2006) 'The Role of Clinical Guidelines in Medical Negligence Litigation: A Shift from the *Bolam* Standard?', *Medical Law Review* 14: 321–66.

Teff, H. (1998) 'The Standard of Care in Medical Negligence—Moving on from *Bolam*', *Oxford Journal of Legal Studies* 18: 473–84.

Woolf, Lord (2001) 'Are the Courts Excessively Deferential to the Medical Profession?', *Medical Law Review* 9: 1–16.

SELF-TEST QUESTIONS

1 Is the *Bolam* test a good one?

2 Brian goes to a hospital and is seen by a nurse. The nurse fails to spot the severity of his condition and so does not immediately refer him to a doctor. He dies shortly afterwards. An expert gives evidence that there was a 60 per cent chance that even if Brian had been referred to a doctor, the doctor would not have spotted the severity of the condition either. Can a successful claim for negligence be brought against the nurse?

3 Would a no-fault system for medical mishaps be preferable to a fault-based one?

4

Consent

SUMMARY

This chapter will consider the role played by consent in medical law. A key legal principal is that a patient with capacity should not be treated without their consent. The Mental Capacity Act 2005 has a complex test which is used to determine whether a patient has capacity to make the decision. Children are generally assumed to lack capacity to make a decision unless it can be shown they are sufficiently mature to make it.

Where a patient does not have capacity, decisions are made on that patient's behalf based on what is in their best interests. While a patient with capacity has the right to refuse treatment, that does not mean a patient has the right to demand tretment. A doctor is always entitled to decide that treatment should not be given.

4.1 It is a cardinal principle of law that a medical professional may only provide treatment to a patient with their consent. To give treatment to a competent patient without their consent could amount to a criminal offence and/or a tort. To have capacity to be able to consent, a person must have a sufficient understanding of the issues to be able to reach a decision about treatment. If a patient lacks capacity then they must be treated in a way which promotes their best interests, as set out in the Mental Capacity Act 2005 (MCA). As we shall see, the notion of best interests is complex and it can be controversial. The 2005 Act does allow people to create an advance directive which will set out what treatment can be offered to them if in the future they lack capacity.

Introduction: the requirement of consent

4.2 One of the cornerstones of medical law is that a competent patient cannot be treated without their consent. Even if a health professional believes that a patient is refusing to consent to treatment for the most foolish of reasons, and even if without the treatment the patient will die, the patient's right to refuse treatment must be respected. The following dramatic case shows these principles well:

> **St George's Healthcare NHS Trust v. S [1998] 3 All ER 673** A woman in labour was told that she needed a Caesarean section. Without it her life and that of her fetus were in danger. She refused consent to the operation, wanting a natural birth. The doctors performed the operation anyway, thereby saving her life and producing a healthy baby. She sued and the Court of Appeal confirmed that the doctors had acted unlawfully. She was competent and so had the right to refuse treatment. The fact that she was pregnant did not affect her capacity.

4.3 Consent does not need to be in writing. It is common before major surgery for a patient to be asked to sign a consent form, but that is not in fact necessary as a matter of law. Consent can be oral and even implied. So, if a doctor tells a patient that he wants to take a mouth swab and the patient opens his mouth wide, that may be taken as consent even though the patient may not have explicitly said he consented to the procedure. However, care must be taken with implied consent. Positive consent is required, a medical professional should not simply rely on the fact that a patient failed to object to treatment as evidence that she consented.

4.4 If a medical professional performs a procedure on a competent patient without their consent, that can amount to a criminal offence (e.g. an assault occasioning actual bodily harm, Offences Against the Person Act 1861, s. 47) or a tort (e.g. a battery). These offences are discussed in Padfield (2010). Forcing treatment on a patient may also involve an interference with their right not to suffer torture or inhuman or degrading treatment under Article 3 of the European Convention on Human Rights (ECHR). If a doctor, knowing that a patient does not consent, then provides medical treatment to that patient this could amount to an assault or an offence under the Offences Against the Person Act 1861. Crucially, these offences require proof that the defendant intended or foresaw that he would be unlawfully harming the victim. So, a doctor who incorrectly decided that the patient was lacking capacity and that she was therefore authorized to perform the procedure, would not be committing the offence. It is very rare for doctors to be charged with criminal offences. The two most common kinds of criminal charges involve cases where a person has committed a sexual assault rather than providing medical treatment (*R* v. *Tabassum* [2000] 2 Cr App R 328) or where the person has caused harm after pretending to be a medical professional when they are not (*R* v. *Richardson* [1999] QB 444).

4.5 While a patient has the right to refuse treatment, that does not mean that a patient has the right to demand treatment. A doctor is entitled to refuse to give treatment that a patient has requested. That may be based on a rationing decision (see Chapter 2) or because she believes it to be treatment which will harm a patient. If the decision not to treat is unreasonable, it is just possible a doctor could face a criminal charge, but that would be most unusual. It might apply if the doctor decided not to treat a relative so that they would die and he would inherit their wealth.

4.6 Where a doctor believes that they are acting lawfully, they are likely to have a defence to any criminal charge. In a case where a patient has not consented it is more likely that a tort action may follow (see Hedley 2011). Here, an important distinction is drawn between the tort of battery and the tort of negligence. The tort of battery can be used where the essential claim is that the medical professional did not have the consent of the patient. The tort of negligence would be more appropriate where it is said that the doctor did not act in accordance with an accepted body of medical opinion (see Chapter 3). The tort of battery is very rarely used in medical law, and where there is a dispute over whether or not there was consent, it is usually the tort of negligence that is relied upon. That may be because claiming that a patient did not consent carries with it overtones that a crime has been committed.

Is it ever permissible to treat a patient without consent?

4.7 As we have seen in *St George's* v. *S* (see 4.2), the Court of Appeal confirmed the principle that a competent patient cannot be operated on without their consent, whatever harm may result from that. Does that mean that it is always unlawful to operate on a competent patient without consent? Not quite. There are a small number of situations where the procedure can be performed even without consent.

- 'Everyday touching' will not amount to an offence. So, jostling someone in the street or a handshake will not amount to a battery (*Collins* v. *Wilcock* [1984] 3 All ER 374).

- A patient detained under the Mental Health Act 1983 can be given treatment for mental disorder.

- If a patient has a notifiable disease, such as cholera or typhus, she or he can be ordered to be detained under the Public Health (Control of Disease) Act 1984. This power is very rarely exercised.

- In *Robb* v. *Home Office* (1994) 22 BMLR 43, Justice Thorpe (as he then was) suggested that in some cases it could be appropriate to force-feed a prisoner if that was necessary to preserve life or protect innocent third parties. However, that was before *St George's* v. *S* and it seems unlikely that what Justice Thorpe said would still be true. That said, it may be that in very exceptional cases, a court would be willing to require a person to be touched against their will, if for example there was a major outbreak of a disease. We do allow those who have been arrested to be searched for drugs or dangerous objects without their consent, and so in other areas of the law we are not as precious about the right to bodily integrity as medical lawyers seem to be.

- If a person is attempting to commit suicide, it is permissible to intervene to prevent them from succeeding (*Savage* v. *South Essex Partnership* [2008] UKHL 274).

The principle of autonomy

4.8 To many medical ethicists, the legal requirement of consent reflects the principle of autonomy (see Chapter 1). It is for the patient to decide whether they want to receive treatment, not the doctor. Individuals should be free to make decisions for themselves, and, providing they have capacity, other people should not make decisions for them. However, as we have just seen, the principle of autonomy is only protected in the law to a limited extent. It does not mean that a doctor must give the treatment a patient demands. In other words, the law protects the right to say 'no' to treatment very strongly; but it gives relatively little weight to the right to say 'yes'.

Who must consent?

4.9 Where a patient is competent their consent is required. No one else's consent will do. A husband is not permitted to consent on behalf of his wife, for example. However, it would be permissible for a person to exercise their autonomy and follow another person's views. So, a wife could consent by agreeing with her husband that she should have treatment. However, a medical professional would need to be sure that the patient was expressing their own views and was not suffering undue influence. In the case of children and incompetent adults, it is possible for someone to have legal authority to consent on their behalf. More on that later.

What is consent?

4.10 There are three main aspects to consent:

- A person must have mental capacity to be able to consent.
- A person must be sufficiently informed to be able to consent.
- A person must be free from undue influence and be able to consent.

Mental capacity

4.11 The starting point is that everyone is presumed to have mental capacity (MCA, s. 1(2)). A person must not assume another lacks capacity because of their age or appearance (MCA, s. 2(3)). So prejudice should not be used to lead to an assumption that someone lacks capacity. Section 2(1) of the MCA states that

> a person lacks capacity in relation to a matter if at the material time he is unable to make a decision for himself in relation to the matter because of an impairment of, or a disturbance in the functioning of, the mind or brain.

Notice that a person only lacks capacity if they suffer from an impairment or disturbance in the functioning of the brain. This would include mental illness, dementia, learning disabilities, and drunkenness. But it would not include the fact that someone is simply eccentric or has unusual views. Indeed, section 1(4) of the Mental Capacity Act 2005 states that 'A person is not to be treated as unable to make a decision merely because he makes an unwise decision.'

4.12 Mental capacity is 'issue specific'. That means that someone may lack the capacity to make some decisions, but not others. A person may, for example, lack the capacity to consent to a complex medical procedure, but have the capacity to be able to decide what kind of ice cream they would like to have. It is wrong, therefore, to talk generally about a person 'who lacks capacity'. It all depends on what the question is. There will, of course, be a small number of people who lack the capacity to make any decisions at all (e.g. if they are in a coma.)

> *Re MM* **[2007] EWHC 2003 (Fam)** M was aged 39. She suffered from paranoid schizophrenia and had significant learning difficulties. She had formed a relationship with K, who also suffered a psychopathic disorder and was an alcoholic. M's social workers thought that K was a bad influence on her. In part this was because he encouraged her not to take her medication and to livee rough. The local authority sought an order to protect M.
>
> It was held that M lacked the capacity to make decisions about herself and where she should live and with whom, although she did have the capacity to consent to sexual relations. There was need to balance M's rights to protection with her rights to respect for her private life, both of which were covered by Article 8 of the ECHR. The correct balance was that M and K could have contact for a minimum of four hours a week, although M was to live in accommodation provided by the local authority. This was to be unsupervised so that they could engage in sex.

4.13 MCA, s. 3(1) provides further guidance on the meaning of incapacity:

> a person is unable to make a decision for himself if he is unable—
>
> (a) to understand the information relevant to the decision,
>
> (b) to retain that information,
>
> (c) to use or weigh that information as part of the process of making the decision, or
>
> (d) to communicate his decision (whether by talking, using sign language or any other means).

4.14 There are a number of elements to capacity decisions. A patient only has capacity if he or she understands the information relevant to the decision.

> *Re C (Adult: Refusal of Treatment)* **[1994] 1 WLR 290** A prisoner was found to have a gangrenous foot. He was told by his doctors that if he did not agree to have his foot amputated he would probably die. He refused to consent because he disagreed with the views of the doctors. He believed he was an excellent foot doctor and that he would survive. He also believed that God would heal him.
>
> Thorpe J held that as he understood the diagnosis of the doctors, and accepted that they were truthfully expressing their views, he understood the relevant information.

The fact that he disagreed with their conclusion did not mean that he was therefore lacking capacity. He was therefore entitled to refuse treatment (strangely, despite the doctors' prognosis, the foot recovered and he lived to tell his tale!). Although that case was decided prior to the MCA coming into force, it is likely that the same result would be reached under the 2005 Act.

4.15 It is important to note that, even though a patient does not understand a relevant piece of information, they do not necessarily lack capacity. That is because a person should not be treated as lacking capacity 'unless all practical steps to help him' reach capacity 'have been taken without success' (MCA Code of Practice). That may involve explaining the things a patient does not understand in simple terms, or even by using sign language or other means of communication.

4.16 Precisely how much information must a person understand before they have capacity to consent? Do they need to understand every aspect of their medical condition and its proposed treatment? Of course not, otherwise you would need a medical degree to be able to consent to any complex surgery. The law is that a patient must understand 'in broad terms the nature of the procedure which is intended' (*Chatterton* v. *Gerson* [1981]). This is not a tough test to satisfy. As long as the patient understands generally what is happening they will be treated as having sufficient understanding to consent. They do not need to know all the gory details.

> **Chatterton v. Gerson [1981] 1 All ER 257** Mrs Chatterton suffered pain as a result of a trapped nerve. Dr Gerson, who specialized in pain management, performed an operation to relieve the pain. He failed to inform her that the operation carried a small risk of permanently affecting the mobility of her leg. Unfortunately, the operation caused permanent immobility in the leg. Mrs Chatterton said that had she been informed of the risk, she would not have agreed to the operation. She sought damages in the tort of battery.
>
> It was held that the claim should be dismissed. She had been informed of the broad nature of the procedure. She was aware it was an operation on her right leg. The failure to disclose the risk of paralysis was not sufficient to mean that she did not consent.
>
> **R v. Tabassum [2000] 2 Cr App R 328** A man purported to be a doctor and a number of women agreed to have their breasts examined by him. In fact, he was examining them simply for his own purposes (presumably sexual). It was found that they had not given consent to the examinations because he had misled them as to the nature and quality of the examinations.

4.17 Capacity, however, involves more than just understanding the information: the person must be able to use that information to make a decision. Where, for example, a person subject to panic attacks whenever the nurse approaches with a needle refuses to consent to an injection, it may be that they are so overcome with panic that they are unable to weigh up the information to make a decision (*Bolton NHS Trust* v. *O* [2002] EWHC 2871 (Fam)).

4.18 An important principle is found in MCA, s. 1(4):

> A person is not to be treated as unable to make a decision merely because he makes an unwise decision.

This does not mean that an irrational decision cannot be evidence of a lack of capacity (notice the statute uses the word 'merely'). It does, however, mean that a medical professional should not jump from the conclusion that the decision of a patient is bizarre to determining that the patient lacks capacity. As Butler Sloss J has held in *Re B (Consent to Treatment: Capacity)* [2002] EWHC 429 (Fam), 'The doctors must not allow their emotional reaction to or strong disagreement with the decision of the patient to cloud their judgment in answering the primary question whether the patient has the mental capacity to make the decision.' Hence, it is well established that an adult Jehovah's Witness can refuse a life-saving blood transfusion, even though others may regard their beliefs as bizarre.

4.19 A patient may be found to understand the information but lack capacity because they are suffering from coercion at the hands of another person. It would not be enough that a patient felt under pressure or uncomfortable making a decision. Often people feel a degree of pressure when they are deciding about medical treatment.

> **Re T (Adult: Refusal of Treatment)** [1992] 4 All ER 649 A young woman (T) had been raised as a Jehovah's Witness, but had not been involved in the religion for several years. She had been involved in a car accident and told that she needed a blood transfusion. It seemed, at first, that she was happy to consent, but following a visit from her mother 'out of the blue' she refused to consent.
>
> The Court of Appeal concluded that T's refusal was not an expression of her own independent decision, but was as a result of improper pressure from her mother. The decision was influenced, in part, by a finding that T was in a weakened and exhausted state.

It might be noted that *Re T* was decided prior to the Human Rights Act 1998. Just possibly the protection to religious rights (Article 9) and respect for private life (Article 8) would justify a different conclusion in that case were it to be heard today.

Children

4.20 In law, a child is a person under the age of 18 (Family Law Reform Act 1969, s. 1). However, section 8 of the Family Law Reform Act 1969 states that a child can consent to treatment and that consent is to be treated in the same way as an adult. At one time it was thought that children under 16 simply lacked the capacity to be able to consent to medical treatment and that their parents had to consent on their behalf. However, this position was changed dramatically with the following decision:

> **Gillick v. West Norfolk Area Health Authority [1986] AC 112** Mrs Gillick was concerned about a Department of Health circular which permitted doctors to provide contraceptive advice and treatment to under-16-year-olds without parental permission. She argued that it should be unlawful for a doctor to treat an under-16-year-old without parental consent. The House of Lords ruled that where a doctor was providing medical treatment which had been determined to be in the child's best interests it could be provided to the child if she consented and was competent. This was true even if the parents had not consented. Indeed, the parents did not even need to be informed; indeed, doing so could breach the child's right to confidentiality.

Before discussing the significance of this case, one side issue needs to be dealt with. A question was raised in the case of whether or not a doctor providing contraception to an underage girl could be committing an offence of aiding and abetting a sexual offence. Their lordships thought not because she or he would not be intending the children to have sexual relations. The issue was put beyond doubt by section 73 of the Sexual Offences Act 2003, which makes it clear that a doctor providing contraceptive treatment or advice will not be guilty of an offence.

4.21 So, what is the significance of the decision in *Gillick*? It is clear that if a child is found to be competent (*Gillick* competent), she can consent to medical treatment without her parent's consent. Some commentators (e.g. Fortin 2009) have detected a difference between the approach of Lord Fraser and that of Lord Scarman in that Lord Fraser emphasized that the treatment could only be offered to a child patient if that treatment was determined to be in the child's best interests, but Lord Scarman did not refer to the best interests requirement. This difference should not be exaggerated. Lord Scarman may well not have mentioned the best interests requirement because it seems obvious. Surely a doctor should not and would not provide harmful treatment: that hardly needs saying. If there is a difference, maybe it relates to medical advice or treatment which is neutral: not harmful, but not beneficial either. Maybe Lord Scarman would permit a doctor to provide treatment, but Lord Fraser would not.

4.22　So what does it mean for a child to be *Gillick* competent? The overall test is whether the child has 'sufficient understanding and intelligence to enable him or her to understand fully what is proposed' (Lord Scarman, *Gillick*). The following are some of the factors the court must take into account:

- The child must understand the relevant medical issues. This means that they must understand what their current state of health is, the proposed treatment, any side effects of treatment, and the consequences of not having treatment. Controversially in *Re E* [1993] 1 FLR 386, a child was found to lack competence because she did not realize the manner of her death if she were to refuse treatment. The case is controversial because the doctors had decided not to tell her how she would die for fear of causing her worry. It seems unfair to be found lacking capacity on the basis that you do not have information the doctors have deliberately decided not to give you.

- The child must have views of their own, and not be simply reflecting the views of others. In some cases where the child has come from a strict religious background the court has not been convinced that the child had the maturity to express her own views. In *Re S* [1993] 1 FLR 376, for example, a child from a Jehovah's Witness family was not able to explain clearly why she did not want a blood transfusion and the court were not satisfied that she had reached a genuine independent decision and were concerned that she was simply reflecting the views of her parents.

- The child must understand the moral and family issues involved, as well as the medical ones. This point was emphasized in *Gillick*. That can be a tricky requirement. In relation to abortion, for example, to what extent must the child be aware of the complex ethical debates? Perhaps the most likely way that this is relevant is that the child must be aware of the possible impact of a decision on her family. It would be most unlikely for a child to have the capacity to understand the medical issues, but not the broader issues.

- The child's competence must be reasonably secure. In *Re R* [1991] 4 All ER 177, the child's understanding fluctuated in and out of competence. The Court of Appeal held that she could be treated as lacking capacity because her ability to understand was fluctuating.

- The court must not reason that because the child's decision is not one the court would make she therefore lacks capacity (*South Glamorgan CC* v. *B* [1993] 1 FLR 673). Despite this, many commentators have claimed that this is precisely how the courts have dealt with these issues (Fortin 2009).

4.23 Let us assume for the moment that it is decided that the child is competent, what if the child then refuses to consent? It might be thought that following the logic of *Gillick*, if a child has the maturity to make the decision, she should be able to refuse to consent to treatment. However, that is not how the case law has developed.

> *Re R* **[1991] 4 All ER 177** A 15-year-old girl was in care after a fight with her father. She suffered mental health problems and became increasingly disturbed. She was put in an adolescent psychiatric unit. While there the doctors sought permission from the local authority to administer anti-psychotic drugs to her. She objected to the administration of the drugs. The Court of Appeal ruled that her mental state was constantly fluctuating: she was *Gillick* competent at one moment and not the next. In such a case she should not be treated as *Gillick* competent. In any event, Lord Donaldson restricted the reasoning in *Gillick* to cases where the child consented to treatment. Their Lordships in *Gillick* had not addressed cases where the child refused treatment. Where a competent child was refusing treatment, the parents could provide effective consent to treatment, despite the child's refusal. So, in this case, even if R had been competent, the doctors could lawfully have provided treatment to her, relying on the consent of the local authority (who had parental responsibility).

> *Re W* **[1992] 4 All ER 627** W, aged 16, suffered from anorexia nervosa. Her condition was deteriorating and it was proposed she be moved from an adolescent residential unit to a hospital specializing in the treatment of eating disorders. W wished to remain where she was. Lord Donaldson used the analogy of the flak jacket to describe consent. He saw consent as providing a doctor with a 'flak jacket' from being sued. He explained that the flak jacket could be provided by either a *Gillick* competent child or a child aged 16 or 17, or by a person with parental responsibility or by a court. In this case, therefore the court could authorize W's treatment.

4.24 The current law, therefore, is that once a doctor has determined that treatment is in the best interests of the child, he or she can provide the treatment as long as consent is provided either by a child aged 16 or 17, a *Gillick* competent child, a person with parental responsibility, or a court. It should be noted that not all parents have parental responsibility, and that it is possible to have parental responsibility without being a parent. An unmarried father who is not registered as the father on the child's birth certificate will not have parental responsibility, unless he has obtained an order from the court granting it to him (Children Act 1989, s. 4). If the court has made a residence order in favour of someone, that will grant them parental responsibility. We can summarize the position as shown in Figure 4.1.

4.25 The current state of the law, as set out above, was recently challenged in the following decision where it was claimed that the law had changed following the Human Rights Act 1998.

> ***R (Axon) v. Secretary of State for Health* [2006] EWHC 37 (Admin)** A mother claimed that Department of Health guidelines, saying that an under-16-year-old girl could receive an abortion without the consent of her parents, were unlawful. In particular, that they infringed a parent's rights under Article 8 of the ECHR to respect

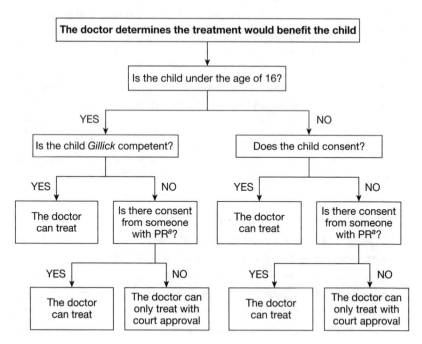

Figure 4.1 Consent and minor patients

Note: [a] *PR* Parental responsibility.

for her family life. Silber J rejected her claim, confirming that the approach taken by the House of Lords in *Gillick* represented the current law. He argued that once a child became *Gillick* competent their parents lose any rights under Article 8 to overrule the child's consent.

Where the court must determine disputes over treatment for children

4.26 If there is no consent from parents or children or there is disagreement, the matter must be taken to a court and the court would be required to make an order, unless there is an emergency (*Glass* v. *UK* [2004] 1 FCR 553). In that case, the court will make the order which best promotes the welfare of the child. Although the courts are willing to place weight on the wishes of the parents, at the end of the day the issue will be seen as one of the welfare of the child. In *Re E* [1993] 1 FLR 386 Ward LJ explained:

> Parents may be free to become martyrs themselves, but it does not follow that they are free in identical circumstances to make martyrs of their children.

Although parents can consent to treatment of children there are limits on their powers. First, the doctor must ensure that the treatment is in the best interests of the child. A doctor could not, for example, rely on parental consent to perform cosmetic surgery if he himself did not think it would promote the child's well-being. Second, there are certain procedures where the approval of the court is required. It is not quite clear which procedures are included. It is probably safe in the following cases to obtain the court's consent:

- Sterilizations for non-therapeutic reasons (i.e. those not medically required).
- Abortion (unless the girl is competent and consents).
- Donation of non-regenerative tissue (e.g. a kidney).
- Refusal of life-saving treatment.

The limits of consent?

4.27 If there is a doctor who is willing to provide the treatment and the patient consents, is there any limit to what treatment can be provided? As emphasized already, the courts have made it clear that just because a patient wants some form of extreme treatment, a doctor is entitled to refuse to provide it. There may be rationing reasons for refusing treatment or the doctor may think the treatment is not beneficial. But what if the doctor is willing to provide it? A good example may be the case of body dysmorphic disorder, where patients seek the removal of healthy limbs which they feel are not part of their body. Most doctors are not willing to provide surgery in a case like that, but some might be. Should it be allowed?

4.28 It might be thought that there should be no objection to it, if both the patient and doctor are willing to proceed. Should not we respect the autonomy of the parties? There is little case law on the issue but in *R v. Brown* [1993] 2 All ER 75, their Lordships stated that it was unlawful to cause another person actual bodily harm or a more serious injury, unless there was a public policy argument justifying the conduct. The actual case concerned sadomasochistic behaviour and their Lordships held (by a majority of 3 to 2) that there was no evidence to say that this benefited the public. By contrast, they thought that there was a public interest in surgery and so that could be permitted. But that leaves the issue of whether some forms of surgery may not be in the public interest. Removal of limbs of those suffering body dysmorphic disorder might be an example of surgery some people would regard as contrary to the public good (Elliott 2009). That said, we do allow cosmetic surgery and gender reassignment surgery. The issue is likely to come before the courts for a clear ruling in the near future.

Failure to provide information

What must be disclosed?

4.29 If a medical professional has not provided adequate information about a medical procedure, that may mean that the patient has not given an effective consent. However, there are cases where the failure to provide information is not such as to mean that there is no consent, because the patient has an understanding of the central nature of the procedure. Nevertheless, the failure to provide the information may mean that the doctor has failed to live up to the standard of a reasonable doctor. In such a case, a claim in negligence may be brought.

> **Sidaway v. Bethlem RHG [1985] 1 All ER 643** Mrs Sidaway's spinal cord had been damaged during an operation, leaving her paralyzed. She brought an action in negligence on the basis that the risks connected with the operation were not properly explained to her. There was no suggestion that the operation itself had been performed

improperly. Expert witnesses agreed that some, but not all, neurosurgeons would have regarded it as acceptable not to inform a patient of the risks of paralysis.

The majority of the House of Lords took the view that the *Bolam* test was appropriate. As long as the failure to inform of the risk was in line with a respectable body of medical opinion an action in negligence would not lie. However, there are indications among the speeches of the majority that there might be some skepticism over claims that a respectable body of opinion existed if the issue involved disclosure of a significant risk. Lord Bridge emphasized that the body of opinion must be respectable. He gave an example of a 10 per cent chance of a stroke being caused by a procedure. Lord Bridge said that no responsible body of medical opinion would hold that a doctor should not disclose such a risk. He held that in this case, as the risk of paralysis was small and there was a body of opinion in favour of non-disclosure, it did not have to be disclosed.

There were two powerful dissenting judgments. Lord Scarman took the view that patients had a right to decide whether or not to agree to treatment and that right could only be given effect to if they were given the relevant information that a reasonable patient would want. Lord Templeman, also dissenting, took the view that the doctor had to inform the patients of the nature of the procedure and any risks that were special to the patient. He held it was then up to the patient to decide whether to ask any further questions, which must be answered by the doctors.

4.30 Later cases seem to have emphasized Lord Bridge's approach: that it should not be assumed that just because some doctors would not have disclosed a risk there is no negligence (Miola 2009). Lord Woolf in *Pearce* v. *United Bristol Healthcare NHS Trust* (1998) 48 BMLR 118 emphasized that the medical opinion not to disclose a risk had to be both reasonable and responsible. Indeed, he suggested that, if there was a significant risk that would affect the judgement of the reasonable patient, then the patient should be informed of the risk. This sounds similar to the 'reasonable patient' test that Lord Scarman supported in the minority in *Sidaway*. Similar, but not quite the same. Lord Woolf referred to the need for the risk to be significant. So it seems that if it is not a significant risk, then even if it is one that a reasonable person would want to know about, it might not be negligent not to disclose it. Lord Steyn in *Chester* v. *Afshar* [2004] 4 All ER 587 also referred to a duty to warn a patient about 'possible serious risks involved in the procedure'. The current position seems to be, therefore, that the *Bolam* test generally applies, but that if a doctor has failed to disclose a significant risk it will be very difficult, perhaps impossible, to persuade the court that a responsible body of medical opinion would support non-disclosure.

***Pearce* v. *United Bristol Healthcare NHS Trust* (1998) BMLR 118** Mrs Pearce had a stillbirth of a baby girl. She claimed that earlier intervention by the medical team would have resulted in a live birth. She had seen a consultant, Mr Niven, when 14 days beyond her due date of delivery and begged to be induced or to have a Caesarean section. Mr Niven had recommended that the pregnancy be allowed to continue until a natural delivery was possible. Seven days later, the mother was admitted to hospital and there was no fetal heartbeat or movement. An ultrasound confirmed the fetus had died. Mr Niven, in discussing the case with Mrs Pearce, had not informed her of the stillbirth. Mrs Pearce was adamant that if she had been told of the risk (between 0.1 and 0.2 per cent) she would have insisted on a Caesarean section.

It was held that the doctor should inform the patient of a significant risk which would affect the judgement of a reasonable patient or of any risk the patient specifically asked about. One expert in this case had said that if the mother had not asked about the risk he did not think a reasonable doctor would mention it because it was a small risk, being less than 10 per cent. The court thought this correct, especially given the distressed state of the mother. The court also held that even if she had been informed of the risk she would still have followed Mr Niven's advice. The claim therefore failed.

4.31 Given the uncertainty in the law, many doctors may be wise to follow the Guidance of the General Medical Council (GMC) (2008), which states that doctors must give patients the information they want or need about

    (a) the diagnosis and prognosis

    (b) any uncertainties about the diagnosis or prognosis, including options for further investigations

    (c) options for treating or managing the condition, including the option not to treat

    (d) the purpose of any proposed investigation or treatment and what it will involve

    (e) the potential benefits, risks and burdens, and the likelihood of success, for each option; this should include information, if available, about whether the benefits or risks are affected by which organisation or doctor is chosen to provide care

    (f) whether a proposed investigation or treatment is part of a research programme or is an innovative treatment designed specifically for their benefit

    (g) the people who will be mainly responsible for and involved in their care, what their roles are, and to what extent students may be involved (*h*) their right to refuse to take part in teaching or research

(*i*) their right to seek a second opinion

(*j*) any bills they will have to pay

(*k*) any conflicts of interest that you, or your organisation, may have

(*l*) any treatments that you believe have greater potential benefit for the patient than those you or your organization can offer.

4.32 Simply disclosing the risk may not be sufficient to satisfy the legal obligation on health professionals. As was held in *Smith* v. *Tunbridge Wells HA* [1994] 5 Med LR 334, the medical professional has a duty to take reasonable steps to ensure that the patient understands the information. So, the court will not only consider whether the risks were disclosed but also whether they were disclosed in a way which made them comprehensible to the particular patient.

4.33 So far we have been looking at the general duty that a doctor may owe a patient. But what if the patient has asked a particular question? That would, of course, change the case. Then it seems that the doctor must provide an answer to the question in a reasonable way. Lord Bridge in *Sidaway* said that where a patient asked questions, these had to be answered truthfully and fully.

4.34 A difficult issue for patients suing after not being told of risks is causation: what loss has been caused by the failure to disclose of the risk? Unless they can show that they would not have agreed to undergo the treatment had they been informed of the risk, it will be very difficult to show that they should be entitled to damages.

> **Chester v. Afshar [2004] 4 All ER 587** Ms Chester was suffering lower back pain and Mr Afshar, a consultant, recommended an operation to remove spinal discs. Mr Afshar discussed the operation but had not revealed the risk of paralysis to Ms Chester, of some 1–2 per cent. It was agreed that this was a risk of which he should have informed her. She agreed to the operation, which was performed in an appropriate way, but sadly it led to severe pain and mobility difficulties for Ms Chester. The House of Lords held that she was entitled to damages for the injuries she suffered.

4.35 Although there was no difficulty in proving the negligence in this case (failing to disclose the serious risk), the problem was in finding that the negligence was the cause of the loss. For the majority, the key fact was that had Ms Chester been informed of the risk of paralysis, although she would still have agreed to the procedure she would have done so having taken some time for thought. This would have meant that she would have had the procedure several days later than she in fact did. Had she had the operation on a later occasion, she might well not have developed the paralysis. Their lordships also made the point that it was important that doctors who failed to disclose serious risks to their patients were liable and they felt that in this case, to allow the doctor to breach the duty but not be liable to pay damages would fail to protect the patient's rights. The minority feared that the majority were departing from a central aspect of the law of negligence: that it had to be shown that the negligence caused a loss. There was nothing in this case to suggest that there were fewer risks attached to the operation at the time it was done and the time it would have been done had the risk been disclosed.

4.36 It is important to appreciate the limits of this decision. Their Lordships did not decide that in every case where there is non-disclosure a patient will be able to recover damages. However, if a patient can show that had the risk been disclosed they would not have had the procedure at the time or place they had it then there was to be a claim. If the court decides that had the disclosure been made the patient would still have proceeded with the operation at the same time and place, then no damages would be awarded. You might think that that will be very common.

4.37 There is some suggestion in *Chester* v. *Afshar* that their Lordships might be willing to make an even more dramatic change in the case law. Lord Hope stated that the law of tort had to protect patients' rights to choose whether or not to have treatment. He went on:

> If it is to fulfill that function it must ensure that the duty to inform is respected by the doctor. It will fail to do this if an appropriate remedy is not given if the duty is breached and the very risk that the patient should have been informed about occurs and she suffers injury. (para. 61)

That seems to suggest a radical approach, namely that if there is not disclosure there should be damages awarded, even if it cannot be shown what loss occurred. The problem is that in a case of non-disclosure, the real loss may be the chance to make an informed decision (rather than the actual injury) and that is a rather vague concept, and certainly one on which it is hard to put a sum of money. The sum that may represent the injury caused by the operation might not accurately reflect the loss that the negligence caused (the loss of a chance to make an informed decision).

The right not to know

4.38 Some patients may not want to know the details of the procedure: they may not want to know the gory details! They simply want their doctor to do whatever is best and do not want the stress of being told all of the risks and given the information. The GMC Guidance states that

> If the patient insists that they do not want even this basic information, you must explain the potential consequences of them not having it, particularly if it might mean that their consent is not valid. You must record the fact that the patient has declined this information. You must also make it clear that they can change their mind and have more information at any time.

Charles Foster (2009) has complained that this goes too far. We need to respect the patients' decisions not to know the details of procedures. For him, the GMC Guidance suggests that doctors should try and pressurize them into agreeing.

The treatment of those lacking capacity

4.39 The law on adults who lack capacity is governed by the MCA. The Act opens with four key principles, found in section 1:

> (1) The following principles apply for the purposes of this Act.
>
> (2) A person must be assumed to have capacity unless it is established that he lacks capacity.
>
> (3) A person is not to be treated as unable to make a decision unless all practicable steps to help him to do so have been taken without success.
>
> (4) A person is not to be treated as unable to make a decision merely because he makes an unwise decision.
>
> (5) An act done, or decision made, under this Act for or on behalf of a person who lacks capacity must be done, or made, in his best interests.

If a person lacks capacity, the first issue is to determine who (or what) can make a decision concerning an individual lacking capacity. This is the list that applies:

- Advance decision
- Lasting power of attorney
- Deputy

- Person caring for the individual
- Court

Figure 4.2 sets out who should make the decision in a case involving a patient who lacks capacity.

Let us consider these separately.

Advance decision

4.40 The definition of an advance decision is found in section 24 of the MCA:

> 'Advance Decision' means a decision made by a person ('P'), after he has reached 18 and when he has capacity to do so, that if—
>
> (a) at a later time and in such circumstances as he may specify, a specified treatment is proposed to be carried out or continued by a person providing health care for him, and
>
> (b) at that time he lacks capacity to consent to the carrying out or continuation of the treatment, the specified treatment is not to be carried out or continued.

4.41 It is important to realize that there are many conditions that must be satisfied before an advance decision can be regarded as binding. Indeed, there are

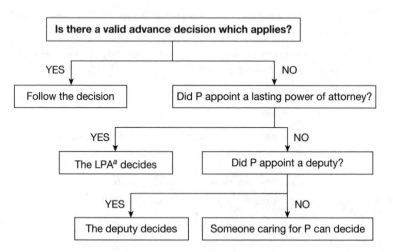

Figure 4.2 Decision-making for patients who lack capacity

Note: [a] LPA Lasting power of attorney.

so many restrictions on when it can apply that it has been suggested that it will be rare that an advance decision will be effective. These are the main requirements:

- When the decision was made P must have been competent and over 18.
- P must currently lack capacity.
- The decision only applies to refusal of treatment and does not apply to positive requests for treatment.
- According to the Code of Practice the decision cannot refuse consent to basic or essential care (e.g. cleaning or food).
- The advance decision must not have been withdrawn.
- P must not have created an LPA after the decision.
- If an advance decision is intended to reject life-saving treatment, the advance decision must explicitly state that it is to be respected even if as a result of it the person will die.
- P must not have done anything inconsistent with the decision (MCA, s. 25(2)(c)).
- The advance decision will not be binding if P had not foreseen matters of significance which have occurred since the making of the advance decision (MCA, s. 25(4)(c)).

4.42 It is these last two factors which offer the most scope for a doctor or court to decide that the advance decision does not apply. The following case (although decided before the Act came into force) gives an example of when it might be decided that P has acted in a way inconsistent with the decision.

> **HE v. A Hospital NHS Trust [2003] EWHC 1017** A patient had signed an advance decision stating that she did not want to receive a blood transfusion. She made it clear that she wanted her wishes followed even if that meant she would die. She made the advance directive while a Jehovah's Witness. However, since signing the advance decision she had ceased to be an active member of that religion and was, in fact, engaged to a Muslim. The court held the advance decision could no longer apply.

It remains to be seen how ready the court will be to find that things said, or changes in lifestyle, since the making of an advance directive will thereby render it invalid. Will family members be able to rely on vaguely remembered dinner conversations as evidence to show that the patient changed his or her mind since making the directive?

4.43 The last factor is significant, too. It will be easy to argue that there exist circumstances which P had not foreseen at the time he or she signed the decision:
there may be new forms of medication available, P may not be in as much pain
as he or she foresaw, or P may not have foreseen how strongly his or her family
opposes following the directive. Whether these will be accepted as sufficient
reasons for departing from the directive remains to be seen (see Michalowski
2005).

4.44 So, there are plenty of ways in which it is open to argue that an advance directive does not apply, but if all these hurdles are jumped, section 26 of the MCA
makes it clear that the refusal is to be treated as an effective refusal and so it
would be unlawful to ignore it. That said, section 26(2) explains that if a person
believes that the advance directive does not apply or does not realize there is an
advance directive, he or she will not incur liability. Perhaps surprisingly there is
no need for the belief to be a reasonable one. There are no cases applying these
provisions to date.

Lasting powers of attorney (LPAs)

4.45 If a person foresees that they will be losing capacity, then they might choose
to make a lasting power of attorney (LPA) (MCA, s. 9). This will appoint someone to make decisions for them if they lost capacity. Someone might wish to
appoint their spouse or child as a donee of an LPA, for example. The donee of an
LPA must be over 18 years of age. It is possible to appoint more than one donee.
An LPA can be revoked at any time while P has capacity.

4.46 The LPA only comes into effect when P loses capacity. The LPA must make
decisions based on what he or she thinks P's best interests are. They should not
ask what decisions they think P would make but rather what would promote P's
best interests. We will discuss this requirement shortly.

Deputies

4.47 If P loses capacity and has not made an advance decision and has not made an
LPA, the court may decide to appoint a deputy who would make decisions on
P's behalf (MCA, s. 19). The deputy can only act if P has lost capacity. It will
only be appropriate to appoint a deputy if there are likely to be a number of
issues concerning P that need to be discussed. If there is a single issue concerning P, then the court can deal with that as a one-off decision.

***G v. E (By His Litigation Friend the Official Solicitor)* [2010] EWHC 2512 (Fam)** E was 20 years old and lacked capacity to make most decisions. G and F were his carer and sister. They applied for orders that they be appointed deputies for his personal welfare and that G and an unidentified professional be deputy to deal with his property and affairs. G and F argued that if they were not appointed deputies they would not have a general authority to act for the purposes of the MCA. That constituted an interference with their right to respect for family life under Article 8 of the ECHR.

It was held that it would be inappropriate to appoint G and F as deputies. The vast majority of decisions were taken by carers and family members without formal authority. Section 5 allowed people caring for a person lacking capacity to act in accordance with what they reasonably believed would be in that person's best interests. It was best that decisions concerning those lacking capacity were taken informally and collaboratively by those interested working together. If there was disagreement or a particularly difficult or grave issue then an application could be made to the court. This meant that the appointment of deputies should be seen as limited to those where the case required regular management. Although it was 'axiomatic' that those who lacked capacity should be cared for by their family, that did not mean that a family member should automatically be appointed a deputy.

Other carers

4.48 If there is no LPA or deputy then decisions can be taken by P's carers based on P's best interests (MCA, s. 1). There is no need to consult the LPA, deputy, or court over every issue that concerns P. For day-to-day care issues, as long as those dealing with P act in accordance with his or her best interests, they will be acting lawfully.

Limits on the power of decision-makers

4.49 Where someone is making a decision on P's behalf, they must act in P's best interests. There are, however, limits on the kinds of decisions that these substitute decision-makers can take. There are some things they cannot consent to on behalf of P. These are listed in section 27 of the MCA:

- Consent to marriage or a civil partnership
- Consent to sexual relations
- Consent to divorce or dissolution of a civil partnership

- Consent to a child being placed for adoption or the making of an adoption order
- Discharging parental responsibility
- Giving consent for the purposes of the Human Fertilisation and Embryology Acts 1990 and 2008.

Best interests

4.50 If P has made an advance decision and it applies it must be followed. If, however, a decision is made on behalf of P by a deputy, the donee of an LPA, or a court, then the decision will be made based on an assessment of the person's best interests. This test must be exercised with care. The Code of Practice states:

> When working out what is in the best interests of the person who lacks capacity to make a decision or act for themselves, decision makers must take into account all relevant actors that it would be reasonable to consider, not just those that they think are important. They must not act or make a decision based on what they would want to do if they were the person who lacked capacity.

4.51 The following principles can be used when ascertaining best interests:

- Best interests should be considered widely and not limited to medical interests, but consider ethical, social, normal emotional, and welfare interests (*Re MM* [2007] EWCA 2003 (Fam)).
- If a person is likely to have capacity in the future it may be appropriate to delay the decision until they are able to make the decision for themselves (MCA, s. 4(3)).
- P's current views and feelings must be taken into account. This is so even though P has lost capacity.
- P's past views should be taken into account as well as his beliefs and values.
- The views of anyone caring for P or a donee of an LPA or deputy as to what would be in a patient's interests will be taken into count.

4.52 Of these different points it is worth exploring three of them a little further. In all of these discussions it should be remembered that the points listed are to assist the decision-maker in determining what is in the best interests of P. It is never permissible to take someone else's views or interests into account, save as to how they may impact on an assessment of P's best interests.

4.53 First, there is the requirement to consider the current wishes and feelings of P. These may be relevant in choosing between two courses of action, both of which would benefit P. If P found one disturbing and the other not, then it would, of course, be wise to follow the course of action which would not perturb P. It might be said to promote P's dignity to follow P's wishes unless doing so would cause them clear harm. In *Re S and S (Protected Persons)* [2009] WTLR 315, HHJ Marshall QC stated that P's current views should carry great weight. Academic commentators (Donnelly 2009*a*; Herring 2008) have also suggested that P's wishes should be followed unless serious harm will result. Herring (2008) argues that even though the patient lacks capacity, the principles of dignity and liberty require that respect be paid to the patient's views. However, not everyone agrees with those views. HHJ Lewison in *Re P* [2009] EWHC 163 (Ch) suggested that in *Re S and S*, HHJ Marshal had overstated the importance of P's current views. Indeed, given that P's views are the views of someone who has lost capacity, it might be thought they should carry little weight. The issue is likely to be receiving attention in the case law for some time to come.

4.54 The following are useful cases discussing the relevance of the current wishes of the person lacking capacity in determining their best interests.

> ***A Primary Care Trust* v. *AH* [2008] EWHC 1403 (Fam)** P was an adult man who suffered from epilepsy. He lived with his mother (H) who was his primary carer. P suffered frequent fits which posed a risk of serious brain damage. H believed that his medication made his condition worse and sometimes disagreed with medical advice and refused to follow it. P was found to lack capacity to make a decision about where he lived or his care. The Primary Care Trust wished to assess his general health and social care needs. There were various places where this could be done. H was happy with the assessment at a particular unit, but objected to the assessment at a local hospital. P took the same view. The Trust took the view that the assessment should be done at the local hospital because there would be a delay if the assessment was done elsewhere.
>
> The court ruled that P and H were close. It was not possible therefore to determine whether P's views were his own or simply a reflection of H's. The court agreed that it was important to assess P as a patient on his own, free from H's influence. However, removing P from his home against his and H's wishes would be distressing and make

assessment harder. The case involved a difficult balancing of the welfare factors. It was best if P was assessed within a week, but only if H would cooperate. If within a week P had not started the assessment then he should be admitted immediately to the local hospital, using a reasonable degree of force if necessary.

DH NHS Foundation Trust v. PS [2010] EWHC 1217 (Fam) PS suffered a severe learning disability. An expert reported that she lacked capacity to make decisions about her medical treatment. She suffered from cancer of the uterus and her doctors recommended a hysterectomy and removal of her fallopian tubes and ovaries. Because of her fears of hospital and needles, PS would not permit the operation to take place. The NHS Trust sought court permission to use force or sedation if necessary.

It was held that it was well established that it was in PS's interests to undergo the operation. It was true that there were risks of death attached to the operation, but these were the kinds of risks attached to any major operation. The risks, therefore, did not mean that the operation should not be performed. The court was persuaded that there were no alternatives to carrying out the procedure. It was justifiable to sedate her to enable the operation to be carried out. If necessary, PS should be detained in the hospital to aid her recovery.

Dorset County Council v. EH [2009] EWHC 784 (Fam) EH was 82 and suffering with Alzheimer's disease. She was supported by her brother and his wife and the local community health team. EH had become disorganized and confused and had problems managing her food intake and medication. The Dorset County Council (supported by EH's brother) sought an order authorizing her removal to a secure residential home and for the use of reasonable force to do so. The Official Solicitor expressed concern that the loss of autonomy and independence would not be in her best interests.

Parker J held that EH lacked capacity to decide where to live. The best interests test applied. There was conflicting evidence as to her best interests. On the one hand, there was evidence that leaving her at home exposed her to risks of cold, malnutrition, and risks of fire. But on the other hand, moving her to the home would restrict her freedom and autonomy. Parker J held that the balance came down in favour of placing her in the care home and thereby protecting her from the risks of harm.

4.55 Second, we should say a little more about a person's past views. Although these are to be taken into account, English law does not rely on a substituted judgement approach, as some American courts have done. So, the test is not what would P have decided had P had the capacity to decide, but simply what is in P's best interests. So, if what P would have decided would clearly harm P they will not be followed, but if there are alternatives and there is little to choose between them then P's views may become relevant.

> **Ahsan v. University Hospitals Leicester NHS Trust [2006] EWHC 2624 (QB)** A, a Muslim woman had been seriously injured in a car crash. She had no real awareness of her surroundings. She was due compensation for her injuries, but there was a dispute over what kind of care she should receive. Her family wished her to be treated in accordance with Muslim tradition, but that was more expensive that normal care. It was argued that it would not be in her best interests to be cared for in accordance with Muslim tradition, because she would not know how she was being treated. Hegarty J had no difficulty in finding that it was in A's best interests to receive Muslim care.

4.56 This case shows how the past views of P can play a significant role in determining what is in P's current interests. However, it is submitted that P's past views can never be relied upon to justify doing something to P which is contrary to his current best interests. If, for example, a devout Roman Catholic has always received Mass once a week, but having lost capacity, found receiving Mass distressing, his prior religious beliefs could not justify giving him Mass.

4.57 Third, there is the issue of P's relatives and carers. Notice that the views and interests of carers and family members are only relevant in so far as they are about what is in P's best interests. So the decision-maker can listen to the arguments of P's spouse: 'I think it would be better for P to receive this care' but not an argument 'It would be best for me if P received this care.' The following case is instructive, although it was heard prior to the 2005 Act.

> **Re Y (Mental Patient: Bone Marrow Donation) [1997] 2 FCR 172** Y was aged 25 and had very limited mental ability. She lacked capacity to make medical decisions. Y's sister suffered a serious medical disorder and was facing death without a bone marrow donation. Y was the only person that could be found as a suitable donor. Connell J granted a declaration authorizing the donation. He held that Y would benefit from the donation. He explained that if Y's sister were to die that would cause serious distress to Y's mother. Y had a close emotional tie with her mother and distress to her would harm Y. The bone marrow donor would suffer only a small amount of detriment from the operation.

Notice that even though the procedure was in the sister's interests, the court could not place weight on that. What can be argued is that what will benefit a member of P's family could in the long run benefit P if it assists in his or her care (Herring 2008). Critics of *Re Y* argue that in reality the courts were using Y to save her sister's life. Talk of this being in Y's best interests was a fiction.

What is not to be considered when assessing best interests

4.58 The MCA mentions two particular factors that should not be taken into account when considering best interests. First, the assessment should not be made based on 'unjustified assumptions' based on a person's age, appearance, or medical condition. For example, it should not be assumed that because the person is old they do not like listening to rock music. An assessment must be made of the best interests of the particular person and not based on generalizations of 'people like that'.

4.59 Second, section 4(5) of the MCA states that

> when the determination relates to life-sustaining treatment [the decision-maker] must not, in considering whether the treatment is in the best interests of the person concerned, be motivated by a desire to bring about his death.

This rather strange provision was inserted to protect the principle of sanctity of life. The Code of Practice makes it clear that the provision should not lead doctors to feel that they are under an obligation to keep providing treatment when that is not in the best interests of the individual. It makes it clear, perhaps, that the question should be whether the treatment is in the person's best interests, rather than whether they would be better off dead.

Use of force

4.60 There are special rules governing where force or restraint is needed against P. The following conditions must be satisfied before D can use force against P (a person lacking capacity):

- The use of force or restraint must be in P's best interests.
- D must reasonably believe that the use of force is necessary in order to prevent harm to P.
- The act must be a proportionate response to the likelihood of P suffering harm and the seriousness of that harm.

There is a special Code of Practice and provision where P is to be deprived of liberty.

Ethical issues surrounding autonomy

4.61 To many medical ethicists, autonomy has become one of the central ethical principles. Gone are the days when paternalism ruled the roost. Patients are not expected simply to agree to whatever the doctors tell them. We now accept that as the great American Judge Cardozo J stated:

> Every human being of adult years and sound mind has a right to determine what shall be done with his own body; and a surgeon who performs an operation without his patient's consent, commits an assault. (*Schloendorff* v. *Society of NY Hospital* 105 NE 92 (NY 1914), 92–3)

It is important that we have control over our bodies and what is done to them. We should be involved in decisions made and our refusal must be accepted.

4.62 The move to autonomy has gone too far for some, with Charles Foster (2009) complaining that medical ethics has become boring, because autonomy is widely regarded as the sole principle. He adds 'any society whose sole principle is autonomy is unreflective, shallow and dangerous' (Foster 2009: 1). John Keown (2002) has argued that the flaw in supporting autonomy is the idea that we should respect all autonomous decisions. He argues that we should only respect decisions that promote human flourishing. So, while he would be happy to respect your autonomy if you wished to spend your time trainspotting, if you wished to engage in activities that caused you harm or were degrading, he would argue then that autonomy should not be respected. The difficulty with such a view is what one regards as being degrading or contrary to human flourishing. Once we move away from saying that each person must decide what is best for them, we open up room for other people to decide what is best for a particular person and to interfere in their life choices.

4.63 One powerful challenge to autonomy as it is commonly presented is that promoted by supporters of relational autonomy (see, e.g. Herring 2009). They argue that we should not view people in isolation. We cannot consider what is in the best interests of a person without considering all those that they are in relationship with. Our interests and plans for our lives are often interconnected with our families and those with whom we are in caring relationships. So we need to find ways of protecting not just individual patients' autonomy, but the autonomy of those they are in relationship with. This theory has much theoretical attraction but can prove very difficult to operate in practice. Many will find any suggestion that a patient must receive treatment in order to protect the autonomy or interests of their friends and family unacceptable.

4.64 An important issue concerns which decisions we are to count as 'autonomous decisions'. If a patient refuses treatment on the basis of fear or ignorance, are they fully autonomous? Do we require patients, as some philosophers have suggested, to have weighed up carefully and thoughtfully their higher order preferences in reaching a decision? If so, very few patients will truly be able to make autonomous decisions. Most people make decisions based on a rather bad basis (relying on instinct or poor logic). Or are we to say any decision made is autonomous, however bad the reasoning process? The difficulty is that the stricter we are about which decisions are autonomous, the fewer people will be able to benefit from the right to autonomy. But the looser we are about which decisions count as autonomous, the harder it is to justify lending great weight to protecting the right to make autonomous decisions.

CONCLUSION

In this chapter we have seen that English medical law takes very seriously the right of a competent patient to refuse medical treatment. Only very exceptionally is it permissible to treat a competent patient without their consent. Although this reflects the right to autonomy, it does not mean that a patient has a right to insist on treatment. Where a patient lacks capacity then a patient will be treated on the basis of what is in that person's best interests. Advance decisions are respected to a limited extent, but there is plenty of scope in the Mental Capacity Act 2005 for them to be found ineffective in the circumstances of the particular case.

FURTHER READING

Boyle, A. (2008) 'The Law and Incapacity Determinations', *Modern Law Review* 71: 433–63.

Donnelly, M. (2009a) 'Best Interests, Patient Participation and the Mental Capacity Act 2005', *Medical Law Review* 17: 129.

Donnelly, M. (2009b) 'Capacity Assessment under the Mental Capacity Act 2005: Delivering on the Function Approach', *Legal Studies* 29: 464–85.

Dresser, R. (2003) 'Precommitment: A Misguided Strategy for Securing Death with Dignity', *Texas Law Review* 81: 1823–47.

Elliott, T. (2009) 'Body Dysmorphic Disorder, Radical Surgery and the Limits of Consent', *Medical Law Review* 17: 149–82.

Foster, C. (2009) *Choosing Life, Choosing Death: The Tyranny of Authority in Medical Ethics and Law* (Oxford: Hart).

Gilmore, S. (2009) 'The Limits of Parental Responsibility', in R. Probert, S. Gilmore, and J. Herring (eds), *Responsible Parents and Parental Responsibility* (Oxford: Hart), pp. 63–89.

General Medical Council (GMC) (2008) *Consent: Patients and Doctors Making Decisions Together* (London: GMC).

Fortin, J. (2009) *Children's Rights and the Developing Law* (Cambridge: Cambridge University Press).

Hedley, S. (2011) *Tort Law* (Oxford: Oxford University Press).

Herring, J. (2008) 'The Place of Carers', in M. Freeman (ed.), *Law and Bioethics* (Oxford: Oxford University Press), pp. 274–93.

Herring, J. (2009) 'Relational Autonomy and Rape', in S. Day Sclater, F. Ebtehaj, E. Jackson, and M. Richards (eds), *Regulating Autonomy* (Oxford: Hart), pp. 79–101.

Keown, J. (2002) *Euthanasia, Ethics and Public Policy* (Cambridge: Cambridge University Press).

Lewis, P. (2002) 'Procedures that are Against the Medical Interests of the Incompetent Person', *Oxford Journal of Legal Studies* 12: 575–618.

Maclean, A. (2009) *Autonomy, Informed Consent and the Law: A Relational Challenge* (Cambridge: Cambridge University Press).

Michalowski, S. (2005) 'Advance Refusals of Life-Sustaining Medical Treatment: The Relativity of an Absolute Right', *Modern Law Review* 68: 958–82.

Miola, J. (2009) 'On the Materiality of Risk: Paper Tigers and Panaceas', *Medical Law Review* 17: 76–108.

Padfield, N. (2010) *Criminal Law* (Oxford: Oxford University Press).

SELF-TEST QUESTIONS

1 Alf arrives in hospital looking rather dazed. The doctor is concerned that he may have a serious illness and wishes to take a blood sample. He refuses, saying he

hates needles. The doctor tries to discuss the issue with him, but he simply repeats his refusal. Can the doctor force treatment on him?

2   Susan is in labour. She tells the doctors to do everything they can to save her baby, but that she only wants to be treated by women doctors. Only male doctors are available. Without immediate treatment, her life and that of her baby are in serious danger. Should the male doctors simply treat her?

3   Charles has an absolute terror of 'pins and needles'. He needs an operation without which he will be paralyzed. There is a risk with the operation that he will have pins and needles. His doctor, who knows him well, knows that if he mentions this Charles will not consent, so he does not disclose it and Charles consents to the operation. Can Charles sue the doctor if he does indeed develop pins and needles? What if he does not? What if the doctor discloses a risk of paraesthesia (the technical name for pins and needles), a term that Charles does not understand and does not ask the doctor to explain?

4   Is there anything to which a patient should not be able to consent?

5

Confidentiality

SUMMARY

Most people assume that what they tell their doctor will be kept confidential. That seems like an obvious principle, but it has proved a difficult one to put into legal effect. This chapter sets out the circumstances in which information can be protected by the principle of confidentiality. It also considers when it is justifiable to breach confidentiality. The area is now also influenced by the law on Data Protection, which is summarized here.

Introduction

5.1 Some people seem to like to put as much information in the public domain as possible through social networking websites such as Facebook. But for most people, there is information which they would want to be kept quiet. This is especially true of medical information. Medical professionals can be privy to some of the most personal information about a person and they are expected to keep that private. Hence, the principle of medical confidentiality: health care professionals must keep their patients' confidential information secret. As Lord Phillips MR stated in *Ashworth Security Hospital* v. *MGN* [2000] 1 WLR 515, 'when a patient enters a hospital for treatment...he is entitled to be confident that details about his condition and treatment remain between himself and those who treat him'. This is not just a legal obligation, it is also in the

Hippocratic Oath (the ancient oath seen by many to underpin the obligations of doctors):

> Whatsoever things I see or hear concerning the life of men, in my attendance on the sick or even apart therefrom, which ought not to be noised abroad, I will keep silence thereon, counting such things to be sacred secrets.

So, both law and ethics agree: patients' personal information must be kept confidential. Despite this apparent agreement, there is much disagreement as to the details of the law on confidentiality.

5.2 One of the remarkable things about the law of confidentiality is the large number of potential sources of the legal obligation. We shall be looking at the following candidates:

- Equity
- Human rights
- Contract law
- Tort law
- Property
- Criminal law
- Statute
- Professional regulation

This is a long list, and all of them will be considered now, but it is the top two—equity and human rights—which are the most significant.

Equity

5.3 The law of equity has developed to impose an obligation not to disclose confidential information. This applies not only in the context of medical cases, but in a wide range of different kinds of cases involving personal information and relationships of trust. For example, it has been said to apply between people in an intimate relationship (*Stephens* v. *Avery* [1988] Ch 449). If the obligation is to be imposed, the following must be shown:

- The information is of a personal or private nature or the information was passed on in circumstances indicating confidence.

- The information was disclosed to an unauthorized person.
- There is no justification for the disclosure.

5.4 Looking at these requirements separately, let us first consider the requirement that the information is of a personal or private nature. Nearly all medical information will be regarded as private. Perhaps some information that a doctor discovered about a patient would not be included. For example, trivial information (what colour tie the patient was wearing) or non-medical information (e.g. what television programmes the patient enjoyed watching) would not be protected by the duty of confidentiality. In *R (Stevens)* v. *Plymouth* [2002] EWCA Civ 388, it was stated that 'straight-forward descriptions of everyday life' would not be regarded as confidential. Quite where the line between protected and non-protected information should be drawn may be debatable. Would information about the patient's favourite tipple be covered? Or what about the mere fact that a patient visited the doctor? Baroness Hale in *Campbell* v. *MGN* [2004] UKHL 22 stated:

> Not every statement about a person's health will carry the badge of confidentiality or risk doing harm to that person's physical or moral integrity. The privacy interest in the fact that a public figure has a cold or a broken leg is unlikely to be strong enough to justify restricting the press's freedom to report it. What harm could it possibly do?

This is a controversial statement. It might suggest that only important medical information is covered by confidentiality. However, it may be that what Baroness Hale was suggesting was that with well-known figures, it is likely that a breach of confidentiality concerning minor ailments would be easily justified in the name of press freedom. Alternatively, she may have been suggesting that in relation to public figures, the fact that they have, for example, a broken leg will soon be obvious to the public.

5.5 It must also be shown that the information was imparted in circumstances of confidentiality. There are two ways that this may be so. First, it may depend on the relationship between the parties. Where a member of the public tells their solicitor or doctor information during a formal appointment, we would expect the professional to keep confidence. The same might not apply to things said to a medical professional in a casual conversation in a supermarket queue. There the circumstances would be different and an expectation of confidentiality would not arise. Second, the information is such that its nature is confidential. So, if a member of public found a medical record in a bin, they would be covered by the equitable obligation.

5.6 A breach of equitable obligation requires that an unauthorized person received the information. Technically, therefore, if a person put confidential information in a public place, but it was removed before anyone saw it, there would be no breach. It also means that the obligation is breached even if the information is not made public; if it is disclosed to one person.

5.7 A major drawback with equitable breach of confidence concerns the remedy. The primary remedy is an injunction. That may be an effective remedy if it is known that a breach is soon to occur and one wants to prevent it. In that case, if the person still publishes in breach of the injunction then they will be guilty of contempt of court and could face imprisonment. But an injunction is of limited use if the information has already been put in the public domain. It is little use once a breach has already occurred. Even if breach of confidence is combined with the tort of negligence, there is rarely a financial loss resulting from a breach of confidence and so any damages are likely to be limited.

> **Mosley v. News Groups Newspapers [2008] EWHC 687 (QB)** Max Mosley sought damages from a newspaper publisher after the publication of an article headed, 'F1 BOSS HAS SICK NAZI ORGY WITH 5 HOOKERS'. The article was accompanied by a photograph and described M's sadomasochistic role play with five women. M complained that the material was inherently private in nature. It was alleged that one of the women had breached confidence in secretly recording what had happened and revealing what had happened to the newspapers. He also argued that the participants had a relationship of confidentiality as the activities had taken place on the understanding that they were private and none of them would reveal what had taken place. The newspapers responded that there was no reasonable expectation of privacy and that the public interest in freedom of expression out-weighed any rights to privacy.
>
> It was held that the law of confidence applied to information in respect of which there was a reasonable expectation of privacy. There was no need to show there was a pre-existing relationship between the parties. In this case, although the activities might be regarded as unconventional, they were sexual activities in private between consenting adults and so there was an expectation of privacy. The court rejected an argument that there was still a principle that 'there is no confidence in iniquity'. So, even in the cases of fetishist activity, if performed between consenting adults, it could be pro-tected by confidence. The court also rejected the argument that privacy rights could be trumped by the right to freedom of speech. Interest in people's private sexual lives did not justify invading their privacy. £60,000 damages were awarded.

Human rights

5.8 In recent years, it has been the law of human rights which has shaped the approach to confidentiality.

> **Campbell v. MGN [2004] UKHL 22** The *Daily Mirror* published a photograph of Naomi Campbell leaving a meeting of Narcotics Anonymous. The newspaper praised Ms Campbell's attempts to battle addiction. She sued for breach of confidence. The House of Lords upheld the claim. Interestingly, their Lordships did not seem concerned to specify which legal source they were relying on. They considered that the law, whatever its source, was shaped by the European Convention on Human Rights (ECHR). Article 8(1) protected confidential information as part of the right to respect for private life. Article 8(2) could justify interference in that right, if the interference was necessary for one of the reasons listed in paragraph 2, such as the interests of others.
>
> Applying the principles to the facts of the case, it was accepted that although information about her drug use was in the public domain, the information that Naomi Campbell was receiving this particular treatment for drug addiction was confidential information. However, it was necessary to balance her right with the public interest, in this case press freedom. Their Lordships did not seem to think of this as a straightforward case. Baroness Hale described the case as 'a prima donna celebrity against a celebrity-tabloid newspaper'. In the end, they decided that the public interest in the case did not justify the interference and so Ms Campbell was entitled to damages. However, they only awarded the small sum of £3,500, which suggests that the court did not think the breach was very serious.

5.9 Lord Nicholls in the subsequent case of *Douglas* v. *Hello!* [2007] UKHL 21 suggested that the law on breach of confidence had developed in light of the Human Rights Act 1998. He argued that there were two separate causes of action: privacy and confidential information. He thought that some information would fall into both categories. This distinction may be less relevant for medical lawyers than others. Medical information is likely to be both private and confidential. This was confirmed in *McKennit* v. *Ash* [2006] EWCA Civ 1714, where it was noted that information given to a doctor was protected by the law of confidentiality for two reasons. First, because it was given in a relationship where there was an expectation that confidence was kept and, second, because it was private information.

5.10 Article 8 of the ECHR protects the right to respect for private and family life. This right includes protection for confidential information (Z v. *Finland* (1998) EHRR 371). It is permissible to interfere with that right if 'necessary in a democratic society' in the interest of 'national security, public safety or the economic well-being of the country, for the prevention of disorder or crime, for the protection of health and morals, or for the protection of the rights and freedoms of others'. In deciding whether the breach is justified, the word 'necessary' is important because it shows that there must be a sufficiently strong reason to justify an interference. In Z v. *Finland* it was held that the disclosure of a woman's medical records, which revealed her HIV status, could be justified. They were disclosed as part of a criminal trial in which her husband was charged with rape. Although the breach of her rights was grave, it was justified because of the importance of prosecuting serious criminal offences. Nevertheless, the court accepted that there was a breach in this case because the court publicly disclosed her identity and HIV status in the judgment, which it did not need to do. This case makes the important point that under a human rights analysis even though some disclosure could be justified, if there was a broader disclosure than was strictly necessary a breach may be proved.

> ***Z v. Finland* (1997) 25 EHRR 371** While investigating the husband for rape, medical records of the wife were seized without her consent. These included the fact that she had been infected with HIV. She objected to the publication in criminal proceedings of her name and her HIV status.
>
> The European Court of Human Rights (ECtHR) held that it was especially important to keep confidential health information about individuals. This was especially important in relation to HIV infection. Where the state sought to disclose such information without the individual's consent there had to be strong justification. While the use of her medical information as part of the prosecution was justified, there was no compelling reason why, in the publication of the judgment, her name and status had to be disclosed. Her rights to respect for her private and family life were, therefore, justified.
>
> ***MS v. Sweden* (Application No. 20837/92) (ECtHR, 27 August 1997)** A woman was required to release her medical records in order to claim social security following a back injury at work. The medical records disclosed that she had had an abortion as a result of her back problem. Although the requirement of disclosure did breach her rights, it was a proportionate means of pursuing a legitimate state interest in ensuring that a person could indeed claim the benefit.

5.11 The Human Rights Act 1998 does not provide for a straightforward enforcement of the ECtHR. Claims based on the ECHR can be used in two main ways. First, it can be used to interpret statute, or more relevantly here to shape the development of the common law, such as the equitable law on confidence (see *Campbell* v. *MGN* [2004] UKHL 44). Second, section 7 allows a person to sue a public authority which has infringed their Convention rights. So, a claim could be brought against an NHS Trust, but not against an individual doctor. That could include a claim for damages. However, as the Campbell case suggests, the level of damages may not be high, unless a financial loss can be shown.

Contract law

5.12 Revealing confidential information could be a breach of contract with a patient. However, there is no contract between the NHS and its patients. So, a contractual claim could only be made where a patient is receiving private treatment. Where there is a contract, there may be an express term of the contract that confidentiality will be protected, but even if there is no such term the courts may well imply a term into it. An injunction could be available to prevent an imminent breach, or damages may be awarded where a breach occurred. But the absence of a proven financial loss as a result of the breach means that it is unlikely that any damages will be substantial.

Tort law

5.13 A breach of confidence could amount to negligence. If it could be shown that the disclosure of confidential information was one that no reasonable body of medical opinion would support, then a negligence claim could follow (see further Chapter 3). However, the difficulty would be in relation to damages. Generally, the law of tort protects financial or physical loss, but does not protect emotional loss or feelings of embarrassment. A tort law claim is only worth making if it can be shown to have caused identifiable physical harm or financial loss.

5.14 An alternative argument is the new tort of breach of privacy. This tort is still in the early stages of development (see *Murray* v. *Big Pictures* [2008] EWCA 446).

It will be particularly useful in a case where there is no duty of care between the patient and the person making the disclosure. For example, if someone finds medical records in a bin it may not be possible to rely on the tort of negligence because there would probably not be a duty of care. However, using the developing tort of breach of privacy would be possible. In *Campbell* (see 5.8) and *Murray* it was stated that the ECHR would be used to shape the development of the tort.

Property

5.15 A claim might be made that private information can be regarded as property. If that were accepted then it would open up a range of remedies, including the tort of conversion. However, in *R* v. *Department of Health ex p Source Informatics Ltd* [2000] 1 All ER 786, the Court of Appeal rejected an argument that a patient owns medical information about themselves. It suggested that an NHS Trust owns the medical records it produced. That said, there has been little case law on the issue and it is not unforeseeable that the law will develop to recognize some kind of property claim.

Criminal law

5.16 Sometimes, a disclosure of medical information could amount to a criminal offence. If information is accessed from a computer without authorization, that could amount to an offence under the Computer Misuse Act 1990. Removal of paper medical records could involve the offence of theft of the paper. However, there cannot be theft of information and so just looking at a paper medical record and making its contents public would not be a crime.

Statutory obligation

5.17 Statute imposes obligations in relation to information in certain circumstances. For example, the Data Protection Act 1998 imposes a wide range of duties relating to information stored and protected. We shall be discussing these in more detail shortly.

Professional regulation

5.18 Perhaps for many professionals it is the guidance offered by their professional bodies which governs their approach to confidentiality. Understandably, they trust that as long as they comply with their professional guidance they will be in compliance with the law. The most significant professional guidance is that produced by the General Medical Council (GMC). Their Guidance, issued in 2009, states that confidentially must be preserved and that if disclosure is necessary it must be kept to a minimum. They state clearly that 'patients have a right to expect that information about them will be held in confidence by their doctors'. There are similar statements that are found in the professional bodies of other medical professionals. The GMC Guidance states:

> Confidentiality is central to trust between doctors and patients. Without assurances about confidentiality, patients may be reluctant to seek medical attention or to give doctors the information they need in order to provide good care. But appropriate information sharing is essential to the efficient provision of safe, effective care, both for the individual patient and for the wider community of patients. (para. 6)

It is interesting to note that in this paragraph, having set out the principle of confidentiality, the GMC immediately goes on to emphasize the importance of sharing the information. This highlights the tension between protecting confidence and ensuring that that does not hinder patients receiving the best treatment.

Denying breach of confidentiality

Loss of confidentiality

5.19 One defence available to a person charged with breaching confidence would be to deny that the information disclosed was confidential. For example, in *Campbell* v. *MGN* (see 5.8) it was argued that because Naomi Campbell had made public comments about drug-taking the information about her attending Narcotics Anonymous was no longer confidential. This argument failed, however, because it was held that Ms Campbell had never made public comments about the details of the treatment she was receiving. That makes it clear that although some aspects of a person's medical care may be public, that does not mean that all the details are.

> **BBC v. Harper Collins Publishers Ltd and Ben Collins [2010] EWHC 2424 (Ch)** The BBC sought an injunction to prevent Harper Collins and Ben Collins from disclosing the true identity of Stig (a character in the TV show *Top Gear*). Collins had played the role of Stig from 2003 to 2010. It was made clear to him from the outset that it was important that his identity was concealed. In his autobiography, to be published by Harper Collins, Ben Collins was going to reveal that he played the part of Stig. The BBC claimed that disclosing the information would amount to a breach of contract and breach of confidentiality. Ben Collins claimed that there was so much speculation in the media concerning his identity that it had ceased to be a confidential matter.
>
> It was held that the contractual claim failed as Ben Collins was not a party to the contract with the BBC as it had been entered into with his company. However, the claim in confidence could be made. The issue, the court held, was whether or not the identity of Stig was still confidential. It was held that there was considerable coverage in the press of the speculation that Stig was Collins. Anyone who had any interest in finding out who Stig was could have found out the information as it was generally accessible (e.g. through the Internet). It was therefore no longer confidential.

Consent to disclosure

5.20 Obviously, if there is consent to the disclosure then this will not breach confidentiality. For example, a wife might agree that her doctor can discuss her medical condition with her husband. Or a patient may agree that a doctor can write about their case in an article for a journal. The most common circumstances involving consent must be where a patient consents to one doctor passing on information to another doctor (e.g. where a patient is referred to a consultant).

Anonymized information

5.21 This case concerns anonymized information:

> **R v. Department of Health ex p Source Informatics Ltd [2001] QB 424** Source Informatics Ltd sold medical information to pharmaceutical companies. They made an agreement with GPs and pharmacists under which patients' information would be sold. However, the name of the patient would not appear on any of the information. The Department of Health issued guidelines stating that passing on this information

breached the professionals' duty of confidentiality. The company challenged the guidelines. The Court of Appeal held that the guidelines were incorrect and that as long as the information was anonymized there was no breach of confidentiality. Simon Brown LJ explained that the reasonable pharmacist's conscience would not be troubled as long as the information was anonymized. It was held that the giving of the information to Source Informatics Ltd was a fair use of the information.

5.22 *R* v. *Department of Health ex p Source Informatics Ltd* holds that if the information is anonymized then disclosure of it will not breach the law. The decision has proved controversial. A person may feel that their privacy was violated if private information was disclosed, even if their name was hidden. People may feel their privacy has been invaded if naked photographs of themselves have been made public, even if they were not identified. Patients may not want their information used in research to which they object. While many patients may happily consent to anonymized information being used for research, that does not mean that consent should not be sought.

> **Common Services Agency v. Scottish Information Commissioner [2008] UKHL 47** The Common Services Agency (CSA) appealed against a decision of the Scottish Information Commissioner that the CSA had breached its duty under the Freedom of Information (Scotland) Act 2002, s. 15 in failing to provide information to a Member of the Scottish Parliament. The Member had asked for the incidents of leukaemia in a thirteen-year period for a certain postal area. The Agency had refused to provide the information, regarding it as personal data and therefore exempt for the purposes of the Data Protection Act 1998. The Commissioner had suggested that 'barnardisation' (a process which makes the information anonymous) be used so as to camouflage the information.
>
> The House of Lords held that data would still be personal data even if 'barnardised', as taken with other information they would enable a living individual to whom the data related to be identified. To fall outside the scope of personal data it would need to be data which was anonymous, such that the information to which the data related was no longer identifiable.

5.23 Critics (e.g. Beyleveld and Histed 2000) have sought ways to limit the impact of *Source Informatics*. It is noticeable that the Court of Appeal assumed that the fact that the information was anonymized meant that it was impossible to discover whose information it was. It would be very different if it was possible to identify the individuals even though their names were removed. So it might be argued that if the condition was very rare, or if the combination of conditions was unusual, the information was not truly anonymous, then it might be argued that disclosure of it breaches confidence. Second, the reference to the conscience of pharmacists suggests that there might be cases where even though the information was anonymized, the conscience of the pharmacists was affected and/or was not fair use.

Justification

Consent

5.24 As already mentioned, if there is consent then any disclosure is justified. This can be expressed or implied. For example, if a patient agrees that her GP may refer her to a consultant, this impliedly consents to the disclosure of medical confidential information to a consultant. Indeed, the GMC Guidance says that patients should realize that medical information provided to someone in the NHS is likely to be shared with others in their health care team.

5.25 Where a patient is unable to consent because she lacks mental capacity, then her treatment is covered by the Mental Capacity Act 2005. A disclosure of confidential information about a person lacking capacity would be permitted if doing so would be in the interests of the person lacking capacity. In the case of a child, consent could be provided by a parent with parental responsibility.

Proper working of the hospital

5.26 Simon Brown LJ suggested, obiter, that the use of confidential information for legitimate NHS purposes was legitimate. This echoes comments in the NHS Constitution that the sharing of patient information was an essential part of the working of a modern national health care system. The sharing of information may be necessary for the purposes of audit, research, and good practice. Indeed, it may even be that a patient is taken to impliedly consent to the sharing of information. The GMC Guidance is interesting on this:

> You should make sure that information is readily available to patients explaining that, unless they object, their personal information may be disclosed for the sake of their own care and for local clinical audit. Patients usually understand that information about them has to be shared within the healthcare team to provide their care. But it is

not always clear to patients that others who support the provision of care might also need to have access to their personal information. And patients may not be aware of disclosures to others for purposes other than their care, such as service planning or medical research. You must inform patients about disclosures for purposes they would not reasonably expect; or check that they have already received information about such disclosures.

This advice might suggest that although patients should be informed about how their information will be used, their consent is not required. Indeed, the Guidance later states that:

You must respect the wishes of any patient who objects to particular personal information being shared within the healthcare team or with others providing care, unless disclosure would be justified in the public interest. If a patient objects to a disclosure that you consider essential to the provision of safe care, you should explain that you cannot refer them or otherwise arrange for their treatment without also disclosing that information.

This suggests that patients should be informed that their information may be shared with other health care professionals. If they do not object then consent can be assumed. However, if they object then that objection should be respected, unless there is a public interest reason for overruling it.

A threat of serious harm to others

5.27   The following illustrates a case about the threat of serious harm to others:

W v. *Egdell* **[1990] 1 All ER 835**   W had been convicted of a number of violent killings and was detained under the Mental Health Act 1983. Dr Egdell prepared a report for a Mental Health Review Tribunal, which had to consider whether or not W should be released. W's report expressed serious concerns about W's propensity to violence and was concerned that those caring for him did not appreciate it. W decided not to pursue his application to the tribunal. Dr Egdell wanted to disclose his report to the Home Office and to those caring for W. The Court of Appeal held that the disclosure of the report would breach confidentiality, but that the disclosure was justified. There was a real risk of significant harm to others and this justified the disclosure.

Where there is a risk that without the disclosure of the confidential information there would be a real risk of significant harm to others, the disclosure would be justified. The risk must be a real one and not a fanciful one. Further, it must be of serious risk of danger to the public. Importantly, the disclosure needs to be limited to the extent necessary to protect from the risk. Hence, in *W* v. *Egdell*, the Court of Appeal indicated that the sharing of the report with the Home Office and those caring for W was justified, but disclosure to the press would not be.

5.28   What if a public authority does not disclose confidential information and as a result someone is harmed? This is the leading case:

> ***Tarasoff* v. *Regents of the University of California* (1976) 131 Cal Rptr 14 (Cal Sup Ct)** Poddar and Tarasoff were students at the University of California. Poddar believed they had a serious relationship, but Tarasoff told him that she was not interested in entering a serious relationship with him. Poddar started to stalk her and developed a wish for revenge. Poddar entered into an emotional crisis and sought assistance. He became a patient of a Dr Moore at the university's hospital. Poddar told Dr Moore of his intent to kill Tarasoff. He determined that Poddar was suffering from acute and severe paranoid schizophrenia and recommended Poddar be detained. Poddar was detained but later released, as he appeared better. Later, he killed Tarasoff. Tarasoff's parents sued Moore, claiming that Moore should have warned Tarasoff of the threats.
>
> The California Supreme Court held that a mental health professional owes a duty of care towards individuals who are specifically threatened by a patient. Justice Tobriner held that
>
>> the public policy favoring protection of the confidential character of patient–psychotherapist communications must yield to the extent to which disclosure is essential to avert danger to others. The protective privilege ends where the public peril begins. (at 442)
>
> ***Palmer* v. *Tees Health Authority* [2000] PIQR 1**   A health authority was caring for a man who was suffering from a personality disorder. They decided to release him from detention and care for him in the community. He subsequently abducted a four-year-old girl, sexually assaulted, and killed her. The girl's parents claimed that the hospital was negligent in releasing the man, or, at least, for not warning those who lived close by. It was held that there was no reason for the local authority to believe that the man posed a risk to the girl. The health authority did not owe her, or her parents, a duty of care. The court contrasted an American decision, *Tarasoff* v. *The Regents of the University California* (1976) 131 Cal Rptr 14. The Palmer decision was different as the danger was not directed towards an identified person.

There is a particular obligation to breach confidence in cases where a patient may have been or is about to cause harm to children. Note that issues over child protection not only justify a breach of confidentiality, but can actually require it. In the *Palmer* case, even though the tort action failed, it might have led to disciplinary proceedings if appropriate steps had not been taken to ensure the appropriate authorities were aware of any particular risks. A failure to inform the authorities that a child is being abused by her parents or that a woman is the victim of domestic violence at the hands of her partner could expose a professional to liability in tort law.

Assisting police investigations

5.29 You probably expect to read that if a health care professional is asked by the police whether a patient has given them information relevant to a police investigation, then they are under a duty to inform the police. But that, in fact, is not the law. There is no general obligation to breach confidence to help a police enquiry. Of course, medical professionals must not obstruct a police investigation, but there is no general requirement to assist the police by answering questions. There are a few circumstances in which disclosure of confidential information is permitted. Most notably under section 115 of the Crime and Disorder Act 1998, the disclosure of confidential information to a Chief Officer of Police is permitted where there is a strong public interest for doing so. The Department of Health has suggested it would only apply in relation to serious offences and where the prevention or detection of crime will be seriously delayed or prejudiced without the disclosure.

Press freedom

5.30 The courts have accepted that in some cases freedom of the press can justify a breach of confidence.

> *X* v. *Y* **[1988] 2 All ER 649** A hospital sought an injunction to prevent a newspaper publicizing the fact that two doctors were being treated for AIDS. The newspaper accepted that the publication would breach confidence, but argued that doing so was justified because it was important to have a public debate on the issue. It was emphasized that there was a difference between things that the public were interested in and what was in the public interest.

The Court of Appeal held that newspapers could not publish the information. In this case, the issue was one of genuine public interest, but it was an issue about which there was already much debate in the media. This had to be weighed up against the general principle that medical records should be kept confidential; that people should not be encouraged to give confidential information to newspapers; and that AIDS suffers should feel free to seek treatment for AIDS, without fear that their condition would be made public. Weighing up the different arguments, it was held that the newspapers should not publish the information.

H (A Health Worker) v. *Associated Newspapers Ltd* **[2002] LL Rep 210** A health care authority proposed to notify all the patients of H, a health care professional, that H was HIV positive. H sought an injunction to prevent that. He argued that as he posed a very low risk to his patients, they should not be informed. The newspaper, the *Mail on Sunday*, learned of this and wanted to publish details of the dispute.

The Court of Appeal agreed that H's name should not be published, but that his specialization could be. They rejected an argument that naming his specialization would reveal his identity; but on the contrary argued that revealing the specialization raised particular issues that were relevant to the public discussions taking place.

Associated Newspapers Ltd v. *His Royal Highness the Prince of Wales* **[2006] EWCA Civ 1776** The Prince of Wales had kept handwritten journals recording his impressions and views during overseas tours. In breach of her contract, one of his employees had passed on a copy of the journals to a newspaper. The Prince had obtained a summary judgment against the newspaper for breach of confidence and infringement of copyright. The newspaper appealed.

The Court of Appeal held that the information in the journal was obviously confidential and private. The Prince had a reasonable expectation that the contents of the journal would remain private. The contracts of employment made it clear that copies of the journal were to be treated as confidential. The key issue was whether the public interest could justify interference in the rights. The public interest was insufficient to outweigh the confidential nature of the information.

As these three cases show, a breach of confidentiality can be justified in order to promote freedom of the press and public debate. The courts will consider carefully the importance of the issue being discussed, whether the disclosure would add to the debate, and how much information needed to be disclosed in order for the debate to take place. A further factor, mentioned in the *Campbell* case, is whether the individual is in the public eye. *Murray* v. *Big Pictures* [2008] EWCA 446 suggests that where a child is involved, the courts will be particularly protective of privacy. Notably in *H (A Health Worker)* v. *Associated Newspapers Ltd*, the court placed weight on Article 10 ECHR, which protects the right to freedom of the press. The weight attached to this right means that the burden rests on those who would seek to restrict the freedom of the press.

Specific statutory provisions

5.31 There are some specific statutory provisions requiring or permitting the disclosure of confidential information. For example, the Public Health (Control of Disease) Act 1984 requires doctors to inform the Home Office of details of people with certain infectious diseases. Another example is the controversial National Health Service Act 2006, s. 251(1) which permits the disclosure of medical information for research purposes without consent.

Other public interests

5.32 Most commentators agree that there is a 'catch-all' category of disclosure in the public interest. Even if the disclosure does not fall into one of the categories above, then disclosure could be justified in the public interest. In *R (Axon)* v. *Secretary of State* [2006] QB 539, it was argued that the public interest required a doctor to disclose to a parent the fact that her child had sought an abortion. Silber J firmly rejected the argument that such a requirement would promote the public interest. The GMC Guidance suggests the following as a guide to deciding whether to make a disclosure in the public interest:

> Personal information may, therefore, be disclosed in the public interest, without patients' consent, and in exceptional cases where patients have withheld consent, if the benefits to an individual or to society of the disclosure outweigh both the public and the patient's interest in keeping the information confidential. You must weigh the harms that are likely to arise from non-disclosure of information against the possible harm, both to the patient and to the overall trust between doctors and patients, arising from the release of that information.

> **R (Stone) v. South East Coast Strategic Health Authority [2006] All ER (D) 144 (Jul)** Michael Stone had been convicted of two murders and one attempted murder and was now in prison. He sought a judicial review of the decision to publish an independent inquiry into his care, treatment, and supervision. He objected to the report being published in full.

The court held that although the protection of personal data was of fundamental importance and was protected by Article 8 of the ECHR, this had to be weighed against Article 10. The court had to undertake a 'close and penetrating examination' of the competing rights. The court had to consider if there was a compelling case to justify the publication of the full report. Stone was entitled to protection of the private information he disclosed to his doctors and there was also a public interest in assuring people that information disclosed to doctors would be kept quiet. However, in this case, it was significant that Stone had accepted that at least part of the report should be published; further, that there was a strong interest in the public knowing of the issues raised by the case and learning lessons from it. The court noted that the publicity surrounding Stone had arisen solely from his own criminal acts. The interference in his rights inherent in publishing the report was necessary and proportionate.

R (S) v. *Plymouth CC* **[2002] 1 FLR 1177** S sought a judicial review of the decision by the local social services authority to refuse her information about her adult son (C) who was in the council's care. S was entitled to make applications about C, as his nearest relative. The council were willing to disclose the information about C to the experts appointed by S. The experts could communicate to her such parts as they thought proper. However, the council did not agree that S should herself have direct access to the information. It argued there was a need to protect C's rights to confidentiality. This needed to be balanced with S's right to information so that she could exercise her capacity as his nearest relative.

The Court of Appeal held that the information should be disclosed to S. Although C had an interest in protecting information that was confidential, S had a statutory role to protect his interests. That role could only be performed if the information was provided.

5.33 Another difficult area concerns genetic information (Laurie 2002; Gilbar 2005). If a doctor discovers that a patient has a genetically related disease and that this means it is likely that the patient's siblings also have the disease, can the doctor contact the patients to warn them? Of course this is not a problem if the patient gives consent, but it is a problem if the patient does not. The difficulty is that by informing the relative of the risk, this in effect discloses that the patient has the condition. One response to such cases is that information is shared (Gilbar 2005; Skene 2001) and so the patient cannot claim it is theirs. It belongs to the family. Yet another difficulty in this scenario is that the relative may claim a right not to know (Andorno 2005). They may not want to know if they have a condition. The trouble is that a doctor cannot know if a patient wants to know a piece of information without telling them that there is something to know!

Data protection

5.34 The Data Protection Act 1998 covers the processing of personal data. It covers all personal data and not just medical information. It covers all data stored in systems, be that electronic or paper. The Act is based on the following key principles:

(1) Personal data shall be processed fairly and lawfully and, in particular, shall not be processed unless—

(a) at least one of the conditions in Schedule 2 is met, and

(b) in the case of sensitive personal data, at least one of the conditions in Schedule 3 is also met.

(2) Personal data shall be obtained only for one or more specified and lawful purposes, and shall not be further processed in any manner incompatible with that purpose or those purposes.

(3) Personal data shall be adequate, relevant and not excessive in relation to the purpose or purposes for which they are processed.

(4) Personal data shall be accurate and, where necessary, kept up to date.

(5) Personal data processed for any purpose or purposes shall not be kept for longer than is necessary for that purpose or those purposes.

(6) Personal data shall be processed in accordance with the rights of data subjects under this Act.

(7) Appropriate technical and organizational measures shall be taken against unauthorized or unlawful processing of personal data and against accidental loss or destruction of, or damage to, personal data.

(8) Personal data shall not be transferred to a country or territory outside the European Economic Area unless that country or territory ensures an adequate level of protection for the rights and freedoms of data subjects in relation to the processing of personal data.

There are special regulations governing sensitive personal information, which would include health records. If sensitive personal data is to be used, the following special conditions must be satisfied:

(a) The patient has given explicit consent to the information being used.

(b) It is necessary to process the information to protect the vital interests of the patient.

(c) Where the data is in the public domain.

(d) A health care organization or professional needs to use the information to obtain legal advice or in the course of legal proceedings.

(e) The processing of the information is necessary for the purposes of statutory or government functions.

(f) It is necessary for medical purposes and the information is used by a health care professional.

(g) Processing of medical data or data relating to ethnic origin for monitoring purposes.

(h) Processing in the substantial public interest, necessary for the purpose of research whose object is not to support decisions with respect to any particular data subject otherwise than with the explicit consent of the data subject and which is unlikely to cause substantial damage or substantial distress to the data subject or any other person.

Keeping safe

5.35 The GMC Guidance (2009) makes it clear that it is not just a matter of ensuring that information is not disclosed, but also of ensuring that there is not unintentional disclosure:

> You must make sure that any personal information about patients that you hold or control is effectively protected at all times against improper disclosure. The UK health departments publish guidance on how long health records should be kept and how they should be disposed of. You should follow the guidance whether or not you work in the NHS. (para. 2)

This is relevant because it indicates that a professional can breach their professional regulations (and be subject to disciplinary proceedings by their professional body) if they leave medical records in an inappropriate place, even if in fact no one discloses them.

Children and confidentiality

5.36 There is no real difficulty in establishing that medical information about children should be kept confidential. The real issue is whether doctors can tell the parents of a child confidential information about their child. In the *Gillick* decision, Lord Fraser was clear that the doctor did not need to obtain the parents' consent and indeed the parents did not even need to know about the issue. That approach was taken further in the following case:

> **R (Axon) v. Secretary of State for Health [2006] QB 539** Mrs Axon challenged Department of Health guidance on abortion. In particular, she argued that health professionals should inform parents of advice on sexual matters relating to their children. She was willing to accept that there might be exceptions to this, where, for example, the child's physical or mental health was under threat. She further argued that her rights as a parent under Article 8 of the ECHR required that she be informed of medical discussion, unless there was a good reason not to. This was rejected by Silber J who confirmed that where a child was *Gillick* competent, then her parents ceased to have Article 8 rights. Although doctors should encourage young people to discuss issues with their parents, it would be a breach of confidentiality to inform parents without the young person's consent.

This makes it clear that where a child is *Gillick* competent she has the same rights to confidentiality as an adult. A doctor who informed parents that he had been seeing their competent daughter to discuss contraceptive advice would be clearly breaching a duty of confidence. *Axon* does not tell us the position where the young person is not *Gillick* competent. It seems in that case that the parents should be informed unless there is a strong reason not to be informed (*Re C* [1990] Fam 39).

5.37 The courts, however, are aware that protecting confidence in some cases will interfere in the obligation to protect children from abuse and the administration of justice. This can justify breaching the confidence.

> **A County Council v. (1) SB (2) MA (3) AA [2010] EWHC 2528 (Fam)** X, a 16-year-old was the subject of care proceedings after her parents' disapproval of her relationship with a man. Proceedings were brought under the Forced Marriage (Civil Protection) Act 2007, as there were concerns that X's family were trying to force a marriage upon her. An expert produced a report which concluded that X was not at immediate risk of marriage, although the current orders should remain. At the court hearing, the expert revealed that after she had given assurances of confidentiality, X

had provided other information. However, that information was not in her report, but it had influenced her report. The expert was required in court to disclose that evidence (including allegations of domestic violence by her father towards her mother) and produce a second report which included that information. The issue then arose as to whether the second report should be disclosed to the parties' legal advisers only or to the clients as well.

It was ordered that the report be produce for all the parties. The rights of the parents under Article 6 of the ECHR to a fair hearing outweighed the risk to X from disclosure of the report. The court emphasized that experts in Children Act 1989 cases could not receive information in confidence from everyone. All information would have to be disclosed to the court. The information could be kept confidential to the court and the parties to the proceedings. In some cases, the court could decide not to order full disclosure if there was a real risk of harm. There was none here.

Dead patients

5.38 If a patient has died, does any information a health professional held cease to be confidential? A patient might well want to keep information private even after their death. A devout Muslim might not want her family to know that she once had an abortion, for example. There is little case law on the issue but that which there is suggests that the duty of confidentiality does survive death (*Lewis* v. *Secretary of Health for Health* [2008] EWHC 2196 (QB)). It is submitted that this is correct. If part of the purpose of the law on confidentiality is to encourage honesty between patients and doctors, then that would be inhibited if the patient thought that the information would be disclosed. Also, as Foskett J indicated in *Lewis*, most patients would expect that their medical details would be kept private, even after death. It may, however, be that a breach of medical confidence of a dead person would be easier to justify than the breach of confidence for a live person.

Access to records

5.39 What about the flip side of confidentiality: may a patient know what is in their records? One route for doing this is section 8 of the Data Protection Act 1998. That gives a patient a clear right to information from a data controller. A written request and payment of a fee is required. However, regulations permit a health professional to withhold access to medical records if it would be likely to cause serious harm to the physical or mental health of any person, including the patient requesting the information. In relation to the health records of a deceased person, a claim can be made under section 3(1)(f) of the Access to Health Records Act 1990. The Freedom of Information Act 2000 also enables individuals to claim access to data held by public authorities. The Act applies not only to the Department of Health and NHS Trusts but also to independent medical practitioners. The Act applies to all recorded information. A public authority can be exempt from disclosing information under the Act if the public interest in non-disclosure justifies not providing the information. Indeed, the Equality Act 2010 outlaws unjustified discrimination on the grounds of disability.

Ethical arguments

5.40 The arguments over confidentiality tend to break down into two main kinds: those that focus on the harms that flow from confidentiality (consequentialist arguments), and those that are a matter of principle (deontological arguments). We will look at these separately.

Consequentialist arguments

5.41 It might help to think about what would happen if we did not have laws protecting medical confidentiality. This might mean that people would be less honest with their doctors. They might not disclose all their symptoms or past behaviour. That could mean that patients would not receive the best diagnosis or treatment. That would not be good for the individual or for the general public. It might also mean in a broader way that we lose a sense of private or intimate life. John Eekelaar (2006) has written on the way that protection of an intimate sphere is necessary for the values of love and friendship to flourish. If we know everything there is to know about each other that might hinder social interaction. There is a further issue here: suspicions of illness or predisposition to illness can lead to prejudice. If people know that someone has been told that they have a predisposition to depression, this may mean that people will treat them unfairly. Protection of medical confidentiality plays a part in ensuring that people are not unfairly discriminated against on the basis of their medical condition. In short, the consequentialist argument states that a wide range of undesirable consequences will flow from not protecting medical confidentiality.

Deontological argument

5.42 These arguments claim that as a matter of principle confidential information should be kept private. A common way of putting this is to regard protection of confidence as an aspect of autonomy. As part of protecting the right to control our lives and live them as we want to, we are entitled to control information which is private, and which shapes our sense of self, and the way that others perceive us. This explains why if you want to disclose your medical information you can, but you also have the right not to disclose it. It should be your choice. Another way of putting this argument is that the confidential information is property which belongs to the individual. However, information is not normally regarded as property in the law.

5.43 A slightly different argument is to emphasize privacy. The argument is that we have a right to have areas of solitude which are outside the public gaze. Having a sphere of intimacy is important to a wide range of activities. It reflects a deep human need to have areas of life where we can be completely honest and need not put up any pretence. In *Campbell* v. *MGN*, the House of Lords referred to a mixture of privacy, dignity, and autonomy as the basis for medical confidentiality. This suggests that there is a range of different justifications that support the protection of confidentiality.

5.44 Another way of supporting the law on confidentiality is to see it as an obligation that is imposed on professionals. As someone in a privileged position, who is well paid and highly respected, they have obligations not to misuse their position for gain. Protecting confidentiality means that doctors and other health care professionals are prevented from taking advantage of the position they are in and misusing the information they have been given in a professional capacity.

CONCLUSION

As we have seen in this chapter, there is a clear principle that medical information should be kept confidential. However, despite the rhetoric, there is little substance in the right. A breach of medical confidentiality rarely results in serious legal consequences, unless it is done in breach of an injunction. Although the legal remedies are effective in a case where the breach has not yet occurred, where it has already occurred only very limited remedies are available. We have also seen that there are many cases in which breach of medical confidentiality is breached. A visit to a hospital is likely to lead to at least 100 different medical professionals having access to your medical records. The reality is that in this day and age it has become very difficult to keep anything truly secret.

FURTHER READING

Andorno, R. (2004) 'The Right Not to Know: An Autonomy Based Approach', *Journal of Medical Ethics* 30: 435–9.

Beyleveld, D., and Histed, E. (2000) 'Betrayal of Confidence in the Court of Appeal', *Medical Law International* 4: 277–311.

Brazier, M., and Cave, E. (2007) *Medicine, Patients and the Law* (London: Penguin).

Eekelaar, J. (2006) *Family Law and Personal Life* (Oxford: Oxford University Press).

General Medical Council (GMC) (2009) *Confidentiality* (London: GMC).

Gibbons, S. (2009) 'Regulating Biobanks: A Twelve-Point Typological Tool', *Medical Law Review* 19: 313–46.

Gilbar, R. (2005) *The Status of the Family in Law and Bioethics: The Genetic Context* (Aldershot: Ashgate).

Laurie, G. (2002) *Genetic Privacy: A Challenge to Medico-Legal Norms* (Cambridge: Cambridge University Press).

Kipnis, K. (2006) 'A Defense of Unqualified Medical Confidentiality', *American Journal of Bioethics* 6: 7–18.

Skene, L. (2001) 'Genetic Secrets and the Family', *Medical Law Review* 9: 162–9.

SELF-TEST QUESTIONS

1 A doctor tells her husband over supper that a particular celebrity came to see her that day. She does not give details, but says it was an 'intimate' issue. Has she breached confidentiality?

2 Mary goes to see her doctor and tells him that she is being beaten by her husband. She asks the doctor not to tell anyone about this. The doctor is concerned about her. Can he inform the police? Must he?

3 Bobby tells his doctor that he has become obsessed about a newsreader. He keeps imagining that he will do her harm. The doctor decides that he probably poses no danger, but is not sure. She writes to the newsreader informing him about her patient. Has she acted unlawfully?

4 What are the best justifications for protecting confidentiality?

6

Regulation of abortion and pregnancy

SUMMARY

Chapter 6 will discuss the issues of abortion, pregnancy regulation, and contraception. It will set out the law, but also outline the ethical disputes around these topics. The legal and moral status of the fetus will also be examined. The chapter will consider the arguments that have been put forward on either side of the debate over the fetus.

Introduction

6.1 The issues raised in this chapter are among the most controversial in medical law and ethics. In a way that is surprising. Abortion and contraception have become almost routine procedures. In the UK, abortion is not really a hot political topic and is certainly rarely raised in elections or political debates. In the US, by contrast, abortion continues to be a major political and social issue. While it would be unimaginable that in the UK abortion would become illegal or very strictly controlled, that is not so in the US.

6.2 The reason for the heat in the debate is that for both sides the stakes are high. For opponents of abortion (and for some opponents of contraception) these practices are nothing short of murder (Beckwith 2007). While for those supporting the right of access to abortion or contraception they are central to ensure women's equality and should be regarded as a basic human right (Boonin 2002). For the law, there is the difficulty in determining what response to take given the lack of consensus over these issues.

Contraception

6.3 At one time, contraception was seen as contrary to the public interest. In *Bravery* v. *Bravery* [1954] 1 WLR 1169, Lord Denning famously stated that sterilization was done 'so as to enable a man to have the pleasure of sexual intercourse, without shouldering the responsibilities attached to it'. He regarded it as contrary to the public interest and degrading to the man. Of course, time has moved on and a more representative view is that of Munby J in *R (Smeaton)* v. *Secretary of State for Health* [2002] 2 FCR 193, para. 215, who concluded that contraception 'Is no business of government, judges or the law,' but rather a decision for individuals to decide for themselves.

6.4 In fact, Munby J is not quite right. Contraception is the law's business because contraceptives are medical products and need to be licensed by the European Medicines Agency before use. Further, in the National Health Service Act 1977, s. 5(1)(b), the Secretary of State is under a duty to arrange to meet the reasonable requirements for advice and supply of contraception.

6.5 In practice, there are some important restrictions on the access to contraception. The oral contraceptive pill is only available on prescription from a doctor. However, condoms and post-coital contraception (the morning-after pill) are available without a prescription. Despite the access to contraception, England and Wales still have the highest teenage pregnancy and parenthood rates in Europe, three times that of France and six times that of the Netherlands. Three issues concerning contraception have troubled the courts in particular and we will examine these next.

The distinction between contraception and abortion

6.6 While contraception is largely unregulated, abortion is controlled through the Abortion Act 1967, as we shall see. It is, therefore, important that a clear line is drawn between contraception and abortion. The leading case is the following:

***R (John Smeaton on behalf of the SPUC) v. Secretary of State for Health* [2002]
2 FCR 193** The Society for the Protection of the Unborn Child (SPUC) sought to challenge the legality of SI 2000/3231, which allowed for the sale of the morning-after pill
without prescriptions. They argued that the morning-after pill procured a miscarriage
and therefore was illegal unless its supply was to be justified under the Abortion Act
1967. In essence, their claim was that a contraceptive prevented fertilization, while
the term 'abortion' covered all procedures which operated on a conceptus. Munby
J spent some time in his judgment going over the biology explaining that there was
a distinction between fertilization which took place hours, or occasionally days, after
sexual intercourse and then implantation, when the fertilized egg has moved into the
womb. The morning-after pill operated to prevent implantation. Munby J rejected the
argument that preventing implantation amounted to a miscarriage. This he thought
was the current understanding of the term 'miscarriage'; in any event, the thought that
the operation of the morning-after pill would not be seen as producing a miscarriage
by medical professionals, nor by members of the public. He also took into account the
social benefits of the availability of emergency contraception. Indeed, he noted that
the normal contraceptive pill can operate to prevent implantation of a fertilized egg
and if SPUC's argument was accepted, even the contraceptive pill would have to be
regulated under the Abortion Act 1967.

In short, the effect of this judgment is that it is implantation which distinguishes
contraception and abortion, rather than fertilization.

Contraception and children

6.7 Can a doctor or medical professional give advice about contraception to a child
without the consent of her parent? The leading case on this is the decision in the
following:

***Gillick v. West Norfolk and Wisbech AHA* [1986] AC 112** Mrs Gillick sought to
challenge the legality of a Department of Health circular which allowed doctors to
provide contraceptive advice and treatment without parental consent. The House
of Lords upheld the guidelines. A doctor could give such advice, but only if the child
was sufficiently mature to understand the medical, social, and family issues involved.
Where the child was sufficiently competent to make decisions about contraceptive
treatment the doctor or health professional could give that advice, if doing so was in
the child's best interests, without the consent of the parents. Further, doctors would
owe such a child a duty of confidentiality and so should not inform the parents of the
child's visit.

There has been some discussion of whether a doctor who provided a minor with contraception could be regarded as aiding and abetting a sexual offence. Section 73 of the Sexual Offences Act 2003 has now made clear that no such crime is committed as long as the doctor is acting to protect the child's health or well-being.

Contraception and those lacking capacity

6.8 When does someone have capacity to consent to receive, or not to receive, contraception? When is it in someone's best interests to be given contraception? These were the key questions at the heart of the following important decision:

> *A Local Authority* v. *Mrs A and Mr A* **[2010] EWHC 1549 (Fam)** Mrs A was aged 29, but had an extremely low level of intellectual functioning. She had previously had two children removed from her at birth because there were real concerns that she would not be able to provide adequate care for them. Later, she had married Mr A. He, too, had a learning difficulty and a significant impairment of intellectual functioning. Before her marriage, Mrs A had been receiving daily support from the local authority's community living team and had received contraception by means of a monthly injection, to which she consented. Since her marriage, she had not consented to receive any form of contraception. Indeed, Mr A did not want the social services to be involved in their marriage at all. There were reports that Mr A had bruised Mrs A regularly. The only reason given by Mrs A for her refusal to contraception was that her husband objected to it.
>
> Applying the Mental Capacity Act 2005 (see Chapter 4), Bodey J found that Mrs A had sufficient understanding of the facts to have capacity because she understood the basic facts about what contraception did. She understood the effect of contraception. The fact that she did not fully appreciate what it would be like to look after a child did not mean that she lacked capacity to make the decision about contraception. The issue of child rearing was said to be 'remote' from the question of contraception. However, he concluded that she lacked capacity because she was not able to make a free decision. Mr A's influence over her was so strong that she was not in a position to make a free decision. However, that still left the difficulty of what order to make. Although he thought it was in her best interests to receive contraception, he did not think it appropriate to force her to have it. He therefore made no order, but encouraged her social workers to persuade her to agree to use the contraception.

This case demonstrates the difficulties in forcing contraception on those who do not want it, even if they lack capacity. It has been criticized for failing to place weight on the fact that the evidence suggested that but for her husband's pressuring she would have consented (see Herring 2010).

Sterilization

6.9 Where a patient with capacity wishes to be sterilized, there are no special legal provisions beyond the normal rules of negligence and the law of consent. However, in two categories of cases legal issues do arise. First, there is the question of whether it is ever appropriate to perform a sterilization on a patient who lacks capacity. Second, there is the question of whether a claim can be brought if after a sterilization a patient becomes pregnant.

Adults lacking capacity

6.10 As we saw in Chapter 4, where a person lacks capacity then the Mental Capacity Act 2005 states that decisions should be made on their behalf based on what is in their best interests. However, unlike other procedures, if it is thought that sterilization is in the patient's best interests, the approval of the court is required first. If the patient is an adult then a declaration can be sought under the inherent jurisdiction, or, preferably, under the Mental Capacity Act 2005, s. 15; while if the patient is a child then an order can be made under the Children Act 1989. It may well be that if there are therapeutic reasons for the sterilization (i.e. the patient has an illness and the appropriate treatment is sterilization) court approval is not required.

> *A Trust* v. *H (An Adult)* **[2006] EWHC 1230 (Fam)** H was a patient who was detained under the Mental Health Act 1983. She suffered schizophrenia and had delusional beliefs, in particular that she had no children. A cancerous cyst developed on her ovaries. The condition caused her pain and discomfort. The doctors recommended a total abdominal hysterectomy, which would render her infertile. H refused because she wished to have children.
>
> It was held that H lacked the capacity to decide about the operation. Her delusional beliefs about her circumstances, her failure to appreciate the severity of her condition, and that her life was threatened meant that she lacked capacity to make the decision. In this case, it was in her best interests to undergo the operation, as it was therapeutically necessary. If necessary, restraint could be used to enable the operation to proceed.

6.11 Much debate has centred on when, if ever, it will be in the best interests of a patient to be sterilized for non-therapeutic reasons (e.g. to prevent the person having children). The following case gives guidance on the approach taken by the courts:

> ***Re B* [1987] 2 ALL ER 206** B was 17 years old, but had the mental functioning of a 5- or 6-year-old. The key issue before the court was whether or not it would be lawful to sterilize. The House of Lords emphasized that the key focus must be on the best interests of the patient. The wider interests of society or eugenic concerns had no role to play. They also rejected an argument that the approach should consider B's human rights. Rather, the focus was simply on what was in the child's best interests. In this case, a key factor was that B would not understand what was happening to her if she fell pregnant. She would find it a distressing and frightening experience. She would not be able to care for any resulting child. It was, therefore, in her best interests for the procedure to be performed.

6.12 Subsequent cases have developed this approach and the following points emerge. The question is what is in the best interests of the patient, and not whether there is a respectable body of opinion in favour of the sterilization (e.g. a form of the *Bolam* test). So, if the parents are wanting their adult child sterilized, the question is not 'is it a reasonable view that the child should be sterilised?'; but rather 'is it in this child's best interests to be sterilised' (*Re F (A Mental Patient: Sterilisation)* [1990] 2 AC 1).

> ***Re SL (Adult Patient)* [2002] FLR 389** SL had severe learning difficulties. It was accepted that she did not have capacity to consent to medical treatment. Her mother wished a sterilization and/or hysterectomy, due to the risk of pregnancy and SL's heavy periods. Wall J granted the order, despite evidence from a doctor that sterilization was not necessary in this case. On appeal this was overturned. It was held that insufficient weight had been attached to the expert's evidence that alternative forms of contraception could be used and that treatment for the heavy periods could follow in the future. The judge should have addressed why the less intrusive measure of contraception could not have been attempted. While it was true that it was for the judge to weigh the value of the medical evidence and that it was for the judge to determine what was in a patient's overall best interests, due weight had to be attached to the view of the experts. In this case, it was the unanimous evidence from impressive experts that less intrusive forms of contraception should be used. The patient had a right not to have drastic surgery imposed upon her, unless that could be demonstrated to be in her best interests. The judge had erred by asking whether the sterilization would be acceptable according to the standards of a responsible body of medical opinion (the *Bolam* test). Instead, he should have made an assessment of what was in SL's best interests.

6.13 The case law indicates that the following are two irrelevant factors that should not be considered when determining what is in a patient's best interests:

- Eugenic considerations should not be taken into account: The fact that any child that the patient gives birth to may suffer a disability should not be a factor that is considered (*Re X (Adult Sterilisation)* [1998] 2 FLR 1124).

- The interests of the parents or carers: In some cases, carers have made arguments that if the patient becomes pregnant or produces a child then their burdens will become excessive and have therefore sought sterilization. Or they have argued that the work in dealing with menstruation is so significant that the sterilization is necessary to ease their burden. The courts have generally been very reluctant to take such arguments into account (*Re B* [1987] 2 All ER 206). The focus must be on the best interests of the patient, rather than what is best for the carers. It may be that if the court was persuaded that without the sterilization the carers could not carry on and that that would cause the patient serious harm, then the burden on the carers would carry weight.

6.14 The following are relevant factors which the court will take into account in deciding whether a sterilization will be in a patient's best interests:

- The views of professionals: it would be a most unusual case for the court to approve sterilization of a patient lacking capacity, without the support of the professionals involved. There have been a few cases where there has been divided professional opinion and in these the court has refused to grant the declaration (*Re LC* [1997] 2 FLR 258.)

- It must be shown that sterilization is a last resort (*Re B* [1987] 2 All ER 206): it needs to be shown that there are no less interventionist ways of protecting the patient from the dangers. For example, if the concern is pregnancy, it might be asked whether it is not possible to use other forms of contraception, short of sterilization (*Re P (A Minor) (Wardship: Sterilisation)* [1989] 1 FLR 182). It might also be asked if supervision cannot prevent sexual intercourse taking place. This approach could be justified on the basis that sterilization without consent interferes with a patient's rights under the European Convention on Human Rights (ECHR) Articles 3 and 8. Therefore, any interference must be justified as necessary in order to protect the patient from serious harm.

- The courts have been willing to take into account distress or pain connected with menstruation as a reason for justifying sterilization (*Re Z (Medical*

Treatment: Hysterectomy) [2000] 1 FCR 274): however, the court is likely to require clear proof of serious difficulties before relying on this ground.

- Where fears over pregnancy are relied upon, the fears must be realistic: in *Re LC* [1997] 2 FLR 258, Thorpe LJ found that the carers were constantly supervising the woman in question and so concerns over pregnancy were unfounded. Successful applications often refer to the fact that the patient is involved in a relationship or has shown an 'interest' in patients of the opposite sex or even that she is 'attractive' (*Re P (A Minor) (Warship: Sterilisation)* [1989] 1 FLR 182; *SL* v. *SL* [2000] 2 FCR 452).

6.15 The courts' approach has proved controversial. Some critics feel that the courts have been too ready to approve sterilization (Keywood 2002). In particular, the complaint is made that the courts have failed to recognize that sterilization is a major interference in the rights of patients, and the best interests test fails to recognize adequately the severity of that interference. It is an interference not only of bodily integrity, but also of reproductive choices.

6.16 A rather different point is that the current law enables a 'cover-up' of sexual abuse. If we are talking about people with serious mental illness, it is unlikely that they are able to consent to sexual intercourse. The sterilization 'protects' them from pregnancy, whereas perhaps we should be protecting them from the rape.

6.17 It can also be pointed out that nearly all the cases involve women. Perhaps this is because if a man makes a woman pregnant through sexual intercourse this will not be contrary to his best interests (*Re A (Medical Treatment: Male Sterilisation)* [2000] 1 FCR 193). However, critics would note that the burden of avoiding pregnancy tends to fall on the women involved.

6.18 Some commentators have suggested that the current law fails to protect the rights of patients in these cases (Keywood 2002). Not everyone is convinced by these arguments. If a patient is not able to understand the nature of pregnancy or childhood, it is sensible to talk in terms of her right to make reproductive choices. And have the courts been too harsh on the carers in these cases? Given the huge sacrifices that the carers have made, it is unreasonable that an operation be performed which will greatly benefit the carers without causing significant pain to the individual.

Re Eve [1986] 2 SCR 388 (Supreme Court of Canada) Mrs E sought permission from the court for sterilization of her daughter Eve. Eve was an adult but suffered from a mental disorder which made it extremely difficult to communicate with others. Mrs E, who was nearly 60, was concerned that if Eve became pregnant, she, Mrs E, would have the burden of caring for the child.

The Supreme Court held that any order under the *parens patriae* jurisdiction had to be made for the benefit of the person in need of protection. It could not be used to benefit others. The jurisdiction had to act with great caution. Sterilization should never be authorized for non-therapeutic purposes. In the absence of the person's consent it can never safely be found to be for their benefit. Sterilization involved a grave intrusion on a person's rights and its physical damage outweighed any possible advantages. La Forest noted that it 'removes from a person the great privilege of giving birth, and is for practical purpose[s] irreversible. If achieved by means of a hysterectomy, the procedure approved by the Appeal Division, it is not only irreversible; it is major surgery.' (para. 79)

Tort and failed contraception

6.19 If a woman has become pregnant after a failed sterilization an action in negligence could be brought. This can raise a number of issues.

Was a duty of care owed?

6.20 There will be little difficulty in finding that a doctor owes a duty of care to a patient upon whom he performed a sterilization. However, in *Goodwill* v. *BPAS* [1996] 2 All ER 161, a doctor negligently performed a sterilization of a man. Three years later, the man had sex with a woman and she became pregnant as a result. It was held that the doctor could not be said to owe her a duty of care.

Was the doctor negligent?

6.21 There are two arguments that could be used here. It could be said that the procedure was performed improperly (in which case the ordinary *Bolam* test, set out in Chapter 3, applies). Alternatively, it may be claimed that the doctor was negligent in failing to make it clear that there was a risk that the operation would fail and to encourage the parties to use contraception until tests had confirmed that the operation had been a success. It might also be claimed that the doctor had been negligent in stating that the operation was a success when it had not. Again, in such a case, the general law on failure to disclose statements are applied (see Chapter 3). Given that professional bodies state that patients should be warned of the risk that the procedure will not work, it is very likely that it will be found to be negligent not to disclose the risk of pregnancy.

Is there a loss?

6.22 This has proved the most difficult issue. Looking first at what losses a woman can recover for. She can seek damages for her pain and suffering in the pregnancy and labour; and for any medical expenses incurred during the pregnancy and childbirth. A claim for loss of earnings can also be brought.

6.23 A woman cannot recover for the fact a child was born. A child will be regarded as a benefit and not a loss, even if the pregnancy was not wanted. The courts have declared it contrary to public policy to regard a child's birth as a loss to the parents. While the parents will no doubt incur expenses in caring for the child, the joys of looking after the child will outweigh these disadvantages. If the child were later to find out that the court had regarded their birth as a harm to the parents that could cause the child serious emotional harm. This was established in the following case:

> **McFarlane v. Tayside Health Board [1999] 3 WLR 1301** The McFarlanes, a married couple, already had four children. They decided not to have further children and so the husband underwent a vasectomy. The husband was told his sperm count was negative and he no longer needed to take contraceptive precautions. However, the wife became pregnant. They sued in negligence. The House of Lords held that the cost of raising the child could not be recovered. Although the wife could recover for the pain, discomfort, inconvenience, and cost of the pregnancy, the couple could not recover for the cost of raising the child. It would not be fair, just, or reasonable for the health board to be liable. Lord Millett explained:
>
>> if the law regards an event as beneficial, plaintiffs cannot make it a matter for compensation merely by saying that it is an event they did not want to happen. In this branch of the law at least, plaintiffs are not normally allowed, by a process of subjective devaluation, to make a detriment out of benefit.

6.24 That seems a straightforward approach. However, more complex cases have still troubled the court:

> **Rees v. Darlington NHS Trust [2004] AC 309** A sterilization was performed on a woman with severe visual impairment. A healthy child was born. The House of Lords upheld the *McFarlane* approach even on such facts. This time they accepted that the approach taken was not in accordance with the normal rules of tort law. She could receive damages for the pain and cost of pregnancy, but not the costs of raising the child. The one concession was that the majority awarded her £15,000 to recognize the breach of her autonomy. This was to compensate her for the loss of opportunity to live her life as she wished, rather than the loss caused by having the child.

Parkinson v. St James and Seacroft University Hospital NHS Trust [2002] QB 266 Following a negligently performed sterilization, a woman gave birth to a disabled child and the court were asked whether *McFarlane* was still to be followed. Hale LJ emphasized that in cases where a woman becomes pregnant despite being assured that she could not, was a violation of her bodily integrity. As the case was in the Court of Appeal she could not overrule *McFarlane*, but her disapproval of the approach taken is barely disguised. The solution in that case is to award the costs of raising the disabled child over and above those for a non-disabled child.

The *Parkinson* decision was discussed, obiter by their Lordships in *Rees* where three of their Lordships seem to approve it, although the powerful voices of Lords Bingham and Nicholls did not. In *Groom* v. *Selby* (2002) 64 BMLR 47, *Parkinson* was followed and so it seems to represent the current law.

6.25 These decisions have engendered quite some debate. This will be presented through two speakers.

Speaker 1 (opponent of the current law)

6.26 The current law is unacceptable. At the heart of my objection is that the courts seemed to have overlooked the point that the whole purpose of a sterilization is to prevent having children, maybe particularly due to the expense. If the doctor negligently performs the operation and causes the very loss that the parents have tried so hard to avoid, it seems hard to justify why they should not be compensated for the loss. Emily Jackson (2001) has put the argument well:

> Where a patient has decided to have an operation in order to irrevocably remove the possibility of conception, it seems perverse to argue that they should regard the failure of this surgery as a blessing.

To use an example from a different field of law: if I hire a decorator to paint my room blue and instead he paints it pink, surely I am entitled to damages. Even if most people would think the pink a preferable colour, it is not the colour I requested. It should be regarded as a basic principle of law that I should be entitled to what I expected.

6.27 One of the arguments emphasized by the House of Lords in *McFarlane* was very weak. That was that the level of damages (the cost of raising a child) would be out of proportion to the wrongdoing of the doctor (Lord Clyde emphasized this point). However, that is a regular feature of tort law. A moment's inadvertence by a driver can cause catastrophic injuries to a pedestrian and millions of pounds worth of damages can be claimed.

Speaker 2 (supporting the current law)

6.28   The courts have taken a realistic and appropriate stance. When assessing damages for a loss we must consider not only the losses caused by the negligence, but also the gains. In this case, the losses for the parents will be financial, while the gains will be the relationship with the child. Nearly all parents will quickly say that the joys children bring outweigh their financial costs. To assess the creation of the child simply in terms of the financial costs is to ignore the non-economic benefits.

6.29   This point becomes all the stronger when the broader picture is looked at. Parents will have the joy of raising a child, should we give them money from the NHS coffers to do this, when the money could be used to save lives or cure terrible illnesses?

Abortion

The legal structure

6.30   The structure of the law on abortion is a surprise to many students. The starting point is that abortion is a crime. The Abortion Act 1967 creates circumstances in which a defence may be available. So, at least as a matter of technical law, abortion is seen as a justified crime.

The criminal offences

6.31   Section 58 of the Offences Against the Person Act 1861 states that

> Every woman, being with child, who, with intent to procure her own miscarriage, shall unlawfully administer to herself any poison or other noxious thing, or shall unlawfully use any instrument or other means whatsoever with the like intent and whosoever, with intent to procure the miscarriage of any woman, whether she be or not with child shall unlawfully administer to her or cause to be taken by her any poison or other noxious thing, or shall unlawfully use any instrument or other means whatsoever with the like intent, shall be guilty of an offence.

The offence can be committed by the woman who procures her own miscarriage or another person who procures her miscarriage. The offence is only committed if there is an intent to procure a miscarriage, so someone who accidentally procures a miscarriage will not be committing an offence. There is also an offence under section 59 of the 1861 Act where a defendant supplies or procures any poison or instrument, knowing it will be used in unlawful abortions.

> *R* **v.** *A* **[2010] EWCA Crim 1949** A was convicted of the offence of procuring a miscarriage contrary to section 59 of the Offences Against the Person Act. He had taken his pregnant wife (W) to an abortion clinic. His wife did not speak English, but A offered to act as an interpreter. Concern was expressed after a nurse, who was also able to act as an interpreter, spoke to the wife. It transpired that W thought she was attending the clinic for a minor operation and that she had no wish for an abortion.
>
> It was held that A's conviction was wrong. The section 59 offence only covered procuring or supplying something intended for use in procuring an unlawful miscarriage. The particulars of the charge laid against A were that he had intended unlawfully to bring about the use of procedures on W to procure a miscarriage. However, that was not something covered by section 59. As he had not procured any poison, noxious thing, or any other instrument, he could not be convicted. There was no evidence that any particular instruments had been selected by the clinic, or even if they had that A had procured them.

6.32 Another offence is found in the Infant Life (Preservation) Act 1929, s. 1:

> (1) Subject as hereinafter in this subsection provided, any person who, with intent to destroy the life of a child capable of being born alive, by any wilful act causes a child to die before it has an existence independent of its mother, shall be guilty of felony, to wit, of child destruction, and shall be liable on conviction thereof on indictment to penal servitude for life:
>
> > Provided that no person shall be found guilty of an offence under this section unless it is proved that the act which caused the death of the child was not done in good faith for the purpose only of preserving the life of the mother.
>
> (2) For the purpose of this Act, evidence that a woman had at any material time been pregnant for a period of 28 weeks or more shall be prima facie proof that she was at the time pregnant of a child capable of being born alive.

This makes it an offence intentionally to destroy the life of a child who is capable of being born alive (understood to be from 28 weeks from conception). This would make late abortions criminal, unless justified under the Abortion Act 1967.

The Abortion Act 1967

6.33 The Abortion Act 1967 sets out the circumstances in which an abortion is lawful. Before the Act was passed, the courts used the common law of necessity as a defence in extreme cases (*R* v. *Bourne* [1939] 1 KB 687). However, it is generally accepted that it is very unlikely that an abortion which was not permitted under the Abortion Act would be justified under the defence of necessity.

6.34 The Abortion Act 1967 sets down four requirements that must be satisfied if an abortion is to be lawful (save in emergencies):

1 Two medical practitioners must agree that one of the statutory grounds permitting abortion is present. These will be discussed shortly.

2 Abortions may only be carried out under the authority of a registered medical practitioner. This is not to say that nurses, or other health professionals, cannot perform the abortion, but if they do so they must be acting under the authority of a doctor.

3 All abortions must take place in an NHS hospital or other approved place. Private health clinics are often approved. This requirement means that 'back-street' abortions are not permitted.

4 All abortions must be notified to the relevant authorities.

The statutory grounds for an abortion are the most controversial of these requirements and we need to discuss these further.

6.35 For the abortion to be justified under the Act, it is necessary to show that the doctors are of the opinion that the grounds are made out. It does NOT need to be shown that the grounds were actually made out. So, if a doctor mistakenly believes that say, ground (d), is made out because the fetus is disabled and he performs an abortion, the abortion will be lawful, even if in fact he had made a misdiagnosis. This makes it extremely hard to prove that an abortion was unlawful. Even though it might be proved that the ground justifying abortion was not present, it would be hard to show that the doctor did not believe that it did.

6.36 One of the very few cases where an illegal abortion was found was *R* v. *Smith* [1974] 1 All ER 376. There the doctor seems to have made no internal examination of the patient and had taken no personal history or heard about her situation, save for a note that she was depressed. It seems that the doctor who gave the second opinion had not even examined the patient. But that is the exception. In *Paton* v. *BPAS* [1978] 2 All ER 992, George Baker P suggested it would it be a 'foolish judge' who would declare that an abortion would be unlawful, unless there was clear bad faith.

Grounds for abortion

6.37 We will now look at the grounds for abortion.

Risk to physical or mental health

6.38 Abortion Act 1967, s. 1(1)(a) states:

> that the pregnancy has not exceeded its twenty-fourth week and that the continuance of the pregnancy would involve risk, greater than if the pregnancy were terminated, of injury to the physical or mental health of the pregnant woman or any existing children of her family.

The first point to emphasize is that this ground only applies to pregnancies of under 24 weeks. It requires the medical practitioners to consider the risk posed to the mental or physical health of the pregnant woman or any existing children. These must be considered: first, if the abortion does not occur; and second, if the abortion does occur. If the risk to the health without the abortion is greater than the risk to the health with the abortion then this ground is satisfied.

6.39 The term 'mental health' is generally interpreted in a wide way and not restricted to medically recognized disorders and could therefore include emotional upset. However, we have no case specifically saying that it might be open to a court to take a more restrictive interpretation of the term.

6.40 The reference to the existing children of the women presumably means that if it could be shown that the continuation of the pregnancy would impact negatively on her care for those children, that could be a factor to be taken into account. Section 1(2) of the Abortion Act 1967 indicates that the doctors should consider the woman's 'actual and foreseeable environment' when considering the impact of the continued pregnancy. This suggests that the doctors can consider the woman's social, housing, and family situation when considering the impact of the continued pregnancy.

6.41 This ground is the most commonly relied upon ground, by some way. Some have complained that if the woman wants an abortion, it is easy for a doctor to conclude that her mental health will be better if the abortion goes ahead. In effect, this ground is no more than saying that the woman requests the abortion. That may well be how the ground operates in the real world, but whether that is a bad thing or not is a matter of opinion.

6.42 In 2008, there was a debate in Parliament over whether the 24-week time period should be reduced. Those supporting the lowering argued that technology had improved so that a fetus could be viable at less than 24 weeks. The proposed amendment failed.

Grave permanent injury

6.43 Section 1(1)(b) of the Abortion Act 1967 states:

> that the termination is necessary to prevent grave permanant injury to the physical or mental health of the pregnant woman.

The differences between ground (a) and (b) are important. First, there is no time limit on ground (b). Abortion can be performed up until just before birth based on it. Second, ground (b) is harder to prove than ground (a): it needs to be shown that the harm was grave, permanent, and involves an injury. Third, it must be shown that the termination is necessary. This suggests that if there are other ways of avoiding the injury then these should be used.

Risk to life

6.44 Section 1(1)(c) of the Abortion Act 1967 states:

> that the continuance of the pregnancy would involve risk to the life of the pregnant woman, greater than if the pregnancy were terminated.

This ground, too, has no time limit to it and can be used to justify an abortion up until the time of birth. Notably, it only requires a belief in a risk of death. There is no need to show that the risk is a high one.

Abnormalities

6.45 Section 1(1)(d) Abortion Act 1967 states:

> that there is a substantial risk that if the child were born it would suffer from physical or mental abnormalities as to be seriously handicapped.

This ground, too, has no time limit. It should be noted that the risk of the handicap must be a substantial risk. A slight risk will be insufficient. The handicap must be a serious one. Gillian Douglas (1991) has suggested that the two elements are linked: in cases of a very serious handicap, a lower risk might be acceptable. Not everyone will agree and it might be argued that the word 'substantial' should not take on different meanings depending on the nature of the handicap. It has been suggested that a substantial risk is one that is over 50 per cent (Royal College of Obstetricians and Gynaecologists 2008). Another issue which has generated some debate is whether the mother's views of the seriousness of handicap are relevant. One study (Statham et al. 2006) found a wide variation in the attitude of doctors as to what amounts to a serious handicap in this context.

6.46 There has been quite some debate over its basis (Scott 2005). One argument is that if the child was born, it would suffer such appalling handicaps that it would be better for the child not to have been born. If that is the basis, then it is not clear that a serious handicap sets the hurdle high enough. The second ground is that the raising of a severely disabled child will impose such a heavy burden on the parents that they should not be compelled to take it on.

Other provisions in the Abortion Act 1967

6.47 There are some detailed provisions elsewhere in the Abortion Act 1967. In section 1(4), if termination is immediately necessary to save the life or prevent grave permanent injury to the mental or physical health of the pregnant woman, then there is no need to have the opinion of two registered practitioners.

6.48 Some medical practitioners have conscientious objections to the procedures. Abortion Act 1967, s. 4 makes it clear that if someone has a conscientious objection to abortion, they are not under a legal duty to participate in any treatment authorized by the Act. However, that is subject to limitations. Section 4 does not affect the duty of a doctor to perform an abortion if necessary to save the life or prevent permanent injury to a pregnant woman. If he or she were to fail to act in such a case, they could be open to legal claims (presumably surrounding negligence, and perhaps even gross negligence manslaughter), or to professional claims. The issue has not arisen, presumably because a colleague can always be found in such a case to provide the necessary care.

6.49 It is noticeable that the Act removes the duty to participate in treatment, but not necessarily to advise. This means that if a GP has a conscientious objection, he or she must refer the patient to another practitioner.

> *Janaway v. Salford AHA* **[1989] AC 537** The applicant was a secretary at a health centre. She was asked to type a letter referring a patient to a consultant for an abortion. As a Roman Catholic, she refused to type it and her contract of employment was terminated. She argued that she was protected by section 4. The House of Lords held that section 4 did not apply to her because it only applied to those actually taking part in the treatment.

Legal actions to prevent abortion

6.50 There have been a number of attempts by men to prevent women from having abortions. In short, these have all failed. A number of avenues have been tried:

> **Paton v. Trustees of the BPAS [1979] QB 276** A husband sought an injunction to prevent his wife from having an abortion without his consent. This failed. Sir George Baker explained that the Abortion Act did not even require that a father or husband be notified, let alone consent, before an abortion could take place.

> **C v. S [1988] QB 135** A claimed that his partner's proposed abortion would be unlawful and sought an injunction to prevent it. Sir John Donaldson MR, in rejecting the application, stated that any such application should be brought by the DPP or the Attorney General.

> **Jepson v. CC of West Mercia [2003] EWHC 3318** A curate learned of a case of an abortion carried out on the disability ground where the child had had a cleft palate. She argued that this was unlawful because a cleft palate was not a serious disability. The Crown Prosecution Services (CPS) decided to prosecute. The CPS agreed to reinvestigate the case but found that there was no evidence that the doctors had not formed the view, in good faith, that the child would be seriously handicapped.

Abortion and those lacking capacity

6.51 The courts have, as we have seen, tried to stay clear of the tricky area of abortion. However, it is difficult to do that where the individual lacks capacity. The court will seek to determine what will be in the individual's best interests.

> **Re SS (Adult: Medical Treatment) [2002] 1 FCR 73** A pregnant woman suffering from schizophrenia was detained under the Mental Health Act 1983. It was held that she lacked the capacity to make the decision of whether or not to abort. S was in favour of a termination. She would not be able to look after any child that was born. There was conflicting evidence, however, of what would be in her best interests. Justice Wall in deciding against ordering an abortion ordered that S was 24 weeks pregnant and that the abortion procedure would be painful and traumatic, especially given that the patient would understand the issue.

Debates on the abortion law

6.52 One point to emphasize is that the abortion law in England does not reflect the idea of a 'right to choose'. The legality of abortion depends on the views of the medical professionals rather than on the wishes of the woman. Indeed, the Act does not even mention the consent of the woman, although under the standard law on medical treatment her consent would of course be required.

6.53 The reason for this is, no doubt, historical. It was easy to get the Abortion Act 1967 passed: abortion was portrayed as a medical procedure, better left to the medical professionals than to outside intervention. This was seen as a more acceptable way of justifying the law than references to the choice of the woman. Indeed, the image of the pregnant woman driven to despair by the pregnancy was the one commonly raised in the debate over the Act.

6.54 It is not surprising then that pro-abortion campaigners have objected to the portrayal of the pregnant woman as a sidelined figure, with the focus being on 'expert' medical opinion rather than on choice. However, despite the validity of those concerns, there may be something to be said in favour of the way the law is presented. First, as Marie Fox (1998) notes, it makes it harder for outsiders to challenge the decision of the doctors. As the *Jepsom* case shows, it is very hard to challenge an abortion because it seems due to a medical decision by the doctors concerned. If the law put the issue more in terms of a woman's right, it might be more readily open to challenge (see Sheldon 1997). Second, whatever the law says on paper, the reality is that, at least in the early stages of pregnancy, a woman seeking an abortion will be able to get one: the law operates as abortion on demand, even though the Act is not worded in those terms. So the Act is in a sense a benign fiction.

The legal status of the fetus

6.55 The fetus holds an uneasy status in English law. The judicial pronouncements are somewhat ambiguous and contradictory. It seems that there are some statements that can be made with confidence:

- A fetus is not a person. Therefore a fetus cannot be the victim of murder or enforce contracts (*Attorney-General's Reference (No. 3 of 1994)* [1997] 3 WLR 421).

- The fetus is not a 'nothing' (*St George's Healthcare NHS Trust* v. *S* (1998) 44 BMLR 160), nor simply a part of the mother (*Attorney-General's Reference (No. 3 of 1994)*).

As Lord Mustill stated in *Attorney-General's Reference (No. 3 of 1994)*, the feuts is '*sui generis*', a 'unique organism'. However, it would be misleading to suggest that the fetus is given a significant level of protection. The fetus cannot be made a ward of court (R*e F (In Utero)* [1988] Fam 122) and proceedings cannot be brought 'in the name of the fetus' (*Paton* v. *BPAS* [1978] 2 All ER 987).

> ***Re MB* [1997] 2 FLR 426** MB was 40 weeks pregnant when it was discovered that the fetus was in the breach position. This meant that a vaginal delivery posed serious risks to the child. A Caesarean section was recommended and she consented to have this. However, she withdrew her consent when the doctor was about to inject her, due to her irrational fear of needles. The patient was in labour and was not responding to the midwives. The health authority sought an order that it would be lawful to operate on her without her consent. A psychiatrist gave evidence that MB lacked capacity to see beyond the immediate situation because of her fear of needles.
>
> The Court of Appeal confirmed that it would be a crime and a tort to perform treatment on a person without their consent. A competent patient had an absolute right to refuse treatment, for any reason, even if it led to her death. The reason for refusal could be irrational; it still needed to be respected. The interests of the fetus did not justify overriding her rights. Fear and panic could render a person incompetent. That was so in this case because her fear meant that she was unable to make a decision. As she lacked capacity, the decision as to whether to authorize the Caesarean section depended on an assessment of her best interests. It was in her best interests to give birth to a healthy baby because if the baby had died or been injured that would have caused her long-term harm. It was therefore lawful to perform the Caesarean section and if necessary use force to enable that to happen.

6.56 On the other hand, the interests of the fetus seem protected in two ways:

1 The criminal law protects the fetus through the offences of procuring a miscarriage (see above). The fact that these offences can be committed by the woman indicates that they are not designed to protect her interests, and that suggests that the offences are designed to protect the fetus. Further, the fact that the law does not allow unlimited abortion indicates that there is some recognition of the fetus.

2 The law allows a child to sue for injuries caused while she/he was a fetus. However, such injury cannot be sued for until birth, which indicates that at best these are seen as a contingent interests. The interests of the fetus have crystallized on birth.

Attorney-General's Reference (No. 3 of 1994) **[1997] 3 WLR 421** The appellant stabbed his girlfriend who, as he knew, was 22 to 24 weeks pregnant. He stabbed her in the face, abdomen, and back. The child was born seventeen days later and survived 120 days before dying as a result of the premature birth. The mother recovered. The appellant was convicted with wounding with intent to cause grievous bodily harm against the mother. There was no issue over that conviction. He was also charged with murder of the child. The judge ruled that he could not be guilty of murder or manslaughter.

The House of Lords confirmed that to be guilty of murder a defendant must do an act which causes the death of the victim, intending to kill or cause grievous bodily harm to the victim. Under the doctrine of 'transferred malice' a defendant who intended to kill A, but in fact killed B, could be convicted as the intent to kill A could be 'transferred' to enable a conviction for the murder of B. Except for the specific statutory offence, a fetus-in-utero could not be the victim of murder or any violent crime. However, violence to a fetus-in-utero which caused harm after birth could give rise to criminal responsibility. It would stretch these principles too far to convict the appellant of murder. It was not possible to transfer the intent to harm the girlfriend to the fetus as the foetus was not a person in the eyes of the law. The fetus was best regarded as a unique organism which was not a person, but not simply a part of the mother. The appellant could be guilty of manslaughter as that offence did not require there to be an intention directed at the victim.

6.57 In the following case, the European Court of Human Rights had to determine whether a fetus had rights under the ECHR:

Vo v. France **[2004] 2 FCR 577** Ms Vo, who was pregnant, attended a routine antenatal appointment. There was a mix-up over the name and the doctor thought she was present for the removal of a contraceptive coil. In attempting this, he ruptured the amniotic sac and the pregnancy had to be terminated. Under French law, the doctor had committed no offence and Ms Vo claimed that the absence of a criminal remedy to punish the destruction of a fetus meant that French law failed to protect the right to life of a fetus under Article 2. The majority of the court concluded that there was no violation. The court refused to rule on the precise status of the fetus under the convention. It was accepted that the fetus was not a person and so was not directly protected by Article 2, but it was left as an open question whether the fetus had a version of a right protected by Article 2. The court held that even if such a view were adopted, in the case of abortion the mother's interest would trump any claim by the fetus. The majority took the view that the issue of the status of the fetus was best left to individual countries. The minority wanted a clear holding that a fetus was protected by Article 2, although in the abortion context the interests of the woman would override those.

One can understand the feelings of Ken Mason (2005), who on reading the case, said that it was like 'a long journey to the pub with no beer!'

6.58 The Canadian Supreme Court has also considered the issue of the status of the fetus in this significant judgment:

> **Winnipeg Child and Family Services (Northwest Area) v. G (DF) [1997] 3 SCR 925** G was five months pregnant with her fourth child. She was addicted to sniffing glue. This addiction had meant that two of her previous children had been born permanently disabled and were in state care. The local Family Services sought an order that G be detained for treatment until the birth of her child. The Superior Court judge granted the order.
>
> The majority of the Supreme Court held that the order should not have been made. Canadian law did not recognize the unborn child as a legal person with rights. Once the child is born then his or her existence before birth can be recognized for limited purposes, but that is dependent on the child being born. The Family services were seeking to act on the interests of the fetus, but the fetus had no legal rights. The application must fail.
>
> The majority rejected an argument that the case showed that the law needed to be changed by the court. The issue involved a conflict between fundamental interests and rights. The court could not assess the possible ramifications of determining that a pregnant woman's rights might be infringed in order to protect the fetus. If any such change was to be made it would need to be done by the legislature.
>
> In a dissenting judgment, Sopinka and Major JJ held that the *parens patriae* jurisdiction existed to protect those who could not look after themselves. A fetus suffering from a mother's abusive behaviour fell within this class. Modern technology showed that a child had human characteristics before birth and so the rule that a child only acquired rights on birth could no longer be supported.

Abortion ethics

Speaker 1 (pro-choice)

6.59 I reject the view that the fetus has any moral or legal status until birth. In order to decide if something has the moral status of being a person we need to ask what it is that makes a person valuable and unique (Warren 1997). It is surely their capacity for rational thought, their ability to interact with other people and be part of a community, and their ability to be self-conscious. These do not occur until birth, and indeed perhaps some time afterwards. I realize that there are some religious people who see the essence of personhood to be a soul, but that is a religious concept and we cannot rely on it as the basis of a legal approach. Although it might be a rather unpleasant analogy, imagine a woman gave birth to something that had no head. We would probably not regard that as a person. That is because we recognize that the capacity for thought and interaction is central to humanity.

6.60 The best argument that might be made against my view is that the fetus is a potential person and therefore is worthy of respect (Marquis 2006). But that is not really convincing. A sperm or egg is a potential person, but we dispose of those without concern. A pencil and blank piece of paper is a potential master-piece of art but we do not show them the respect of a masterwork of art.

6.61 As a fetus is of no moral value it is best regarded as simply part of the mother. Professor Warren (1997), supporting a similar view to mine, suggests that abortion should be seen in a similar light to clipping a toenail or cutting hair. That might be a rather offensive analogy to opponents of abortion, but she is right! There should, therefore, be no restriction on abortion, save that the woman has given her consent.

Speaker 2 (pro-life view)

6.62 I take the view that a fetus is a person from the moment of conception. Many who take that view do so because their beliefs follow the teachings of a particular religion, but I do not rely on religious arguments because we are discussing what the law should be. I would make my case with the following points.

6.63 First, at the point of conception the entire genetic make-up of the person is complete (Beckwith 2007). There is no new genetic input that takes place. The unique DNA of the individual is fixed at conception. We are increasingly recognizing the significance of DNA to identity and we should therefore recognize the significance of this point as the start of unique genetic identify.

6.64 Second, there must be a point at which personhood begins. Others might point to birth or viability, but these are arbitrary lines. Is the baby just before birth any morally different to the baby just after birth? The only clear point in time at which we can draw a sharp line is conception: before then there is no genetically unique person, but after then there is.

6.65 Third, even if the above arguments are rejected, we should recognize that the fetus has the potential to become a person (Marquis 2006). We are, in killing fetuses, destroying the lives they would have had in the future. That might at first sound like a stretched argument, but it is not. We view the killing of a child as a graver wrong than the killing of someone aged 90, in part because the child has been deprived of all their future life, whereas the loss of potential life to the 90-year-old (although tragic) is less. We are therefore familiar with the concept of the loss of potential life as a marker of a wrong (see particularly Marquis 2006).

6.66 Just one final point, in case I have not convinced you so far. We should play it safe. We don't know for sure when a fetus becomes a person. In such a case, should we not choose the earliest possible time? If we treat a fetus who is not a person as a person, we have not done a serious wrong. But if we treat a fetus as a non-person who is a person, that is a terrible wrong.

6.67 So, if it is accepted that the fetus has the same status as a person, the question of the legality of abortion must be faced. The fetus deserves the same protection as any other person. The location of a person does not affect their legal rights. This is why opponents of abortion describe abortion as murder. That may be inflammatory, but it recognizes that abortion is killing a person. The only circumstance in which murder can be justified is in self-defence. Although even there, self-defence is only available where there is an attack by the victim, and that is hardly appropriate. There may, possibly, be a justification for abortion if the choice was between an abortion or the death of the mother. So, in short, abortion should be unlawful, except in the most unusual of cases.

Speaker 3 (Jarvis Thomson view)

6.68 I agree with much of what Speaker 2 has said. I agree that we must regard the fetus as having the same status as a person. However, where I disagree with Speaker 2 is that it follows that abortion should be unlawful.

6.69 I have found particularly helpful an article by Judith Jarvis Thomson (1971). She considers a hypothetical scenario where you find yourself hooked up to a famous unconscious violinist. He has a fatal kidney ailment and you have been kidnapped and hooked up to his circulatory system. You are told that if you unplug yourself, the violinist will die. Are you required to remain plugged in? Jarvis Thomson suggests that the answer is 'No', and I agree.

6.70 Her point in effect is this. The law does not require you to keep other people alive. If a parent, whose child is in need of a sample of the parent's blood, refuses to provide the sample, resulting in the death of the child, there is nothing unlawful in that. The principle of bodily integrity is strongly protected in the law. Of course, many people would feel it is immoral for the parent not to give the blood or even to unplug oneself from the violinist, but it is not the job of the law to impose high moral standards. If we protect the rights of people not to have organs or material taken from them without their consent, even if that means others will die, it is unfair to deny that right to pregnant women.

6.71 It is true that Jarvis Thomson's hypothetical scenario involved being kidnapped and so it might be argued that at best that is an analogy with rape. However, her essential point that you cannot be obliged to have your bodily integrity interfered with, even without your consent, stands. In an amusing comment, she points out that she has no right to demand the touch of the hand of Henry Fonda (a film star) on her fevered brow, even if it will save her life. If that is true, a fetus cannot demand that the woman keeps her or him alive.

Speaker 4 (the liberal pro-lifer)

6.72 I, too, agree with Speaker 2. The fetus is a person from the moment of conception. However, I accept that that is because I am a Roman Catholic and that is what the Church teaches. I myself could therefore never engage in an abortion. However, I find it much harder to decide what the law should be. I strongly believe that I should not impose my views on others.

6.73 I find it difficult to know what the law should be. Perhaps the fairest view to take would be that the fetus should be regarded as a 'possible person' (Brazier 1988). As a society, we don't know what the fetus is. People have different views and the best thing we can say is that a fetus is a possible person. Adopting that line, we need to ask whether it is reasonable to compel women to go through an unwanted pregnancy in order to protect a possible person. This is not an easy question to answer, but my own view is that at the early stages of pregnancy it would be too much to expect someone to go through all that pregnancy and birth entails just for a possible person. However, once it gets close to birth and so less is required of the pregnant woman, abortion would become harder to justify.

Speaker 5 (a neutral stance)

6.74 There is a wide range of legitimate views on abortion. I respect those who regard a fetus as having a right to life and those who do not. The law, however, cannot take sides on what is a highly controversial issue. It must seek to take a neutral stance. No one can prove if the fetus is a person or not. That reflects profound moral and religious issues. The law then should simply not intervene and leave this as a matter of individual conscience and personal choice. The ethical debates are all very interesting, but for lawyers, at the end of the day, we fall back on the principle that the law should not be used to enforce morality.

Speaker 6 (a relational view)

6.75 The way the debates over abortion are often presented is misleading. Both sides of the debate present this as a clash between the interests of the fetus and the interests of the woman. With the 'pro-choice' side preferring the rights of autonomy of the woman, and 'pro-life' the rights of the fetus. That, however, is to misrepresent the issue.

6.76 The better view is to see moral obligations as arising from a relationship. We cannot view the fetus and woman in isolation from each other. Rather, we need to look at the relationship between them and what obligations arise from them. As Dworkin (1993: 142) puts it:

> her fetus is not merely 'in her' as an inanimate object might be, or something live but alien that has been transplanted into her body. It is 'of her' and is hers more than anyone's because it is, more than anyone else's, her creation and her responsibility; it is alive because she has made it come alive.

So the fetus cannot be regarded as an abstract entity with its own rights. We need therefore to ask whether in the light of the relationship between the parties, what obligations, responsibilities and rights arise.

6.77 In applying this approach, I would argue that given all the woman has done for the fetus and all that she would need to do to give birth, it would not be fair to expect her to continue a pregnancy against her wishes, save in a case of a very late-term pregnancy.

CONCLUSION

As these arguments show, there is a broad range of views that can be held on abortion. Reaching a decision on them can depend on your religious, political, and ethical views. It is not surprising that there is so much disagreement on the issue and that the debates are unlikely ever to be resolved.

FURTHER READING

Beckwith, F. (2007) *Defending Life: A Moral and Legal Case Against Abortion Choice* (Cambridge: Cambridge University Press).

Boonin, D. (2002) *A Defense of Abortion* (Cambridge: Cambridge University Press).

Brazier, M. (1988) 'Embryo's "Rights": Abortion and Research', in M. Freeman (ed.), *Medicine, Ethics and Law* (London: Stevens), pp. 9–22.

Douglas, G. (1991) *Law, Fertility and Reproduction* (London: Sweet and Maxwell).

Dworkin, R. (1993) *Life's Dominion* (London: Harper Collins).

Ford, M. (2005) 'A Property Model of Pregnancy', *International Journal of Law in Context* 1: 261–93.

Fox, M. (1998) 'Abortion Decision-Making—Taking Men's Needs Seriously', in E. Lee (ed.), *Abortion Law and Politics* (Basingstoke: Palgrave), pp. 147–78.

Herring, J. (2010) 'The Right to Choose', *New Law Journal* 160: 1066–7.

Jackson, E. (2001) *Regulating Reproduction* (Oxford: Hart).

Jarvis Thomson, J. (1971) 'A Defense of Abortion', *Philosophy and Public Affairs* 1: 47–66.

Keywood, K. (2002) 'Disabling Sex: Some Legal Thinking about Sterilisation, Learning Disability and Embodiment', in A. Morris and S. Nott (eds), *The Gendered Nature of Health Care Provision* (Aldershot: Dartmouth), pp 134–70.

Marquis, D. (2006) 'Abortion and the Beginning and End of Human Life', *Journal of Law, Medicine and Ethics* 19: 17–26.

Mason, K. (2005) 'What is in a Name? The Vagaries of Vo v France', *Child and Family Law Quarterly* 16: 97–121.

Royal College of Obstetricians and Gynaecologists (RCOG) (2008) *Abortion and Mental Health* (London: RCOG).

Scott, R. (2005) 'Interpreting the Disability Ground of the Abortion Act', *Cambridge Law Journal* 64: 388–412.

Seymour, J. (2000) *Childbirth and the Law* (Oxford: Oxford University Press).

Sheldon, S. (1997) *Beyond Control: Medical Power and Abortion* (Bristol: Pluto).

Sperling, D. (2006) *Management of Post-Mortem Pregnancy: Legal and Philosophical Aspects* (Aldershot: Ashgate).

Statham, H., Solomou, W., and Green, J. (2006) 'Late Termination of Pregnancy: Law, Policy and Decision Making in Four English Fetal Medicine Units', *British Journal of Obstetrics and Gynaecology* 113: 1402–11.

Tooley, M., Wolf-Devine, C., Devine, P., and Jaggar, A. (2009) *Abortion: Three Perspectives* (Oxford: Oxford University Press).

Warren, M. (1997) *Moral Status: Obligations to Persons and Other Living Things* (Oxford: Oxford University Press).

SELF-TEST QUESTIONS

1   Abby is just a few weeks pregnant when she seeks an abortion. She tells the doctor that she does not feel like having a baby at this stage in her life because she is still looking for a husband. Is the doctor allowed in law to perform the abortion? What should the law say?

2   Is it possible to have a 'morally neutral' law on abortion?

3   If it became possible to create an artificial womb so that embryos could be removed from a pregnant woman and gestated, would that alter the ethics of abortion? Should it alter the law?

4   Would it be ethically sound to say that a fetus has a right to life, but that abortion is permissible?

Assisted reproduction

SUMMARY

This chapter will look at the issues around assisted reproduction. In particular it will examine the controls on who can have access to these technologies, and how it is determined whose the child is that is born as a result of any procedure. Another theme is whether it is permissible to use assisted reproduction to select children with or without particular characteristics.

Introduction

7.1 Many couples can have children without the assistance of medicine. There is, unsurprisingly, no regulation on their reproductive activities. The idea that the state should control who can have sex with whom or who is allowed to have children, would appeal only to the most authoritarian and repressive of regimes. However, the issue is less straightforward when we are considering couples who require assistance in reproduction.

Assisted reproduction

7.2 Assisted reproductive technologies are regulated by the Human Fertilisation and Embryology Acts 1990 and 2008 (HFE Acts) (see Deech and Smajdor 2007). The 1990 Act created the Human Fertilisation and Embryology

Authority (HFEA), which has the job of regulating clinics which engage in assisted reproduction. The HFEA inspects clinics working in the area and issues guidance. It has done much to secure public confidence in a field of medicine which, especially in its early years, was seen as dangerous and suspect. In the Coalition government's 2010 cull of the quangos, it was announced that the work of the HFEA may be transferred to the Care Quality Commission. It is unclear how this will affect its work.

7.3 The HFEA has proved to be an independent body to oversee this sensitive area. It can respond quickly to developments in technology in a way that a governmental body would find harder to do (Horsey and Biggs 2007). It also shields the area from political pressure being brought by pressure groups. The regulation offered by the HFE Acts can be divided into three areas:

- Those activities which are unlawful.
- Those activities which are only lawful if performed with a licence.
- Those activities which are lawful and do not require a licence.

Activities which are unlawful

7.4 The following activities are unlawful under the HFE Acts and the HFEA is not permitted to licence them:

1 An embryo cannot be stored for more than 14 days after the mixing of the gametes (HFE Act 1990, s. 4(3)). Fourteen days is chosen as it is the point at which the primitive streak appears. This provision allows research on early-stage embryos, but not beyond 14 days.

2 It is unlawful to place an embryo which is created using the gametes of a non-human animal in a woman (HFE Act 1990, ss. 2 and 3(2)).

3 It is unlawful to place a human embryo in a non-human animal (HFE Act 1990, s. 3(3)).

4 It is unlawful to use eggs taken from embryos in fertility treatment (HFE Act 1990, s. 4(2)).

5 It is unlawful to alter the genetic structure of any cell while it forms part of an embryo (HFE Act 1990, Sch. 2).

6 It is unlawful to keep or store an embryo in breach of regulations issued by the HFE Acts (HFE Act 1990, s. 3).

Activities only permitted with a licence

7.5 The following are activities which are only lawful if carried out under a licence from the HFEA:

1 The storage of an embryo: a private individual cannot store an embryo for their own purposes.

2 It is unlawful to store or use gametes without a licence from the HFEA (HFE Act 1990, s. 4) or for a purpose permitted by the Human Fertilisation and Embryology (Special Exceptions) Regulations 1991, which include teaching or research. This seems surprisingly wide. It would mean that a man storing his sperm in a freezer for fun would be committing an offence. The real significance of the provision is its impact on 'do-it-yourself' assisted reproductive services. In 2009, some men were successfully prosecuted for running an Internet site that offered 'door-to-door' delivery of fresh sperm for do-it-yourself reproduction, at £450 a pot. Doing so was unlawful under the HFE Acts. The aim of the Act is to ensure that assisted reproduction only takes place in licensed clinics, so that good standards can be maintained and to prevent a black market on reproduction.

Activities which do not require a licence

7.6 As long as the activity does not involve the storage of gametes or the creation of embryos outside the body, there are no other restrictions by the HFE Act on what people do with their sperm or eggs. So, if a man went to a woman's house and produced sperm which she immediately used to inseminate herself, there would be no crime. Indeed, it would be difficult to see how such an offence could be policed. As this shows, there are limits to the extent to which the state can control reproduction.

The role of consent

7.7 At the heart of the HFE Acts is the principle of consent. A person's gametes or embryos cannot be used or stored without their consent. That is subject to a limit of 10 years for the storage, after which the clinic can no longer store gametes, unless the couple are infertile or likely to become infertile, in which case an embryo can be stored for up to 55 years. The key case on this issue is the following:

> **Evans v. Amicus Healthcare Ltd [2004] 3 All ER 1025** Ms Evans was suffering from tumours on her ovaries. It was recommended that her ovaries be removed, a procedure which would have rendered her infertile. She had to decide whether to have any of her eggs frozen. She and her financé (Mr Johnson) agreed that embryos should be created using her eggs and his sperm and that these should be frozen. That was because freezing eggs which were fertilized had a much better chance of success then freezing eggs alone. After the medical procedure, the couple separated and Mr Johnson asked the clinic to destroy the embryos.
>
> The Judge at first instance and the Court of Appeal held that the embryos had to be destroyed. A clinic could only store an embryo with the consent of each person whose gametes were used to create the embryo (HFE Act 1990, Sch. 3). As Mr Johnson had withdrawn his consent, the clinic was not permitted to retain the embryos. Consent was required not just for the initial storage but also throughout the period of storage.
>
> The case was taken to the Grand Chamber of the European Court of Human Rights (ECtHR). The court accepted that there was a clash between the rights to the private life of both Ms Evans and Mr Johnson. In essence, Mr Johnson was invoking a right not to be a parent without his consent, while Ms Evans was invoking a claim to be a parent. The court emphasized that there was no common ground between Member States on the correct approach to cases of this kind. The Grand Chamber held, therefore, that each State could decide how to balance the competing rights. It could not be said that the UK's approach was outside the margin of appreciation.

7.8 Not everyone is convinced by the reasoning in the case (Lind 2006; Ford 2008). While the interpretation of the HFE Act 1990 is fairly straightforward, the human rights dimension has attracted considerable debate. According to one view, the essence of the issue should be the right of autonomy: the right to live our lives as we wish (see Morris 2007). If that is the central issue, then we should ask whether Ms Evans's not being able to have a child was a greater interference in how she wished to live her life than it would be for Mr Johnson if a child were produced without his consent. A good case can be made for saying that it would be a far more significant blight on her vision of a good life for Ms Evans not to be able to have a child than it would be for Mr Johnson to have to live with a child without his consent.

7.9 Another criticism of the court's approach is that it discriminated against Ms Evans due to her infertility (Jackson 2008). Had she been fertile and had she and Mr Johnson created the embryo through normal sexual intercourse, then Mr Johnson would have no right to withdraw his consent and demand that the embryo be destroyed. Because she had to use assisted reproduction, she was put in a less advantageous legal position.

7.10 As we have seen, the HFE Acts put much weight on consent, but as the following case shows there may be circumstances where the validity of consent is called into question.

> **Centre for Reproductive Medicine v. Mrs U [2002] EWHC 36 (Fam)** Mr and Mrs U were seeking assisted reproductive treatment. When preparing the paperwork, Mr U originally signed a form giving permission for the posthumous use of his sperm or any embryos created using it. A specialist nurse persuaded him to withdraw that consent. Tragically, he died before Mrs U became pregnant. Mrs U was barred from using his sperm because of his withdrawal of consent. Mrs U claimed that Mr U had been pressurized into withdrawing his consent.
>
> It was held that although there had been pressure on Mr U to change the form and although the sister's request was unexpected, it could not be said that Mr U had not given his free consent. He was aged 47, intelligent, and educated. He was in good health and with a responsible job. It could not really be believed that his will was overborne. Pressure alone was not enough to invalidate a choice. The sperm could not therefore be used after his death.

Restrictions on access to treatment

7.11 The HFE Acts impose restrictions on who can access assisted reproductive treatment. Before offering treatment, the clinic must consider the issues set out in section 13(5) of the HFE Act 1990 (as amended):

> A woman shall not be provided with treatment services unless account has been taken of the welfare of any child who may be born as a result of the treatment (including the need of that child for supportive parenting, and of any other child who may be affected by the birth).

7.12 This provision was amended in the HFE Act 2008. Previously, the clinic had to take account of the child's need for a father. So it is clear now that a single woman or a lesbian couple are entitled to receive treatment, as long as there is a supportive family environment. So clinics should consider whether the applicant or applicants have a wider family or network of friends who will support them as they raise the child.

7.13 The ECtHR has been required to consider whether there can be a right to have access to assisted reproductive treatment.

> **Dickson v. UK [2008] 1 FLR 1315 (ECtHR (GC))** Mr Dickson was serving a minimum sentence of 15 years. He entered into a pen-pal relationship with a woman while serving in prison. The couple married. The couple had never lived together and there was a fourteen-year age difference. Mr Dickson was due to leave prison when his wife would be 51. They therefore sought to use assisted reproduction as that offered them their only realistic chance of having a child. The Secretary of State refused to allow assisted reproductive services to the couple. The reasons given were that the couple's relationship had not been tested in a 'normal environment', that there were inadequate material resources for the child's welfare, that the child would lack a father figure for an important period of childhood, and that the punitive and deterrent element of a life sentence had to be maintained. Mr and Mrs Dickson failed in a judicial review application and applied to the ECtHR on the basis that their rights under Article 8 to the right to respect for their private and family life had been infringed.
>
> The Grand Chamber of the court accepted that Article 8 was engaged. The right to respect for private and family life included the right to become genetic parents. Prisoners did not lose their rights simply on imprisonment and any restriction needed to be justified. While the welfare of any child born could be a factor to be taken into account, in the present case Mrs Dickson would be able to care for the child alone. By requiring proof that their case was an exception, the state had placed too high a burden on the couple. This prevented a proper balancing of the public and private rights.

7.14 The extent to which access to assisted reproduction should be controlled has caused considerable debate.

Speaker 1 (no restrictions view)

7.15 If a couple wish to have children through natural sexual intercourse, there is no investigation into whether they are suitable parents or whether they will have the benefit of a supportive family environment. Why should it be that the law expects clinics to make this assessment of infertile couples? This is nothing short of discrimination against the infertile (Alghrani and Harris 2006).

7.16 But more than that, it asks the impossible. How can a clinic determine how well a child born to a particular woman or couple will fare? It is nothing but guess-work and is likely to depend on prejudice. Even more oddly, it seems to suggest that the treatment should be offered unless it is not in the welfare of the child. But only very usually could it not be in the interests of the child to be born, as Emily Jackson (2001) has pointed out. It is not surprising that research suggests that only very rarely is treatment denied. Emily Jackson has written:

> if we respect the procreative choices of alcoholics, and people with a record of vio-
> lence and abuse, even when we know that their children are likely to be disadvan-
> taged, it is disingenuous to require infertile people to satisfy a conceptually incoherent
> version of the welfare principle prior to reproduction. (p. 195)

As this quotation suggests, the time has come to allow access to infertility treat-ment for all, subject only to any arguments based on rationing.

Speaker 2 (supporting restrictions)

7.17 Speaker 1 has made a strong case against restrictions on access to assisted reproductive treatment, but stop for a moment to think about where that will take us. If a known child abuser and his partner seek treatment, are we really saying that they should be offered assisted reproductive treatment? Or what about a woman who has had all her previous children removed as a result of neglect? To provide treatment, knowing that in all likelihood the child will be removed at birth is ridiculous. It will benefit neither the woman, nor the state, nor the child (Laing and Oderberg 2005).

7.18 Speaker 1 will respond by saying that we allow fertile child abusers etc to pro-duce children. This is true, but the point is that in cases of natural reproduction, there is nothing the state can realistically do to prevent that. But in this case, we can prevent children from being born in such conditions. Indeed, even more to the point, by seeking access to NHS-funded treatment they are seeking the support of the state in producing a child. The state should not be involved in helping a couple produce a child which will immediately be taken into care. The law correctly acknowledges that where a clinic is asked to provide treatment it (the clinic) will be playing a significant role in creating the child and it therefore has responsibilities to him or her.

Parentage

7.19 Who is the parent of a child born as a result of assisted reproduction? The basic approach of the law has always been that the woman who gives birth to a child is the mother and that the father is the genetic father of the child. It is presumed that her husband or the man registered as the father on the birth certificate is the father. These presumptions can be rebutted by DNA tests. However, special rules apply in cases of assisted reproduction.

Mothers

7.20 The woman who gives birth to the child is the mother (HFE Act 2008, s. 33). This is so even where eggs are donated. The donor of the eggs will have no legal relationship with the child (unless she is the mother by virtue of some other provision).

Husbands and civil partners

7.21 Section 35 of the HFE Act 2008 states that the husband of a woman who gives birth having received treatment at a licensed clinic using donated sperm will be treated as the father of the child, unless he can show that he is not the genetic father and did not consent to the placing of the embryo in her. There is a similar provision which applies to a civil partner of a woman (HFE Act 2008, s. 42). The civil partner will be the parent of the child, but not the mother. This reflects the policy of not allowing a child to have more than one mother or one father, which runs through the HFE Acts.

Partners

7.22 If the woman is not married or has not entered a civil partnership, but has a partner (be they male or female), then they too can become parents if they satisfy the 'agreed parenthood conditions' (HFE Act 2008, s. 44). These require that the woman and partner have signed a notice that both consent to the partner being treated as the parent of the child and that the consent has not been withdrawn, and that no other subsequent notice has been signed naming another person, and that the woman and partner are not within the prohibited degrees of relationship with each other (HFE Act 2008, s. 58(2)) (e.g. they are not siblings).

Sperm donors

7.23 A sperm donor will not be treated as the father of any child created using his sperm in accordance with his consent (HFE Act 2008, s. 41). The significance of this is that a sperm donor need not worry that he will become liable to pay child support or otherwise care for any child produced using his sperm. However, this only applies to those who donate sperm to a licensed clinic.

> ***T v. B* [2010] EWHC 1444 (Fam)** T and B were a lesbian couple who had obtained assisted reproductive services together. T was inseminated by an unknown donor and child C resulted. Both T and B were fully involved as the parents of C. Sadly, their relationship broke down. T sought a financial order against B to help with the financial support of C under Schedule 1 of the 1989 Children Act. B denied she was a parent for the purposes of that legislation.
>
> Held that once a person became in law a parent by virtue of the Human Fertilisation and Embryology Acts of 1990 and 2008, they were a legal parent for all statutory purposes. The court refused to draw a distinction between a biological and non-biological parent in this context.

Comments on the allocation of parenthood

7.24 It is notable that the Act is structured to ensure that a child will always have at least one parent. A child could be produced without a father if a single woman gives birth, having given birth using donated sperm. But a child cannot be produced with two mothers or two fathers. Even where a lesbian couple receive treatment, the woman who gives birth will be the mother, her partner will be her 'second parent'. Smith (2006) complains that this will fail to match the expectations of a lesbian couple who may well regard themselves as equal mothers.

7.25 In a case where none of the provisions of the HFE Acts apply, then the court will fall back on the basic rule that the genetic parent is the parent.

> ***Leeds Teaching Hospital v. A* [2003] 1 FLR 1091** By mistake, Mrs A's eggs were fertilized with the sperm of Mr B (rather than Mr A's). The mistake only came to light as Mr and Mrs B were of a different race to Mr and Mrs A. Mrs A gave birth to twins. Mr B had no wish to be regarded as the father of the twins, while Mr A was willing to raise them. While it was clear under the HFE Act 1990 that Mrs A was the mother, it was unclear whether Mr A or Mr B was the father. Mr B argued that he was not the father as he should be treated as a sperm donor. However, as the court noted, that provision (s. 28 as it was then) only applied where the sperm had been treated in line

with the consent of the man. Mr A sought to rely on the provision (s. 28 as it was then) that he was the father as he was married to Mrs A. However, that provision did not apply because he had not consented to the treatment of his wife with the sperm that led to the creation of the child. As none of the HFE Act provisions applied, the court fell back on the general rule that the man who is genetically related to the child is the father. That was not the result that any of the parties wanted, but Mr and Mrs A could adopt the child and that would resolve the issue as thereby Mr and Mrs A would be the only parents of the child.

7.26   Behind these provisions is a larger debate—which is particularly significant in family law—over what makes someone a parent. Traditionally, it has been the genetic link that marks a person as a parent. However, increasingly it is seen to be the practice of caring for the child that generates the parental rights. This is reflected in the provisions of the HFE Act as it means (usually) that the woman who has and will care for the child will be the mother and that the man who will be involved in the child's life will be the father. Consequently, those who are genetic parents, but will play no active role in the child's life (i.e. sperm or egg donors), will not be given the status of parents. However, as we shall see next, that does not mean that the law does not recognize any link between the child and the egg or sperm donors.

Donor anonymity

7.27   In recent years, there has been an increasing interest in the claim that children have a right to know their genetic origins. In the context of assisted reproduction, this means that children should have the right to discover the identity of the man whose sperm was used to produce them or the woman whose eggs were donated. Until recently, there was no way that a child could access such information. However, since the Human Fertilisation and Embryology Authority (Disclosure of Donor Information) Regulations 2004, SI 2004/1511 they can. These apply to children born after 1 April 2005. They can discover the donor's name and address, date and place of birth, notes of their appearance, and a statement (if any) from the donor.

7.28   The change in the law raises the broader issue of the extent to which a child should have a right to discover who his or her biological father was.

> **Re L [2008] EWCA Civ 1388** D was 15 years of age. He suffered from attention deficit hyperactivity disorder and possibly Asperger's syndrome. His father had been imprisoned a few months after D's birth. The mother had then formed a relationship

with another man, whom D had come to believe was his father. Many years later, the father sought contact with D. The father wanted D to be told the truth about his paternity. The judge ordered D to be told.

On appeal, the Court of Appeal asked the judge to rehear the case. A consultant child psychiatrist had reported that the news about his father would have a massive impact on D and would lead to a deterioration in his behaviour at home and at school. This information had not been made available to the judge and the matter needed to be reconsidered. It could not be assumed that it was to D's benefit that he be told the truth now.

Re B (Role of Biological Father) [2007] EWHC 1952 (Fam) The father had agreed to give his sperm so that the mother and her partner could raise a child together. The father had later changed his mind and wanted to see the child (B). B was told that the father was his uncle. B's biological father applied for contact and a parental responsibility order in respect of B. B's mother and her same-sex partner (P) objected.

Hedley J held that the key question was what was in the best interests of the child. It was important that B knew about the truth of his parentage. That was a lesson that had been learned from society's experience of adoption. However, this did not mean that the father should have a full role in B's life. He should not be given parental responsibility. However, contact of four times a year would enable B to know his father.

7.29 Returning to the position of a sperm donor. The provisions allowing access to information about sperm donors, do not render a sperm donor a parent, but are rather seen as a way of recognizing that the child has a right to know what his or her genetic origins are. However, the impact of the provisions are unlikely to be as dramatic as may be thought. This is because children do not have a right to be told that they were born as a result of assisted reproduction. This means they will not know that they can apply for access to this information. In one study (Golombok 2002), less than 10 per cent of those children born following assisted reproduction were told of the fact. The provisions are controversial.

Speaker 1 (the pro-knowledge view)

7.30 It should be regarded as a fundamental human right that children know the identity of their genetic parents. We are only just beginning to realize the importance of genetic information. It is important for medical reasons. More importantly though, it is central to a sense of identity. This is why so many adopted children seek out their genetic parents. To be misled as to one's genetic origins is to lie to a child, and that cannot be acceptable. We should raise children knowing the truth.

7.31 Sometimes it is said that sperm donors are entitled to privacy. This is not a strong argument, as long as it is made clear to donors that their information will be passed on. If a sperm donor wants to keep their identity private then they should not become donors.

Speaker 2 (the pro-secrecy view)

7.32 The case for allowing children to discover the identity of their sperm donor father is exaggerated. A child's real father is the man who is involved in the day-to-day task of raising a child. The sperm donor is probably a student seeking some beer money. Their contribution to the child is negligible and we should not elevate it to some exaggerated importance by saying that there is a right to know one's genetic origins.

7.33 The alleged benefits of the knowledge are not as extensive as claimed by Speaker 1. A person's DNA can be uncovered from their own body; there is little need to find out about their parents. The child's identity should be found in those who care for them and love them, not by some blood tie.

7.34 Not only is providing information about the sperm donor not beneficial, it does harm. Since donors' anonymity has been removed we have seen a major reduction in the numbers of donors. In fact, there has been a severe shortage of donors. There has even been talk of bulk imports of sperm being brought in from Denmark! This has led to UK patients not being able to get fertility treatment or facing long delays (Turkmendag et al. 2008).

Surrogacy

7.35 Surrogacy involves one woman carrying a child for another woman, or a couple, with the intention that after birth the child will be handed over. The child may or may not be genetically related to the commissioning couple.

7.36 The law takes a somewhat ambiguous approach to surrogacy. It does not outlaw it, but it does little to encourage surrogacy arrangements. While it is not illegal to enter a surrogacy arrangement, there are certain criminal offences connected with surrogacy. It is a crime (Surrogacy Arrangements Act 1985, s. 1) to negotiate or arrange surrogacy on a commercial basis, or to advertise surrogacy services or to make an offer for payment for surrogacy (although covering the expenses connected with surrogacy is permitted). This means that surrogacy arrangements have to be made informally and on a non-commercial basis. This makes England very different from, say, the United States where surrogacy is a well-established business, with substantial sums of money changing hands. In England, as a result of its law, surrogacy often involves friends or relatives, rather than strangers.

7.37 Surrogacy contracts are not enforced. Section 1A of the Surrogacy Arrangements Act 1985 states that: 'No surrogacy arrangement is enforceable by or against any of the persons making it.' This, inevitably, leaves open the question of what happens when a child is born following a surrogacy arrangement.

7.38 Let us first imagine that all goes well and the woman hands over the child to the commissioning couple. In that case, the woman who gives birth will be the mother. Her husband (if any) will be presumed to be the father. However, if she hands over the child, the commissioning couple can apply for a parental order so that they will be treated as the parents of the child. To obtain an order it is necessary to show the following (HFE Act 2008, s. 54):

1 Either the sperm, or eggs, or both, came from the commissioning husband or wife.

2 The applicants are married, civil partners, or in 'an enduring family relationship and are not within prohibited degrees of relationship in relation to each other'.

3 The applicants must both be over 18.

4 At least one of the applicants must be domiciled in the UK.

5 The child must, at the time of the order, live with the applicants.

6 The order must be made within six months of the child's birth.

7 The father must give full and unconditional consent to the making of the order.

8 The gestational mother must give her full and unconditional consent to the making of the order, at least six weeks after the birth.

9 The husband of the woman who gave birth to the child must give his full and unconditional consent.

10 Money or other benefits have not been given to the surrogate mother, unless they are reasonable expenses or the court has retrospectively authorized the payments.

11 The pregnancy was not the result of sexual intercourse between the surrogate mother and male applicant.

12 The court must decide to make the order with the child's welfare being the paramount consideration and the checklist of factors in section 1 of the Adoption and Children Act 2002 being applied.

This is quite a restrictive list, most notably because it requires one of the commissioning couple to have a genetic link to the child. Where it is not possible to fulfil these, adoption remains a possibility.

Re X and Y (Foreign Surrogacy) **[2008] EWHC 3030 (Fam)** A married couple sought a parental order under HFE Act 1990, s. 30. They had entered into a surrogacy arrangement with a Ukrainian woman. She was paid a monthly payment during pregnancy and €25,000 at the end. The surrogate was implanted with embryos from anonymously donated eggs and the husband applicant's sperm. Twins were born. The surrogate mother handed them over to the couple.

Two issues were raised before the court. The first was whether the Ukrainian surrogate's husband had to give his consent to the order. Under Ukrainian law, his consent was not needed. The court held that it was, even where the birth had taken place overseas. On the facts of the case the issue was moot, because the husband had in fact given consent. The second issue was the fact that the sums paid significantly exceeded the 'expenses reasonably incurred'. The question was whether the court would authorize these payments. The fact that the Act allowed authorization showed that sometimes there were good reasons to make parental orders even where payments had been made. In this case, there needed to be a balance between the public policy considerations and the welfare of the child. In this case, it was important that the applicants had acted in good faith. There was no suggestion that they had taken advantage of the surrogate mother. There had been no attempt to defraud the authorities. The sums involved were not disproportionate to the 'expenses reasonably incurred'. The welfare of the children was in favour of the order and so it was made.

Re S (Parental Order) **[2009] EWHC 2977 (Fam)** A couple (Mr and Mrs X) sought a parental order in relation to twins born to a surrogate mother in the United States under HFE Act 1990, s. 30. The children were the biological children of Mr X. The surrogate had been paid $23,000. The couple could not explain how the money had been used by the surrogate. The children had been brought to the UK and had lived with Mr and Mrs X since then. The key issue was whether a parental order could be made, given that under s. 30(7) of the Act no money or benefit should be given in consideration of the surrogacy. The Act did permit payment for expenses.

It was held that although part of the $23,000 could be said to cover expenses attributable to the pregnancy, it had not been shown that at least some of the money offended s. 30(7). However, the Act gave the court discretion to decide to make the surrogacy arrangement nonetheless. The key issue was whether public policy would oppose making a parental order in a case such as this. The Act was designed to ensure that commercial surrogacy arrangements were not entered into and to ensure that the courts were not approving the purchasing of children, whether in the UK or overseas. The courts would also be concerned that surrogates were offered such large sums of money as to overbear their will. In this case, the sum was sufficiently low that it could not be regarded as buying children, nor such as to overbear the surrogate's will. The sum involved was not disproportionate to the sums involved. It was in the best interests of the child that a parental order should be made.

7.39 Turning to the case where the surrogate refuses to hand over the child, then she will be the mother of the child. The commissioning couple can apply for a residence order, but unless it is shown that the surrogate mother poses a risk to the child it is unlikely that the court would remove a child from her mother (*Re N (A Child)* [2007] EWCA Civ 1053). In that case, the surrogacy contract would have failed.

Re N **[2007] EWCA Civ 1053** An 18-month-old child (N) was born as a result of a surrogacy arrangement between M and F. F was N's biological father, and M had carried the child. M had given birth to N, but had kept the child with her. The judge found that M had deliberately used deception in order to have further children. Her sole purpose in the surrogacy arrangement was to get another child for herself. The judge ordered M to transfer N over to F, after expert evidence was given that doing so would be best for N. M appealed.

The Court of Appeal upheld the judge's order. The judge had taken into account the fact that early in N's life she had formed an attachment to M, but that her behaviour had indicated that N would be better off with F. F was the biological father and the experts agreed that he and his wife offered the best prospects for N.

What should the law on surrogacy be?

Speaker 1 (pro-surrogacy)

7.40 Surrogacy should be supported and encouraged. The first point to emphasize is that this should be regarded as a matter of autonomy (Jackson 2001). If both the couple and the individual handing over the child are happy, there should be no complaint. No one is being harmed and it is a safe and effective way for a couple to produce children. It is particularly beneficial in that it provides a way for a gay couple to produce children. It opens up the ideas about whom or how many people can be parents. It is true that those with traditional views on families will be concerned about this. But for those who are open to an expanded idea of family it will be welcomed.

7.41 Indeed, surrogacy has a long history and has occurred for centuries. It is unlikely that opponents of surrogacy would succeed in stopping it. More likely, the practice would simply be sent underground.

7.42 Opponents often point to the argument that surrogacy involves degrading conduct in that a woman is 'selling her body'. But, what one person might find degrading, another person will not. To some people, being a surrogate offers a job in which people can give something to others while being self-fulfilling. There are plenty of other jobs that are lawful but which could be regarded as demeaning.

7.43 Opponents also say that surrogacy harms the child. While it might be a slightly unusual situation to be born following a surrogacy arrangement, children can be born in all kinds of unusual circumstances. There is nothing particularly harmful about this. Indeed, a child born by virtue of a surrogacy arrangement can be confident that they were planned for and the result of a careful decision.

Speaker 2 (anti-surrogacy view)

7.44 There are two particular objections to surrogacy which I would highlight. The first is that, in effect, it involves buying babies. The commissioning couple are unable to have children of their own and are seeking to buy a baby. Michael Freeman (1999) tries to argue that any payment is for the labour of the surrogate rather than for the baby, but this is an attempt to disguise the reality and how a child is likely to understand it. When one pays for a painting, one pays for the end result, not the labour.

7.45 The second argument is that surrogacy is exploitative of women. My claim is not that it is always exploitative, but that it is sufficiently often so as to mean that we should be wary of it (Tieu 2009). Surrogacy does not just involve agreeing to do an unpleasant job, it involves the use of one's body. Where surrogacy is undertaken purely for the purpose of making money, that involves behaviour which comes close to slavery.

Preimplantation genetic diagnosis

7.46 Preimplantation genetic diagnosis (PGD) is used to select which embryos to implant. The procedure can be controversial. There is no real controversy if embryos are selected on the basis of which are more likely to survive to birth. But there is more dispute if it sought to select an embryo to avoid a particular disablement or is used on the basis of what the couple see as desirable or undesirable characteristics.

7.47 PGD can only be undertaken under licence from the HFEA (HFE Act 1990, Sch. 2). This only allows PGD in a case where the diagnosis is undertaken to 'establish if an embryo has an abnormality that might affect its capacity to result in a live birth' or 'to avoid a serious medical condition'. This is explained further in the HFEA's Code of Practice:

> PGD can be carried out for a heritable condition only in two circumstances:
>
> (a) Where there is a particular risk that the embryo to be tested may have a genetic, mitochondrial or chromonal abnormality, and the Authority is satisfied that a person with the abnormality will have or develop a serious disability, illness or medical condition, or
>
> (b) Where there is a particular risk that any resulting child will have or develop a gender related serious disability, illness or medical condition. A condition is gender related if the Authority is satisfied that it affects only one sex, or affects one sex significantly more than the other.

This makes it clear that PGD cannot be used simply to ensure one gets a child of a particular sex or particular characteristics such as hair colour. Instead, it is limited to avoiding serious disability. Further, there must be some reason to suspect that the embryo might carry the abnormality.

7.48 Some argue that there should be no limit on why people select embryos (Harris 1998). If a woman would rather have a child with blue eyes, why should anyone else object? After all, there is no objection to a woman choosing to have sex with a dark-haired man in order to produce a child with dark hair. The other embryos have no moral status to object to not being selected.

7.49 However, not everyone is convinced by these arguments in favour of deregulating PGD. It is argued that if a couple choose not to select a child with a particular condition, this says something about people with that condition. For example, if a couple choose not to select an embryo with a gene with cystic fibrosis are they saying that, in effect, the lives of people with cystic fibrosis are not worth living? This is a message that society should not allow parents to send. It promotes the idea that parental love should be conditional and parents are entitled to expect and demand ideal children. However, that point is objected to by some (Asch 2003). There is a difference between saying that a life with cystic fibrosis is preferable to a life without it; and saying that a life with cystic fibrosis is not worth living. The parents in selecting to avoid cystic fibrosis through PGD, are saying the former not the latter. Asch (2003) suggests that parents should be informed of the characteristics of embryos, but it should not be assumed that the parents will choose the 'healthy ones'.

7.50 There have been cases where parents have wanted to use PGD to choose a disability. Most notably where a deaf couple wanted to select an embryo that would develop and be born as a deaf child, so that their child would be accepted as a full member of the deaf community. Supporters of reproductive autonomy might be led to conclude that such a view could be taken, but others argue that parents should not be permitted to produce a child who has a disadvantage, as compared with the average child (see Hull 2006).

Saviour siblings

7.51 One particular use of PGD is where parents try to produce a child specifically so that his or her tissue can be used to provide treatment for a sick sibling.

> **Quintavalle v. HFEA [2005] UKHL 28** The House of Lords was asked whether it was permissible for the HFEA to license the use of human leukocyte antigen (HLA) typing and so test if any embryo could be used for the parents' child Z. The House of Lords held that it was. The HFEA had a wide discretion in licensing these procedures and it could include selection for a sibling.

This is now dealt with by the 2008 HFE Act, para. 1ZA(d) of Sch. 3 which allows testing where

> a person ('the sibling') who is the child of the persons whose gametes are used to bring about the creation of the embryo (or of either of these persons) suffers from a serious medical condition which could be treated by umbilical cord blood stem cells, bone marrow or other tissue of any resulting child, establishing whether the tissue of any resulting child would be compatible with that of the sibling.

7.52 It should be emphasized that the Act imposes important limitations on the creation of 'saviour siblings'. First, the embryo can only be used in the case of siblings. The use of embryos for cousins or other relatives would not be permitted. Second, it can only be used to deal with serious medical conditions. Third, the selection cannot be made if it is planned that a whole organ (e.g. a kidney) is to be donated. The plan must be to use the umbilical cord blood, stem cells, bone marrow, or other tissue from a child. When deciding on the appropriateness of pre-implantation tissue typing in any particular situation, the HFEA Code of Practice requires consideration to be given by the clinic to the condition of the affected child, including

(a) the degree of suffering associated with their condition

(b) the speed of degeneration in progressive disorders

(c) the extent of any intellectual impairment

(d) their prognosis, considering all treatment options available

(e) the availability of alternative sources of tissue for treating them, now and in the future, and

(f) the availability of effective therapy for them, now and in the future.

7.53 In cases of saviour siblings, consideration should also be given to the possible consequences for any child who may be born as a result, including:

(a) any possible risks associated with embryo biopsy

(b) the likely long-term emotional and psychological implications

(c) whether they are likely to require intrusive surgery as a result of the treatment of the affected child (and whether this is likely to be repeated), and

(d) any complications or predispositions associated with the tissue type to be selected.

7.54 Consideration should also be given to the family circumstances of the people seeking treatment, including:

(a) their previous reproductive experience

(b) their views and the affected child's views of the condition

(c) the likelihood of a successful outcome, taking into account:

(i) their reproductive circumstances (ie, the number of embryos likely to be available for testing in each treatment cycle, the number likely to be suitable for transfer, whether carrier embryos may be transferred, and the likely number of cycles)

(ii) the likely outcome of treatment for the affected child

(d) the consequences of an unsuccessful outcome

(e) the demands of IVF/preimplantation testing treatment on them while caring for an affected child, and

(f) the extent of social support available.

The issue of saviour siblings has proved controversial (Freeman 2006).

Speaker 1 (opposing the use of saviour siblings)

7.55 The use of saviour siblings is fundamentally wrong. It leads to the production of a child solely for the purpose of assisting someone else. This breaches the fundamental Kantian principle that a person must not be used as a means to an end. It is hard to see how the removal of the tissue will be for the benefit of the saviour sibling. A fundamental principle of medical law for children is that procedures must be for their own benefit.

7.56 The emotional turmoil for a child who learns that they were created solely as a source of material for their sibling can only be imagined. It will be all the worse if, sadly, the procedure does not work. They will see themselves as having failed in the sole task they were created for. It can only produce an untold impact on family dynamics.

Speaker 2 (supportive of saviour siblings)

7.57 Speaker 1 has misrepresented the issue. Surely no parents will produce a child solely for the purpose of providing bodily material. They will love and treasure their new child (Sheldon and Wilkinson 2004). They only seek to ensure that the embryo selected will carry the necessary gene. They will hardly reject the saviour sibling if the plan does not work out. So, this is not a case of a person being used simply as a means to an end. They will be valued in their own right (Devolder 2005). Further, the suggestion that it will harm the saviour to use his or her material is to use a very narrow understanding of best interests. To provide material for a sibling to save his or her life will be beneficial to the saviour as it will mean he will have a sibling to live with and it will be beneficial in a broader moral sense (see by analogy *Re Y (Mental Incapacity: Bone Marrow Transplant)* [1996] 2 FLR 330).

Hybrids

7.58 The HFE Act 2008 will now bring the following inter-species embryos within the scope of the HFEA. Licences may permit their creation subject to the requirement that the project is necessary or desirable for the purposes described in the legislation. These can assist in medical research in attempts to discover precisely what genes cause an illness or affect the chances of treatment. They can also be used to develop new forms of treatment.

7.59 The 2008 Act inserts a new s. 4A into the 1990 Act:

> (1) No person shall place in a woman—
>
>   (a) a human admixed embryo,
>
>   (b) any other embryo that is not a human embryo, or
>
>   (c) any gametes other than human gametes.
>
> (2) No person shall—
>
>   (a) mix human gametes with animal gametes,
>
>   (b) bring about the creation of a human admixed embryo, or
>
>   (c) keep or use a human admixed embryo,
>
>   except in pursuance of a licence.
>
> (3) A licence cannot authorise keeping or using a human admixed embryo after the earliest of the following—
>
>   (a) the appearance of the primitive streak, or
>
>   (b) the end of the period of 14 days beginning with the day on which the process of creating the human admixed embryo began, but not counting any time during which the human admixed embryo is stored.
>
> (4) A licence cannot authorise placing a human admixed embryo in an animal.

So, the Act only allows the creation of admixed embryos up until the age of 14 days and does not allow such embryo to be placed in a woman. The creation of an admixed embryo is only permitted if done under a licence.

Embryo research

7.60 The HFE Acts allow research to be licensed on embryos until the formation of the primitive streak. That is taken to occur no less than 14 days after fertilization. Baroness Warnock (2002), whose report led to the HFE Act 2008, has explained her view in this way:

> before fourteen days, the embryo, or pre-embryo as it was scientifically known, was a loose cluster of first two, then four, then sixteen cells, undifferentiated. An

> undifferentiated cell could develop into any of the types of cell that go to make up the human body, and some of them would not become part of the embryo at all, but would form the placenta or the umbilical cord. After fourteen days, there begin to appear the first traces of what will become the central nervous system of the embryo, the primitive streak.

The 14-day period has also been supported on the basis that it is close to the time when the embryo may be able to experience pain. It is also the time at which the embryo is a coherent entity and it is clear that there are not going to be twins.

7.61 The HFE Act 2008 imposes a number of important restrictions on the use of embryos in research. These include the following:

(i) An embryo cannot be stored or used for research after the primitive streak has appeared, which is taken to be 14 days from the mixing of gametes.

(ii) The use or storage of an embryo requires a licence and licences can only be issued by the HFEA for certain purposes including promoting advances in treatment of infertility, miscarriages, contraception, or causes of congenital diseases. The Human Fertilisation and Embryology (Research Purposes) Regulations 2001 have added three new purposes to the original five set out in the 1990 Act: increasing knowledge about the development of embryos, increasing knowledge about serious disease, or enabling any such knowledge to be applied in developing treatments for serious disease.

(iii) It is not permitted to mix human and animal gametes or to place a human embryo in a non-human animal.

(iv) The HFEA will only consider licences for research if a research ethics committee has approved the research.

Cloning

7.62 A clone is a group of cells that have identical DNA sequences to the 'parent' group of cells (Harris 2004). Clones are currently created by cell nucleus replacement (CNR). This involves a nucleus from a cell being placed into an egg, thereby activating it. Cloning therefore opens up a number of reproductive possibilities. Because sperm is not required, it offers hope for a man who wants to have genetic offspring, but is unable to produce sperm. It would also enable a lesbian couple to produce a child genetically related to them both.

7.63 There are two main reasons why a person might want to produce a clone:

- Reproductive cloning: here the aim is produce a child. Having produced the cloned embryo, the plan would be to transplant it into the womb to develop.

- Therapeutic cloning: here there is no intent to produce a child. The cloned embryo is created in order to produce cells that will be transplanted for therapeutic reasons into someone who suffers from some kind of disability or condition. The cloned embryo may also be created for research purposes.

7.64 The 2008 HFE Act permits the licensing of some forms of human cloning, but only for the purposes of research. It is not possible for a cloned embryo to be allowed to be implanted in a woman.

Genetic enhancement

7.65 Technological advances are moving apace and soon we will be able to genetically enhance embryos. This means that in the future, it may be possible to improve the characteristics of a child so that they have greater intelligence or strength of other characteristics.

7.66 The current law on this is clear. Schedule 2 of the 1990 HFE Act prohibits the alteration of the genetic structure of a cell which forms part of an embryo, although para. 3(4) states this may be permitted for the purposes of research only. Whether the law should be altered has been fiercely debated.

7.67 Julian Savulescu (2006) has argued in favour of 'procreative beneficence'. He states that this requires parents to do what they can to select and produce the best children they can. He argues, that we criticize parents who do not bother to educate their children, or do not encourage them to undertake exercise. Moral parents do what they can to promote the welfare of their children. He sees a natural extension of this to be that parents should enhance their children genetically. If we can manipulate an embryo to increase intelligence, it would be wrong not to do so.

7.68 For others this is seen as objectionable. It is fashioning children to meet their own needs and aspirations: this is not accepting children unconditionally. Children should be accepted as unpredictable and unique (Sandel 2007).

7.69 Behind this debate is a concern about eugenics. The Nazis were depraved in their appalling attempts to produce a pure Aryan race. To many, this means that there are serious dangers with Savulescu's 'procreative beneficence'. The dangers are in producing a homogenous, perfect human race: we might in fact be creating a 'superhuman' race which would be perfect, but would we be a happier or richer society (see Gavaghan 2007; Pattinson 2002).

Reproductive autonomy

7.70 Throughout this chapter, references have been made to the notion of autonomy (Harris and Holm 2004). Much has been written on the notion of reproductive autonomy, but the phrase is somewhat ambiguous (Murphy 2009). It is more helpful to separate the notions of reproductive liberty and reproductive claim rights.

7.71 Reproductive liberty states that each person has the right to be left alone when making important and intimate decisions. When a person is deciding whether or not to have children and how to have them, these are matters which each person or couple should decide for themselves. The state should not be seeking to interfere in these decisions. 'Keep out' is the message to the government by supporters of reproductive liberty. In particular, the state should not be involved in deciding who will be a good or bad parent (Alghrani and Harris 2006).

7.72 Reproductive claim rights argue that people have the right to services to assist them with fertility issues. Not being able to have children when one would wish to is a similar situation to having an illness or disability. Just as the state takes on obligations to help those with illness or disability, it should do so with infertility. So the claim of reproductive claim rights is a positive one against the state. Its supporters (e.g. Alghrani and Harris 2006) would quickly emphasize that rationing would be relevant and there is no claim to an absolute right to reproductive treatment, but it should take its place alongside other claims for public resources.

CONCLUSION

As we have seen in this chapter, the application of notions of reproductive autonomy in particular situations is far from straightforward. The extent to which these issues should be regarded as private matters and the extent to which they give rise to state interests is a matter of fierce debate (Brownsword 2008). Perhaps the question is best seen as one which raises issues that are both intensely personal and also of great significance to the state. The difficulty for the law is how to strike the correct balance between these public and private interests.

FURTHER READING

Alghrani, A., and Harris, J. (2006) 'Reproductive Liberty: Should the Foundation of Families be Regulated', *Child and Family Law Quarterly* 18: 191–210.

Asch, A. (2003) 'Disability Equality and Prenatal Testing: Contradictory or Compatible?', *Florida State University Law Review* 30: 315–41.

Brownsword, R. (2008) *Rights, Regulation and the Technological Revolution* (Oxford: Oxford University Press).

Deech, R., and Smajdor, A. (2007) *From IVF to Immortality* (Oxford: Oxford University Press).

Devolder, K. (2005) 'Preimplantation HLA Typing: Having Children to Save Our Loved One', *Journal of Medical Ethics* 31: 582–6.

Ford, M. (2008) *'Evans v United Kingdom*: What Implications for the Jurisprudence of Pregnancy?', *Human Rights Law Review* 8: 171–84.

Freeman, M. (1999) 'Does Surrogacy Have a Future after Brazier?' *Medical Law Review* 7: 1–20.

Freeman, M. (2006) 'Saviour Siblings', in S. McLean (ed.), *First Do No Harm: Law, Ethics and Healthcare* (Aldershot: Ashgate), pp. 337–51.

Gavaghan, C. (2007) *Defending the Genetic Supermarket* (Cambridge: Cambridge University Press).

Golombok, S. (2002) 'Parenting and Contemporary Reproductive Technologies', in M. Bornstein (ed.), *Handbook of Parenting* (Hove: Lawrence Erlbaum Associates), pp. 339–60.

Harris, J. (1998) 'Rights and Reproductive Choice', in J. Harris and S. Holm (eds), *The Future of Human Reproduction: Choice and Regulation* (Oxford: Oxford University Press), pp. 5–37.

Harris, J. (2004) *On Cloning* (Abingdon: Routledge).

Harris, J., and Holm, S. (2004) *The Future of Reproduction* (Oxford: Oxford University Press).

Horsey, K., and Biggs, H. (eds) (2007) *Human Fertilization and Embryology: Reproducing Regulation* (Abingdon: Routledge).

Hull, R. (2006) 'Cheap Listening—Reflections on the Concept of Wrongful Disability', *Bioethics* 20: 55–63.

Jackson, E. (2001) *Regulating Reproduction* (Oxford: Hart).

Jackson, E. (2008) 'Degendering Reproduction', *Medical Law Review* 16: 346–84.

Laing, J., and Oderberg, D. (2005) 'Artificial Reproduction, the Welfare Principle, and the Common Good', *Medical Law Review* 13: 328–56.

Lind, C. (2006) '*Evans v United Kingdom*: Judgments of Solomon: Power, Gender and Procreation', *Child and Family Law Quarterly* 18: 576–92.

Morris, C. (2007) '*Evans v United Kingdom*: Paradigms of Parenting', *Modern Law Review* 70: 979–1000.

Murphy, T. (2009) 'The Texture of Reproductive Choice', in T. Murphy (ed.), *New Technologies and Human Rights* (Oxford: Oxford University Press), pp. 195–221.

Pattinson, S. (2002) *Influencing Traits Before Birth* (London: Dartmouth).

Sandel, M. (2007) *The Case Against Perfection: Ethics in the Age of Genetic Engineering* (Cambridge, MA: Harvard University Press).

Savulescu, J. (2006) 'In Defence of Procreative Beneficence', *Journal of Medical Ethics* 33: 284–8.

Sheldon, S., and Wilkinson, S. (2004) 'Should Selecting Saviour Siblings be Banned', *Journal of Medical Ethics* 30: 533–7.

Smith, L. (2006) 'Is Three a Crowd? Lesbian Mothers' Perspectives on Parental Status in Law', *Child and Family Law Quarterly* 18: 231–54.

Tieu, M. (2009) 'Altruistic Surrogacy: The Necessary Objectification of Surrogate Mothers', *Journal of Medical Ethics* 35: 171–5.

Turkmendag, I., Dingwall, R., and Murphy, T. (2008) 'The Removal of Donor Anonymity in the UK: The Silencing of Claims by Would-be Parents', *International Journal of Law, Policy and the Family* 22: 283–310.

Warnock, M. (2002) *Making Babies* (Oxford: Oxford University Press).

SELF-TEST QUESTIONS

1   Is it ever the business of the state how a couple produces a child?

2   Sam agrees to carry a child for Tina and Peter. When the child is born, Sam cannot face handing her over. Can Sam keep the child? What should the law be?

3   Mary has five boys. She would dearly love to have a girl. She asks the doctors to use preimplantation selection to ensure that she has a girl. Would she be allowed to do this? What should the law be?

4 Should the law only allow a child to have one mother and one father?

5 To what extent, if at all, should parents be allowed to select characteristics for their children by using preimplantation genetic diagnosis? Should they be allowed to enhance the characteristics of the embryo if the technology existed? Should they be allowed to harm the characteristics of the embryo if they so desired?

8

Organ donation and the ownership of body parts

SUMMARY

This chapter will consider the regulation of the storage and use of human tissue. It will examine the law set down in the Human Tissue Act 2004. It will also analyse the legal and ethical issues surrounding organ donation. The ownership of the human body raises difficult questions because it straddles the areas of the law of persons and the law of property. Neither branch of the law adequately protects the interests we have in our bodies. The law is still being developed by the courts as we seek to find an appropriate legal regime for governing the use and control of bodies and parts of bodies.

Introduction: the Human Tissue Act 2004

8.1 To appreciate the Human Tissue Act 2004 (HT Act) it is important to understand its background. It was passed in response to scandals at the Bristol Royal Infirmary and the Royal Liverpool Children's Hospital (Alder Hey). There it was discovered that doctors were retaining organs and body parts from dead children. This was usually done without the consent of the parents. Even where consent was provided, this was often done after parents were (unintentionally) misled into thinking that they were donating small samples when agreeing to the retention of tissue. There was outrage when it was discovered what had been done. One mother explained:

> It didn't seem right a heart belonging to my child could be part of a collection like butterflies, or insects, something to be visited and looked at.

8.2 Although many of the parents indicated that had they been asked they would have been ready to consent, what they objected to was the perception that their children's bodies were simply a resource to plunder for the doctors' own uses.

8.3 Interestingly, the doctors were very surprised at the upset their actions caused. The material removed was important to establish the cause of death, to use to refer to in the course of their research, education, or preparation for future operations. If a doctor was performing a particular heart surgery, it would be helpful to have sourced a heart from a deceased child which he could inspect and use to prepare for the operation. Bodily material is regularly removed and disposed of or stored in hospitals. The doctors seemed genuinely surprised that parents might mind if the bodies returned to them were not entirely complete.

> **A and B v. Leeds Teaching Hospitals NHS Trust; Cardiff and Vale NHS Trust [2004] EWHC 644 (QB)** The claimants were parents of deceased children whose organs had been removed post-mortem by medical professionals, without the consent of the parents. They claimed damages for nervous shock or psychiatric injury caused by the removal, retention, and disposal of the organs. They relied on the tort of unlawful interference and breach of the Human Rights Act 1998.
>
> It was held that the removal of the organs was within the terms of the Human Tissue Act 1961. The surgeons had used work and skill on the organs and that gave them rights of possession. There was no right of burial or possession of organs lawfully removed post-mortem. A doctor removing organs from a child could be said to owe a duty of care to the parents of the child. The doctor would need to explain the purpose of the post-mortem. In one case, the claim to psychological harm could be said to be foreseeable and £2,750 damages could be paid.

8.4 The government quickly responded to the scandals with legislation. At the heart of the Bill in its early form was a principle that bodily material could not be stored without the consent of the individual, or in the case of a child, their parents. However, the Act as it was finally passed had moved away from this principle, at least to the extent of creating some significant exceptions (Price 2005).

When the Human Tissue Act 2004 applies

8.5 The HT Act does not deal with the removal of human tissue, rather than the storage and use of material. So, a patient who objects to the removal of material without consent should be bringing a claim in negligence or battery. The Act also only covers certain kinds of human material. It does not deal with sperm, eggs, or embryos. Nor does it deal with material from other animals.

8.6 Surprisingly, the Act only deals with cases where material is stored or used for particular purposes. It does not cover, for example, the storage of bodily material to use in an art project or simply for prurience. This is rather surprising. The legislation might have been thought to give the opportunity to provide comprehensive coverage of the storage of human material.

8.7 Section 1 of the Act states what can be lawfully done with bodily material:

> (1) The following activities shall be lawful if done with appropriate consent—
>
> (a) the storage of the body of a deceased person for use for a purpose specified in Schedule 1, other than anatomical examination;
>
> (b) the use of the body of a deceased person for a purpose so specified, other than anatomical examination;
>
> (c) the removal from the body of a deceased person, for use for a purpose specified in Schedule 1, of any relevant material of which the body consists or which it contains;
>
> (d) the storage for use for a purpose specified in Part 1 of Schedule 1 of any relevant material which has come from a human body;
>
> (e) the storage for use for a purpose specified in Part 2 of Schedule 1 of any relevant material which has come from the body of a deceased person;
>
> (f) the use for a purpose specified in Part 1 of Schedule 1 of any relevant material which has come from a human body;
>
> (g) the use for a purpose specified in Part 2 of Schedule 1 of any relevant material which has come from the body of a deceased person.

This is a rather confusing section at first sight and some of the phrases need an explanation.

8.8 *Human material*: this applies to tissue, cells, and organs of human beings (HT Act, s. 53). It does not apply to gametes, embryos outside the body, hair, or nails.

8.9 *Consent*: a positive consent is required. A failure to object is insufficient. Consent will only provide a defence to a doctor if the consent relates to the actual use made of the organ. For example, consent to the storage of an organ for transplantation will not authorize the storage for research. Consent is defined in the Human Tissue Authority (HTA) Code of Practice:

> To give consent, patients (or the person with parental responsibility) must understand the nature and purpose of what is proposed and be able to make a balanced judgement. They should be told of any 'material' or 'significant' risks inherent in the way the sample will be obtained, how the tissue will be used and any possible implications of its use, e.g., genetic tests.

In the case of a competent adult, HT Act, s. 3 emphasizes that only the adult themselves can provide the consent. In the case of deceased adults, there are three possibilities:

1 The deceased: if they have made their views clear. The consent need not be in writing, unless it concerns public display. There must be no evidence that the deceased had changed his or her views. If there is evidence that the deceased had changed his or her mind, then the transplant should not go ahead.

2 An appointed representative: if the deceased has appointed a representative to make decisions on his or her behalf, then the representative can make the decision.

3 If neither of the other alternatives applies the person who is in the closest 'qualifying relationship' can make the decision. Section 27(4) states that this is the person who is highest up the list for the particular patient:

(*a*) Spouse or civil partner or partner

(*b*) Parent or child

(*c*) Brother or sister

(*d*) Grandparent or grandchild

(*e*) Child of a person falling within (c)

(*f*) Stepfather or step mother

(*g*) Half-brother or half-sister

(*h*) Friend of longstanding

Given category (h), it is unlikely that there will be anyone who does not have someone somewhere on the list. If there are two or more people in the same category, then the consent of only one is required.

8.10 In the case of children, section 2 of the HT Act applies, which means that the child, if competent, can consent, or if the child lacks capacity then a person with parental responsibility for the child can consent. Unlike other areas of the law, the wording of the HT Act indicates that if a competent child refuses to consent, the parent cannot provide alternative consent.

8.11 In the case of incapacitated adults, the law is covered under the Human Tissue Act 2004 (Persons who Lack Capacity to Consent and Transplants) Regulations 2006. These require evidence for believing that the storage is in the best interests of the patient, or is part of an approved clinical trial.

8.12 Schedule 1 purpose: the Schedule divides these purposes into two parts. We shall see why shortly.

Part 1

1   Anatomical examination.

2   Determining the cause of death.

3   Establishing after a person's death the efficacy of any drug or other treatment administered to him.

4   Obtaining scientific or medical information about a living or deceased person which may be relevant to any other person (including a future person).

5   Public display.

6   Research in connection with disorders, or the functioning, of the human body.

7   Transplantation.

Part 2

8   Clinical audit.

9   Education or training relating to human health.

10 Performance assessment.

11 Public health monitoring.

12 Quality assurance.

8.13 The following can be done with appropriate consent for any of the twelve purposes:

(i) The storage of the body of a deceased person (excluding anatomical examination).

(ii) The removal from the body of a deceased person of any 'relevant material' of which the body consists or which it contains.

8.14 The following can be done with appropriate consent for a purpose in Part 1 of Schedule 1:

the storage or use of any 'relevant material' which has come from a human body.

8.15 The following can be done for a purpose in Part 2 of Schedule 2, even without consent:

the storage or use of any 'relevant material' which has come from the body of a deceased person.

8.16 It will be clear from section 1 that where the material is not according to a Schedule 1 purpose then the Act does not apply. So, a person simply storing a relative's body in their attic is not covered by section 1, nor would an artist keeping a body part for a display.

Storage without consent

8.17 While section 1 sets out the basic requirement of consent for storage of human material, the Act in fact includes eight situations where it is permissible to store material without consent.

8.18 (i) The purposes of education, training, and audit: these fall within Part 2 of Schedule 1 and so do not require consent. This is a major exception to the requirement that consent is required for the storage of human tissue. Many people will feel uncomfortable with the idea that parts of their body or organs can be used in education without their consent. It should be emphasized that research is not included within this list. However, it might not always be easy to distinguish research and education. The justification used by the Department of Health is that education, training, and audit is routine and an inherent part of medical treatment and so consent is not required. This argument might be sufficient to argue that consent can be implied, it does not seem to justify the position in the Act, which is that even if a patient objects, their material can be used.

8.19 (ii) Storage for research: the exception we have just discussed does not apply to research but section 1(7–9) allows the storage of human material without consent if the research has been ethically approved in line with regulations issued by the Secretary of State and the material has been 'anonymized' so that it is not possible to identify whose material it is.

8.20 (iii) Coroners' activities: this is another important exception. The removal and retention of organs for the purposes of a post-mortem or to investigate the causes of death is permitted. Again, even if there is evidence that the patient would have opposed this, it can still be permitted. This is because the coroner's role is in effect a judicial one and the lack of consent of an individual cannot be permitted to impede the administration of justice.

8.21 (iv) Imported material: consent is not required where the material has been brought into the country from overseas. That is because it is assumed that any consent that is required will have been obtained in the country of origin.

8.22 (v) The HTA can deem consent: section 7 allows the HTA to deem consent in certain cases. This power can be used where it is not possible to determine from whom the organ originated (e.g. if an organ was washed up on a beach). It can also be used in order to assist in the diagnosis of the condition of a patient. The power to deem consent in such a case can only be made if there is no reason to believe that the patient would not consent to the use of the material.

8.23 (vi) High Court Order: rather oddly, the High Court can deem consent for 'research purposes in connection with disorders, or the functioning of the human brain'. Presumably, a scientist could only seek deemed consent to research in unusual cases. It cannot have been imagined that the High Court would routinely be faced by applications from researchers wanting to use material for which there is no consent. Maybe what is in mind is a case where there is a dangerous epidemic and urgent research is required to find a medical response and in such a case the Court may deem consent to the use of material, even if in fact there is no consent from the individual.

8.24 (vii) Surplus material: if material has been removed in the course of treatment then it can be dealt with as waste. There is no need, for example, to get the consent of the patient to throw away the tumour that was removed during a procedure.

8.25 (viii) Existing holdings: a hospital or surgeon who has material removed before the Act came into force does not need to get consent to retain the material.

8.26 As can be seen from this list, the exceptions to the consent principle are extensive. Indeed, the main impact of the Act seems to be to require doctors to anonymize the samples of material that they have and ensure that they meet any regulations. The Act is better seen as regulating the storage of human material without consent, rather than prohibiting it (Price 2007).

Criminal offences under the Human Tissue Act

8.27 Another controversial aspect of the Act was that it created various criminal offences. The objection to these is that doctors and scientists have to deal with many regulations while carrying out their work. While a breach of the regulations might legitimately incur some professional sanction, the use of criminal law is considered by some to be too heavy-handed (e.g. Herring 2007). However, supporters of the Act's stance argue that the criminal law is necessary to ensure that the requirements of the Act are taken seriously. The following are some of the crimes created.

8.28 (i) Failure to obtain consent: section 5 of the HT Act states that

(1) A person commits an offence if, without appropriate consent, he does an activity to which subsection (1), (2) or (3) of section 1 applies, unless he reasonably believes—

(a) that he does the activity with appropriate consent, or

(b) that what he does is not an activity to which the subsection applies.

Section 1 relates to the storage or use of bodily material without consent. This would mean that some of the storage of material in the Alder Hey case, if it occurred today, would be criminal. However, bearing in mind the extensive exceptions to the consent requirement mentioned above, not all of the retentions would be an offence. Also, notice that there is a defence of 'reasonable belief'. That would cover a case where the doctor mistakenly believed that the deceased had consented.

8.29 (ii) Use or storage of donated material for an improper purpose: a person who stores or uses donated material commits an offence unless it was done for a Schedule 1 purpose, medical diagnosis or treatment, decent disposal, or for purposes set out in Regulations to be made by the Secretary of State. This means that if an artist came across material that was donated for the purposes of research and used it in an art installation, he or she would be committing an offence.

8.30 (iii) False representation of consent: section 5(2) makes it a crime for a person to falsely represent that there is appropriate consent. So, a person who falsely stated that the deceased had agreed that his material could be used for research would be committing an offence.

8.31 (iv) Analysis of DNA without consent: an offence is committed if a person has any bodily material intending that the DNA is to be analysed without 'qualifying consent', unless the results are for an 'excepted purpose'. There are four 'excepted purposes'. These are as follows:

- General excepted purposes:

    (a) the medical diagnosis or treatment of the person whose body manufactured the DNA;

    (b) the purposes or functions of a coroner;

    (c) the purposes or functions of a procurator fiscal in connection with the investigation of deaths;

    (d) the prevention or detection of a crime;

    (e) the conduct of a prosecution;

    (f) the purposes of national security;

    (g) implementing an order or direction of a court or tribunal, including one outside the United Kingdom.

- Under order of the High Court for the purposes of medical research.

- There are complex provisions allowing analysis for certain purposes in respect of existing holdings.

- Where the bodily material is taken from a living person, the DNA can be used without consent for, *inter alia*:

    (a) research;

    (b) clinical audit;

(c) education;

(d) performance assessment;

(e) under direction from the HTA;

(f) for the benefit of another person.

We can see that what the Act is trying to do is to strike an appropriate balance between upholding the principle that consent is required for the storage of material, with a recognition that requiring consent in every case could make life for doctors difficult. It is vital for research and for training that organs are retained.

Organ donation

8.32 A central distinction is drawn in the law between cases where the donor of the organ is alive and where they are deceased.

Living organ donors

8.33 There is little difficulty in cases where what is donated is regenerative tissue (e.g. blood or bone marrow). Then the only real question is whether or not there is consent. There are much more complex issues where the material that is to be donated is non-regenerative (e.g. a kidney or part of a liver).

8.34 The first point to emphasize is that a patient cannot consent to donation which will cause their death or a serious injury. A parent could not donate their heart to save their child's life. To permit that would be to violate the principle that it is not permissible to do an act which causes death (see Chapter 9 and Garwood-Gowers 1999). Live donations of non-regenerative tissue, tends, therefore, to involve the donation of a kidney, a segment of a liver, or a lobe of a lung. These can be removed from the donor without causing death or serious injury.

8.35 It must also be shown that there is consent to the procedure. This requires the patient to have been aware of the procedure and its risks. If a patient lacks capacity, the donation must be shown to be in a patient's interests. It will be rare that it will be found to be in an incompetent patient's interests to donate (Mental Capacity Act 2005 (MCA), s. 4). It may be that the donation can be permitted if the donation is to a person heavily involved in the incompetent person's care, so that without the donation they would suffer if the carer were to die.

8.36 A live donation is only permitted if it complies with the requirement of the HT Act, s. 33. It will be a crime to undertake a live donation, even with consent, unless it complies with the regulations issued by the HTA. A donation is only permitted if there is no 'commercial dealing'. This is defined in section 32:

> Prohibition of commercial dealings in human material for transplantation
>
> (1) A person commits an offence if he—
>
> (a) gives or receives a reward for the supply of, or for an offer to supply, any controlled material;
>
> (b) seeks to find a person willing to supply any controlled material for reward;
>
> (c) offers to supply any controlled material for reward;
>
> (d) initiates or negotiates any arrangement involving the giving of a reward for the supply of, or for an offer to supply, any controlled material;
>
> (e) takes part in the management or control of a body of persons corporate or unincorporate whose activities consist of or include the initiation or negotiation of such arrangements.
>
> (2) Without prejudice to subsection (1)(b) and (c), a person commits an offence if he causes to be published or distributed, or knowingly publishes or distributes, an advertisement—
>
> (a) inviting persons to supply, or offering to supply, any controlled material for reward, or
>
> (b) indicating that the advertiser is willing to initiate or negotiate any such arrangement as is mentioned in subsection (1)(d).
>
> (3) A person who engages in an activity to which subsection (1) or (2) applies does not commit an offence under that subsection if he is designated by the Authority as a person who may lawfully engage in the activity.
>
> . . .
>
> (6) For the purposes of subsections (1) and (2), payment in money or money's worth to the holder of a licence shall be treated as not being a reward where—
>
> (a) it is in consideration for transporting, removing, preparing, preserving or storing controlled material, and
>
> (b) its receipt by the holder of the licence is not expressly prohibited by the terms of the licence.

It should be noted that payment for the transportation and preparation of the organ can be permitted in some cases.

8.37 The HTA has also issued a Code of Practice which must be followed if the live donation is to be lawful. This includes a requirement that the donor is informed of the risks involved in the donation and that there is no guarantee that any transplant will succeed. The donor must meet with a clinical and an independent assessor. If the donor is not genetically or emotionally related to the person receiving the organ, then the donation must be approved by the HTA Panel and have been assessed by a psychiatrist.

8.38 The HTA has also issued specific guidance to deal with cases where the live donor is a child. The Code states that live donations from a child must be approved by the HTA Panel and only rarely will consent be given. In the case of live organ donation, a court order is required. These special procedures are in place because it will be exceptional that it will be in a child's best interests to donate an organ. These provisions apply even in a case where the child is *Gillick* competent. Although in such a case, the competent child's consent may lead the panel and court to grant approval. It should be remembered that the best interests test for children is not limited to medical issues, but can include a consideration of social and emotional factors. Therefore, if a child's sibling or parent needs an organ, it might be said that the family and emotional benefit of providing the organ (and saving the life) will outweigh the physical harm of the procedure. It seems that child live organ donors are very rare in the UK, but not unheard of. Normally adult relatives will be preferred as donors, and only if there is no alternative will a child be able to donate.

8.39 Similar issues arise in relation to a patient who lacks capacity. It needs to be shown that the donation will be in the patient's best interests and that the court has approved the donation.

8.40 It might be argued that consent could be found if a patient has made an advance decision to authorize the removal of the organ. However, an advance directive can only operate to refuse treatment and so it seems unlikely that it can be used to justify removal of an organ for transplantation. Another argument could be that the holder of enduring power of attorney can consent. However, under the terms of the MCA, they are only permitted to consent to 'treatment'. It may well be argued that removal of an organ is not 'treatment', in which case they may lack the power to authorize it. It seems most likely then that the only route to authorization is in showing that the treatment is in the person's best interests.

> **Re Y [1997] 1 FCR 172** Y lacked capacity. Her sister required bone marrow and Y was the only available donor. The court confirmed that it was in Y's best interests

to donate. If her sibling fell seriously ill or died that would impact on the level of care being offered by Y's mother. That would have a serious impact on Y. Therefore it was in Y's interests to donate. Notably Connell J emphasized that if the case had involved invasive surgery and the removal of organs, the case might have been different.

Ethical issues

8.41 To some commentators, the current law on organ donation is far too restrictive. Especially so, given the great shortage of organs for donation from which we suffer. We should, they argue, simply rely on the principle of consent and autonomy. If a person is competent and willing to donate an organ, we should allow it. The restrictive process required by the HT Act is too cumbersome. But how far can we take this? In one case that was discussed in the medical press a man had two sons with kidney failure. He wanted to donate a kidney to each son. That would mean he would be on permanent dialysis, but was willing to suffer this in order to save the lives of his sons. In the end it was decided that he should not be able to donate both his kidneys, although donation of one was permitted. Was this decision correct? After all, allowing the donation would have been in accordance with the wishes of the father and would have produced a good result. In such a case, if a father could only help one child, how could he choose which to help?

8.42 One radical proposal is that we should engage in compulsory organ donation. In a controversial article entitled 'The Survival Lottery', John Harris (1975) suggested that if there are two people needing organs, we could legitimately select a person at random and kill them in order to save the two people. We have the choice of two innocent people dying or one person dying, and to Harris the choice is easy. Opponents of his view would respond that there is a difference between killing someone and letting the two illnesses lead to death. It is notable that few have supported Harris's proposal. It might seem more plausible to use the organs of the deceased first. We turn to that proposal next.

Organs from the dead

8.43 The removal and storage of organs from the deceased is permitted if there is 'appropriate consent' (HT Act, s. 1). Consent can be provided by the deceased if they made a decision while still alive which has not been revoked. That decision can be in writing or oral. Many people do that by registering the wish to donate online (http://www.uktransplant.org.uk) or by having an organ donation card.

8.44 If the deceased has expressed their wishes, be that in favour of donation or not, their view must be respected. So, if the deceased wanted their organs to be used, but the relatives opposed that, then their organs can still be used. Similarly, if the deceased had not wanted their organs used, relatives cannot override their refusal.

8.45 If the deceased has not left views, then the question is whether the deceased has nominated a representative to make decisions. A representative can be nominated in writing or orally, although in both cases the nomination must be witnessed. If a nomination has been made then the representative can make the decision about donation.

8.46 If the deceased has no views and has not nominated a representative, then the person who is the 'qualifying relation' can make the decision. Section 27(4) states that that is the person who is highest up this list for the individual:

1 Spouse or civil partner or partner

2 Parent or child

3 Brother or sister

4 Grandparent or grandchild

5 Child of a person falling within category 3

6 Stepfather or stepmother

7 Half-brother or half-sister

8 Friend of longstanding

If there are two people who rank equally on this list, then it is enough if one of them consents to the donation.

8.47 The list of relatives is controversial. There are some who argue that organ donation is such a personal decision that it should not be made by someone else. That raises issues about the ethical basis for donation, which we will discuss shortly. Others argue that the list puts too much weight on the blood link between an individual and the deceased, as opposed to those who have actually been involved in living with or caring for the deceased (Herring 2007).

8.48 If a surgeon were to remove an organ for transplantation from a deceased person without consent, then that would amount to a criminal offence, with a maximum prison sentence of three years (HT Act, s. 5(1) and (7)). It is, however, a defence if the doctor reasonably believes that he or she has consent. That can raise some tricky issues as to what steps it is reasonable to take to discover whether, for example, the deceased had left an expression of his wishes. It should also be noted that there is no crime if the deceased wished their organ to be used, but it was not.

8.49 There is no clear law where a donor wishes to attach a condition to his donation. In 2000, it was reported that a patient donated an organ on condition that it was only used for a white person. The hospital gave the organ to the person at the top of the queue (who happened to be white in any event). The Department of Health has announced that organs cannot be donated subject to a condition. Controversially, they suggested that if the organ is donated subject to a condition it should not be used. Although it might be thought that it is hard to justify where the person at the top of the queue would, in any event, happen to meet the condition. The policy is not quite clear because in the case of live organ donation a person can donate to a specific individual. Further, paired organ donations are permitted. That is where there is an exchange of organs. For example, where Mr A donates a kidney for use by Mr B, on condition that Mrs B donates part of a liver to Mrs A.

The distribution of organs

8.50 If an organ becomes available for transplant, a decision must be made about who should receive it. The system is shrouded in mystery and there is no publication of strict rules or guidelines of how it is decided who should get an organ. It may be that any such publication would lead to people seeking to manipulate the system to get higher up the list. Or that any published list would be a licence to litigate if a person was not given an organ when they believed that they should have been? The expert group on liver donation (UK Transplant 2007) gave this guidance on how decisions are made:

> Selection of a particular recipient for an individual donor liver depends upon a number of factors. Matching for age, size and blood group are important and, other factors being equal, time on the waiting list will then identify the recipient. However, the condition of patients on the waiting list and the quality of the donor liver must also be taken into account. In contrast to a fitter patient, an unstable recipient will not tolerate a sub-optimal donor liver.

There is no indication of how factors such as age or the number of dependents are taken into account, if at all.

Ethical issues and reform

8.51 The sad fact is that every year people die for want of organs. Around 1,000 people a year die due to the shortage of organs available for transplantation. This has led many to call for a change in the legal approach. Not least because there is good evidence that most people would be happy for their organs to be used, but never get round to registering their wishes. Here are some ways of dealing with organ donation:

1 Opt-in system: this is the current system whereby those wishing to donate their organs can register their desire to do so.

2 Mandated choice: we could have a system which requires citizens to indicate what will happen to their organs on death. This could be done by including a question about organs in every tax return or benefits claim.

3 Opt out: this presumes that everyone wishes to consent to donation, but they can register their objection.

4 No choice: on death, a person's organs can be removed regardless of their wishes.

Let us consider the alternatives further and what ethical arguments might be used in support of them.

8.52 Opt in (the current system): supporters of the current law argue that the opt-in procedure rests on the principle of autonomy (Organ Donation Taskforce 2008). Normally in medical law you cannot treat someone without their consent. The same should be true of organ donation as any other cases. To deal with the shortage of organs we should encourage more people to register, and indeed HT Act, s. 34A requires health authorities to promote awareness of the register. We might even consider offering incentives to those who register. However, they argue, we must stick with the current system based on the consent of the individual.

8.53 Another issue that could be considered is the evidence that under the current system, if a deceased has consented but there is strong opposition from relatives, doctors are reluctant to use the organs. This is understandable. The HTA in its guidance has emphasized that relatives do not have a veto over the use of organs and they should be encouraged to respect the wishes of the deceased. This, too, may be a way of increasing the number of organs available for donation under the current system.

8.54 Mandated choice: this option will appeal to those who support the idea that autonomy dictates that organs can only be used if there is consent, but want to see a large number of organs being donated. The proposal would require everyone to register their views on organ donation, by making it part of the NHS registration system, or part of the tax or benefits system. This makes sure that we know the views of everyone who dies, rather than, as under the current system, having to rely on the views of family members.

8.55 Opt out: this is, perhaps the most popular alternative system. It is assumed that everyone wants to donate, but those who do not can opt out. Supporters allege that the system can fit within the normal principles of autonomy because they are recognizing that people have a choice (British Medical Association (BMA) 2005). Indeed, supporters argue, the current system whereby it is assumed that people do not want to consent works against the autonomy of those who wish to consent but do not get round to registering. As study after study indicates, most people are willing to donate their organs. Having a presumption that people do want to donate is therefore a reasonable starting point (e.g. Department of Health 2002).

8.56 Critics respond that we do not use such an approach in other areas of medical law. Although we might assume that most people would want to consent to the procedure recommended by their doctor, a doctor cannot rely on the fact that the patient did not object as amounting to consent. Rather, we should recognize that organ donation is a controversial issue and we should respect people's choices. We cannot assume people want to consent.

8.57 A rather different argument has been made by some and that is that there is a moral obligation to donate. Most people would be willing to accept an organ if they needed one and so they should be willing to donate. That should be seen as a basic requirement of citizenship. The law is entitled to expect people to comply with their moral obligations, unless they have made it very clear that they do not wish to.

8.58 Supporters of an opt-out system might also point to other countries which have adopted such a scheme and thereby seen an increase in the number of organs available: Belgium, Italy, and Greece; although such an increase was not found in Austria. Indeed, some have said that relatives may be more likely to object in cases where consent is simply presumed and that will mean, in fact, that fewer organs may be freed for transplantation. The Organ Donation Taskforce which reported to the UK government in 2008 could not recommend an opt-out system, because they feared that it would create a lack of trust between patients, relatives, and staff. The principle of autonomy was central to ensuring trust between the NHS and the public. If it was to depart from this, it would destroy a central plank of the principles which underpin trusting relationships between the NHS and patients.

8.59 Mandated donation: this option is the most radical response to the need for organs. It simply requires that organs be removed from the deceased, regardless of their choice. John Harris (2002) makes a straightforward argument. Once a person has died they have no interests that need protection. They cannot be harmed and so there is nothing wrong in removing their organs. Indeed, John Harris points out that post-mortems can be carried out without consent. They are justified in the interests of the state in finding out why people died. He argues that surely the interests of the state in saving the lives of those on the waiting list are even stronger. So, given that we allow post-mortems, we should allow donations. Opponents of this proposal argue that a person can be harmed if their wishes are not followed on their death (Brazier 2002). Further, Harris's view fails to take into account the religious and community interests in how dead bodies are treated. That leads to a broader debate on what weight should be attached to the wishes of a deceased about their body.

The wishes of the deceased

8.60 So far we have assumed that the views of the deceased are the key issue. However, as we have just seen, some, like Harris, argue that the dead cannot be harmed or wronged because they have gone. Not everyone is convinced by this. First, it might be said that the principle of autonomy allows us to direct and shape our lives. That principle should cover the disposal of our body (McGuinness and Brazier 2008). Death and burial are the final chapter of our lives and may create the final memories people think of when we are remembered. Some people put considerable effort into planning how they will be treated once they die. So, following someone's wishes can be respected as a matter of protecting autonomy (Glannon 2008).

8.61 An alternative argument is to suggest that we should follow the wishes of the dead because of the wishes of the living (Chadwick 1994). Relatives will be severely distressed if they see the wishes of the deceased being ignored. Further, other people may be distressed at the thought that they will be treated contrary to their wishes when they die. These concerns justify following the wishes of the deceased. John Harris (2002) argues that even if we accepted these kinds of arguments, they hardly outweigh the interests of the people who need to receive the organs and their relatives.

Selling organs

8.62 The HT Act provides an impressive array of offences connected with the commercial dealing of human material for transplantation. Section 32 contains a series of offences connected with dealing in organs for reward:

> (1) A person commits an offence if he—
>
> > (a) gives or receives a reward for the supply of, or for an offer to supply, any controlled material;
> >
> > (b) seeks to find a person willing to supply any controlled material for reward;
> >
> > (c) offers to supply any controlled material for reward;
> >
> > (d) initiates or negotiates any arrangement involving the giving of a reward for the supply of, or for an offer to supply, any controlled material;
> >
> > (e) takes part in the management or control of a body of persons corporate or unincorporate whose activities consist of or include the initiation or negotiation of such arrangements.

'Reward' here includes giving a financial or other material advantage. It is not therefore possible to bypass these provisions by not paying cash but providing property or other economic benefit.

8.63 There then follows in section 32 an offence dealing with advertising and soliciting commercial dealings in human material:

> (2) Without prejudice to subsection (1)(b) and (c), a person commits an offence if he causes to be published or distributed, or knowingly publishes or distributes, an advertisement—
>
> > (a) inviting persons to supply, or offering to supply, any controlled material for reward, or
> >
> > (b) indicating that the advertiser is willing to initiate or negotiate any such arrangement as is mentioned in subsection (1)(d).

8.64 The prohibitions on payment for organs are not as strict as might first appear. Most importantly in section 32(7), the prohibitions on reward do not apply to expenses incurred in removing, storing, or transporting the organ. Nor does it include payments to cover the loss of earnings of a person donating an organ. It will remain to be seen how generously the terms 'expenses' and 'loss of earnings' might be interpreted. The NHS (2009) suggests that Trusts may decide not to pay for lost earnings if they exceed the average national wage.

Speaker 1 (opposing the sale of organs)

8.65 The prohibition on organ selling is to be welcomed. At the moment in England, the distribution of organs is carried out based on medical need and suitability for transplant. If we allowed organ selling, the rich would be able to acquire organs. Need, not wealth, should determine how organs are dealt with (Andrews and Nelkin 2001). It might be argued that we should allow the sale of organs but only allow the NHS to buy and distribute them, but doing so could only be justified if it was the only way to increase the number of organs available and there are many better ways of doing that.

8.66 Worse, perhaps, allowing the sale of organs will exploit the most vulnerable in society into selling their organs (Dickenson 2009). We know that there are those in the developing world who are driven by poverty and despair to sell their organs for use in Western countries. This largely takes place in a black market (Goodwin 2007), but if we were openly to permit the sale of organs then this would only increase. It is not just that there are questions about whether they are acting autonomously, there is also a matter of dignity. Allowing people to sell their organs is to allow people to infringe their dignity as humans. That is why we oppose slavery: humans should not be reduced to mere objects to be broken up and sold (Cherry 2005).

8.67 The idea of organ selling reflects a broader attitude of commercialization about the body. Donna Dickenson (2009: 217) writes:

> The body both is, and is not, the person. But it should never be only a consumer good, an obscure object of material desire, a capital investment, a transferable resource: merely a thing. Our consciousness, dignity, energy and human essence are all embodied, caught up in our frail bodies. The body is indeed like nothing on earth: not no one's thing, but no thing at all.

Speaker 2 (supporting the sale of organs)

8.68 One key argument in favour of commercial organ-selling is that it allows people autonomy. As long as people are not forced to sell their bodies there should be no objection to doing so. Stephen Wilkinson (2003) refers to a survey of the public which found that 65 per cent of those questioned would be willing to have sex with a stranger for a million pounds. It seems that most people are willing to do something demeaning if the price is right. Quite simply, that is their choice. Organ selling is no different from the things other people are allowed to do for money (e.g. modelling or sport).

8.69 In the case of organ donation, we have the added benefit that not only is a person exercising their free choice, but in doing so they are benefiting another person. And remember, if one person is able to buy an organ then that means that there is one less person on the NHS queue and so it is likely that one person on that queue will get an organ they would not otherwise have got. If organ selling provides a way of increasing the number of organs, and thereby saving lives, we need a good reason not to do it (Stacey Taylor 2005). It is a win-win situation.

8.70 Those who object to the sale of organs suggest that it allows the rich to 'jump' the queue. Well, welcome to the real world. In every area of medicine in the UK a rich person can, by seeking private medical treatment, jump the queue. It is no more objectionable in this area than any other.

8.71 Another common objection is that people are exploited if they agree to sell their organs. What is overlooked is that people are exploited by the poverty that they are in. The possibility of selling their organs increases their options; it can hardly exploit them. In any event, we know that the selling of organs takes place. Having a properly regulated market with proper protection would mean greater protection of the vulnerable, not less.

The body as property

8.72 There has been much academic effort put into answering the question of whether the body should be regarded as property. Gage J in *A and B* v. *Leeds Teaching Hospitals NHS Trust* [2004] EWHC 644 (QB) described the English law on the issue as 'uncertain and unfair' and it would be hard to disagree. In summary, the position is that there are some respects in which the body can be treated as property and other respects in which it cannot.

8.73 The traditional approach has been that a body, be it an alive body or a corpse, cannot be property. It therefore cannot be owned. However, exceptions developed, particularly in relation to separated body parts or products. For the purposes of the Theft Act 1968, hair (*DPP* v. *Smith* [2006] EWHC 94 (Admin); blood (*R* v. *Rathery* [1976] RTR 478); and urine (*R* v. *Welsh* [1974] RTR 478) have all been accepted to be property which can be stolen. In *R* v. *Kelly* [1998] 3 All ER 714 and *Dobson* v. *North Tyneside Health Authority* [1996] 4 All ER 714, the courts developed an exception that if a body part was subjected to the exercise of work and skill then it could become property and then owned. So, if a body part was removed during an operation and then preserved then it could thereby become property.

> *R* v. *Kelly* **[1998] 3 All ER 741** Kelly and another defendant were charged with theft of body parts from the Royal College of Surgeons. Without official authorization, Kelly had arranged for the removal of body parts from the College for use in artistic endeavours.
>
> The Court of Appeal held that parts of corpses could become property for the puporses of the Theft Act 1968 if they had been the subject of skill. That included dissection and preservation. The court added that in future cases, a court might be willing to extend the law so that if a part of a body had a significance beyond its mere existence (e.g. an organ for use in transplantation), then it could become property.
>
> *Dobson* v. *North Tyneside Health Authority* **[1996] 4 All ER 714** Ms Dobson sought the delivery of the deceased's brain. She was considering bringing legal action against the health authority on the basis that it should have been aware of his tumours earlier on and that their negligence had caused his death. The health authority Trust informed her that the brain could not be found and had been disposed of. She sought an action for conversion.
>
> The Court of Appeal held that the claim failed as there was no property in the corpse. Although an administratrix of the estate had the right to possess a corpse until buried, the body had been buried. Although the brain had been preserved, no skill had been exercised upon it and so it was not property.

8.74 However, the whole issue was re-examined in the following case:

> *Yearworth* v. *North Bristol NHS Trust* **[2009] EWCA Civ 37** The case involved six men who had been diagnosed with cancer. Before receiving chemotherapy treatment, it was recommended that they provide samples of sperm for storage because the treatment was likely to affect their fertility. The sperm was stored at the hospital, but due to an error was not kept at the correct temperature and was rendered useless. The men suffered psychological harm when they were informed of what had happened. They sued the hospital.

The court held that because the sperm was not regarded as part of the men's bodies, their claim could not be brought as a personal injury claim. The question was therefore whether or not the claim could be brought on the basis that the sperm was their property and therefore bailment could be used. The court went over the traditional approach of the law towards ownership of the body and body parts. They concluded:

> In this jurisdiction developments in medical science now require a re-analysis of the common law's treatment of and approach to the issue of ownership of parts or products of a living human body, whether for present purposes (viz. an action in negligence) or otherwise.

Although they thought that the case could be brought within the 'exercise of work or skill' exception in *Doodeward* v. *Spence* (1908) 6 CLR 406, the approach in that case should be abandoned:

> we are not content to see the common law in this area founded upon the principle in *Doodeward*, which was devised as an exception to a principle, itself of exceptional character, relating to the ownership of a human corpse. Such ancestry does not commend it as a solid foundation. Moreover a distinction between the capacity to own body parts or products which have, and which have not, been subject to the exercise of work or skill is not entirely logical. Why, for example, should the surgeon presented with a part of the body, for example, a finger which has been amputated in a factory accident, with a view to re-attaching it to the injured hand, but who carelessly damages it before starting the necessary medical procedures, be able to escape liability on the footing that the body part had not been subject to the exercise of work or skill which had changed its attributes?

The court concluded that the sperm was the property of the men for the following reasons:

(i) By their bodies, they alone generated and ejaculated the sperm.

(ii) The sole object of their ejaculation of the sperm was that, in certain events, it might later be used for their benefit. Their rights to its use have been eroded to a limited extent by the Act but, even in the absence of the Act, the men would be likely to have needed medical assistance in using the sperm: so the interposition of medical judgment between any purported direction on their part that the sperm be used in a certain way and such use would be likely to have arisen in any event. It is true that, by confining all storage of sperm and all use of stored sperm to licence holders, the Act has effected a compulsory interposition of professional judgment between the wishes of the men and the use of the sperm. So Mr Stallworthy can validly argue that the men cannot 'direct' the use of their sperm. For two reasons, however, the absence of their ability to 'direct' its use does not in our view derogate from their ownership. First, there are numerous statutes which limit a person's ability to use his property— for example a land-owner's ability to build on his land or to evict his tenant at the end of the tenancy or a pharmacist's ability to sell his medicines—without eliminating his ownership of it. Second, by its provisions for consent, the Act assiduously preserves the ability of the men to direct that the sperm be *not* used in a certain way: their negative control over its use remains absolute.

(iii) Ancillary to the object of later possible use of the sperm is the need for its storage in the interim. In that the Act confines storage to licence holders, Mr Stallworthy stresses its erosion of the ability of the men to arrange for it to be stored by unlicensed persons or even to store it themselves; he also stresses their inability to direct its storage by licence holders for longer than the maximum period provided by the Act. But the significance of these inroads into the normal consequences of ownership, driven by public policy, is, again, much diminished by the negative control of the men, reflected in the provisions that the sperm cannot be stored or continue to be stored without their subsisting consent. Thus the Act recognises in the men a fundamental feature of ownership, namely that at any time they can require the destruction of the sperm.

(iv) The analysis of rights relating to use and storage in (ii) and (iii) above must be considered in context, namely that, while the licence-holder has *duties* which may conflict with the wishes of the men, for example in relation to destruction of the sperm upon expiry of the maximum storage period, no person, whether human or corporate, other than each man has any *rights* in relation to the sperm which he has produced.

(v) In reaching our conclusion that the men had ownership of the sperm for the purposes of their present claims, we are fortified by the precise correlation between the primary, if circumscribed, rights of the men in relation to the sperm, namely in relation to its future use, and the consequence of the Trust's breach of duty, namely preclusion of its future use.

8.75 It must be admitted that *Yearworth* has done little to clarify the law. It seems that the traditional approach that a person cannot claim property rights in their body save through the work and skill exception has been rejected. However, it is far from clear when a property right will arise. The court mentions five factors in their judgment, but which need to be shown? One factor was that 'their bodies alone generated and ejaculated the sperm'. If that is sufficient then it would suggest that most bodily products and parts could be seen as generated by the individual and lay open a broad range of claims to body ownership. However, the court also read the case in the light of the provisions of the HFE Acts, and on a narrow reading it may be restricted to its own facts and not indicate a fundamental shift in the legal nature of the body.

8.76   The significance of *Yearworth* was considered in a recent Australian decision.

> **Bazley v. Wesley Monash IVF [2010] QSC** Ms Bazley's husband had had his semen stored at an IVF clinic. He had since died, without leaving any direct instructions about the semen. The Supreme Court of Queensland found that the sperm could be characterized as property which had belonged to the husband when he was alive, and to his personal representative on his death. As owner of the semen, Ms Bazley could request its return.

8.77   It might at this point be asked why it matters whether we own our bodies or not. It might be an issue of academic interest, but it is of practical significance. The following case shows why it may be an important question.

> **Moore v. Regents of the University of California (1990) 793 P 2d 479** John Moore, who suffered from hairy cell leukaemia, had his spleen removed. Dr Golde discovered that cells from his spleen contained potentially beneficial properties. He developed a cell line from the spleen which he eventually sold for $15 million. The products produced as a result were said to be worth several billion dollars. His research on the spleen was carried out without Moore's consent or knowledge.
>
> Moore brought an action based on conversion, breach of fiduciary duty, and informed consent. The Californian Supreme Court rejected the conversion claim, declaring that there was no precedent on which to base a claim that a person had property rights in their bodies and that it would be inappropriate for the law now to recognize one. Indeed, to recognize one would cause difficulties: it would hinder medical research by restricting access to raw materials and lead to a 'litigation lottery'. The prospect of patients 'shopping around' to find out who would offer them the best price for their bodily parts or products was not an attractive one. They accepted that he might have a claim for breach of fiduciary duty.
>
> Dissenting from the majority opinion in the *Moore* case, California Supreme Court Justice Mosk argued that the law should at least recognize Moore's 'right to do with his own tissue whatever the defendants [including his doctor and the university] did with it: i.e. he could have contracted with researchers and pharmaceutical companies to develop and exploit the vast commercial potential of his tissue and its products'.

As this case shows, considerable sums of money can rest on whether a person can claim property rights in their body. It is an issue about which there has been considerable dispute.

Speaker 1 (against a property analysis)

8.78 The body cannot be property. This is for the simple reason that the owner and owned cannot be the same. The word 'property' is used to describe the relationship between a person and a thing. Our bodies are key to our identity and are part of us. The way to protect bodies is to recognize them as human and protected as a human right to privacy, bodily integrity, dignity, or the like (see Beyleveld and Brownsword (2001) for how the concept of dignity could be used). Here the body is recognized as part of the person.

8.79 It may be that when something is separated from the body then there is a case for recognizing property rights. But even then the claim in relation to the body is based on the claim that it is the body part that reflects us and has some of us in it. This does not match the detachment that is necessary in order for there to be a property right. Again, it is the rights of privacy or autonomy which capture the idea that our bodies are 'us' and so we have an interest in them. Whereas the property view sees the body as 'other' and therefore fails to reflect what we truly see as important about our bodies.

8.80 Property rights tend to reflect commercial and market values (Rao 2000). These are not the kind of values we wish to recognize in the body. The values we wish to recognize in the body are essentially spiritual ones. This is why so many people instinctively recoil at the idea that we own our bodies.

Speaker 2 (in favour of a property analysis)

8.81 We need to start with some practical points. First, take the decision in *Moore*. It is simply unfair that a person can have part of their body sold to make a hugely profitable enterprise and then not be permitted any share of the money on the basis that the body is not theirs. Nor would it have been fair if in *Yearworth* the court had concluded that the men had no legal interest in the sperm. The correct starting point is therefore to ascertain the interests that a person has in their body. So, we want interests which will ensure that if money is made from an abstracted body part, the person whose body was used can claim a share in the proceeds. Or, where someone looking after a body part for someone else damages it, then the person would be entitled to damages. We are looking for a system of legal protection which will ensure that a person can control what happens to a part of their body which is removed. So we are looking for rights of control, rights to compensation if there is damage, and rights to a share in the profits made using body parts. Well, the best legal mechanism for granting those rights is the law of property. The kinds of philosophical nicety that Speaker 1 is engaging in is not very helpful. We need to start with the practical interests we need recognized and then find a legal mechanism which recognizes those interests (Hardcastle 2007). Here, the answer is property.

Speaker 3 (relational bodies)

8.82 Both previous speakers have followed the writing of most commentators on this topic and assume that our bodies are ours. They disagree on whether property rights or other rights capture the sense in which our bodies are ours; but are based on that assumption. In fact, the notion that our bodies are ours is only a partial truth. There are certainly ways in which our bodies are interconnected: during pregnancy, the bodies of fetus and mother are interdependent; even during childhood, the body of the child and and those of the parents can be connected: the child is dependant on the parent to do things; but also the parents' bodies can be connected with the child. In many relations of dependency, the bodies of carer and dependant will be in a relationship of interconnection. If the body of the carer is impaired, then this will impact on the body of the person receiving care. Further, our bodies are connected with the world around us: our bodies take in food, liquid, and air and these are in due course expelled, often in a modified form. Indeed, our bodies are constantly changing: by the time we die, there is little of us left which is the same as when we were born. Neither property rights nor privacy rights capture the fact that our bodies are leaky and interdependent on other bodies. We need a completely different legal regime to recognize the true nature of our bodies (Herring and Chau 2007).

Xenotransplantation

8.83 Xenotransplantation involves the use of the organs of one species to transplant into another (McLean and Williamson 2005). It has been defined by the Department of Health (2006) in this way:

> any procedure that involves the transplantation, implantation, or infusion into a human recipient of either live tissues or organs retrieved from animals, or, human body fluids, cells, tissue or organs that have undergone ex vivo contact with live non-human animal cells, tissues or organs.

8.84 It is at present a complex procedure because of the difficulties of rejection from the recipient. In fact, the procedure is still at an experimental stage (Fovargue 2007). Improvements in drugs which suppress the rejection of the host have meant that only in very recent years has xenotransplantation become a realistic possibility. The Department of Health (2006) has encouraged research into this practice saying that 'it is right to explore the potential of xenotransplantation in a cautious, stepwise fashion...in a controlled research context'.

8.85 Anyone who wishes to use xenotransplantation will need the approval of a research ethics committee. They will only give permission where strict guidelines are followed. The fact that one of the most successful cases of xenotransplantation involved a man who received a baboon's liver, but only lived for 70 days, demonstrates that to permit the practice would be to make participants 'human guinea pigs' (so to speak). Following technological advances, some scientists claim that it is now safe for pig organs to be used in humans; however, so far there have been no xenotransplantations in the UK.

8.86 One concern with xenotransplantation is that it could lead to animal viruses being passed to humans (Fox and McHale 1998). As we do not fully understand the potential consequences of this, it is better not to attempt the practice.

8.87 A further issue is whether there are some animals which should not be used for transplantation. There is a widespread feeling that organs should not be taken from primates because of their special status, even though they, being closest to humans in biological terms, would be the best donors. The pig has therefore become a popular option. There is much debate on whether or not animals have rights (see Fox and McHale 1998). Even if you take the view that animals do not have rights, most people agree that they have interests which deserve some protection (Fox and McHale 1998).

8.88 This still leaves some with a profound distaste for the use of an animal's organs to sustain human life. There are of course those who take a strong line on animal rights and object to the eating of animal meat or for whom there may be religious objections. To those people, the use of animal organs is likely to be objectionable. It could be argued that the eating of animal meat is unjustifiable while there are alternative foods, but if xenotransplantation is the only way of saving the life of a human it may be seen as justifiable. By contrast, others take the view that eating meat is justifiable, but the use of animal organs is not, seeing as one is natural and the other is not. To properly assess this question, it would be necessary to consider the complex issue of animal rights. There is not sufficient space to discuss this in more detail here, but there is further reading on the topic at the end of the chapter.

CONCLUSION

This chapter has revealed the uneasy relationship we have with our bodies. In one sense, they are part of who we are and should not be regarded as objects for us to treat like property that we can dispose of as we wish. In another sense, there are circumstances in which we want to make property-like claims in respect of our bodily material, especially when it has been separated from our bodies. This chapter has shown how the law is struggling to capture in legal terms the correct relationship between us and our bodies.

FURTHER READING

Andrews, L., and Nelkin, D. (2001) *Body Bazaar: The Market for Human Tissue* (New York: Crown).

Beyleveld, D., and Brownsword, R. (2001) *Human Dignity in Bioethics and Biolaw* (Oxford: Oxford University Press).

Brazier, M. (2002) 'Retained Organs: Ethics and Humanity', *Legal Studies* 22: 550–69.

British Medical Association (BMA) (2005) *Organ Donation—Presumed Consent for Organ Donation* (London: British Medical Association).

Chadwick, R. (1994) 'Corpses, Recycling and Therapeutic Purposes', in R. Lee and D. Morgans (eds), *Death Rites* (Abingdon: Routledge), pp. 54–74.

Cherry, M. (2005) *Kidney for Sale by Owner* (Washington, DC: Georgetown University Press).

Department of Health (DoH) (2002) *Human Bodies, Human Choices* (London: DoH).

Department of Health (DoH) (2006) *Xenotransplantation* (London: DoH).

Dickenson, D. (2009) *Body Shopping* (London: Oneworld).

Fovargue, S. (2007) ' "Oh Pick me, Pick me"—Selecting Participants for Xenotransplant Clinical Trials', *Medical Law Review* 15: 176–219.

Fox, M., and McHale, J. (1998) 'Xenotransplantation: The Ethical and Legal Ramifications', *Medical Law Review* 6: 42–61.

Garwood-Gowers, A. (1999) *Key Legal and Ethical Issues in Living Donor Organ Transplantation* (Aldershot: Ashgate).

Glannon, W. (2008) 'The Case against Conscription of Cadaveric Organs for Transplantation', *Cambridge Quarterly of Healthcare Ethics* 17: 330–6.

Goodwin, M. (2007) *Black Markets* (Cambridge: Cambridge University Press).

Hardcastle, R. (2007) *Law and the Human Body* (Oxford: Hart).

Harris, J. (1975) 'The Survival Lottery', *Philosophy* 50: 81–7.

Harris, J. (2002) 'Law and Regulation of Retained Organs: The Ethical Issues', *Legal Studies* 527–49.

Herring, J. (2007) 'Crimes against the Dead', in B. Brooks-Gordon, F. Ebtehaj, J. Herring, M. Johnson, and M. Richards (eds), *Death Rites and Rights* (Oxford: Hart), pp. 121–42.

Herring, J. (2007) 'Where are the Carers in Healthcare Law and Ethics?', *Legal Studies* 27: 51–73.

Herring, J., and Chau, P.-L. (2007) 'My Body, Your Body, Our Bodies', *Medical Law Review* 15: 34–61.

McGuinness, S., and Brazier, M. (2008) 'Respecting the Living Means Respecting the Dead Too', *Oxford Journal of Legal Studies* 28: 297–316.

McLean, S., and Williamson, L. (2005) *Xenotransplantation—Law and Ethics* (Aldershot: Ashgate).

National Health Service (NHS) (2009) *Reimbursement of Living Donor Expenses by the NHS* (London: NHS).

Organ Donation Taskforce (2008) *The Potential Impact of an Opt Out System for Organ Donation in the UK* (London: The Stationery Office).

Price, D. (2000) *Legal and Ethical Aspects of Organ Transplantation* (Cambridge: Cambridge University Press).

Price, D. (2005) 'The Human Tissue Act 2004', *Modern Law Review* 68: 798–821.

Price, D. (2007) 'Property, Harm and the Corpse', in B. Brooks-Gordon, F. Ebtehaj, J. Herring, M. Johnson, and M. Richards (eds), *Death Rites and Rights* (Oxford: Hart), pp. 224–47.

Rao, R. (2000) 'Property, Privacy and the Human Body', *Boston Law Review* 80: 359–413.

Stacey Taylor, J. (2005) *Stakes and Kidneys: Why Markets in Human Body Parts are Morally Imperative* (Aldershot: Ashgate).

UK Transplant (2007) *Liver Organ Sharing Principles* (London: UK Transplant).

Wilkinson, S. (2003) *Bodies for Sale: Ethics and Exploitation in the Human Body Trade* (Abingdon: Routledge).

Wilkinson, T. (2005) 'Individual and Family Consent to Organ and Tissue Donation: Is the Current Position Coherent?', *Journal of Medical Ethics* 31: 587–90.

SELF-TEST QUESTIONS

1 Do you think that once a person has died their views on how they wanted their body to be treated should carry any weight?

2 Dr Smith regularly takes samples from patients' bodies and stores them without consent. He has a large collection and will occasionally select a sample from his collection to discuss with students. He says that all his samples might be used for education, but he cannot say which he might need. Is he acting lawfully?

3 Should the law on organ donation be reformed, and if so how?

Ending life

SUMMARY

This chapter will look at the issue surrounding the end of life. It will consider the circumstances in which it is lawful to hasten death, assist another to commit suicide, or not provide treatment so that someone dies. It will also examine the definition of death. The chapter will highlight the tension between the principle of autonomy (allowing people to make decisions for themselves) and the principle of sanctity of life (respecting the value we place on life).

Introduction

9.1 When do we die? Do we have a right to die? When can a medical professional kill a patient, or help them commit suicide? These are some of the most controversial issues in current medical law and ethics. There are a lot of issues to discuss. We shall start by looking at the definition of death. We shall then consider the legal regulation of end of life decisions. Traditionally, these have been dealt with as a matter of criminal law and we shall start by looking at the law in that way. However, more recently the issue has been seen as one involving human rights and we shall be looking at that later.

The definition of death

9.2 The courts have not often discussed the definition of death. Where they do (*Airedale NHS Trust* v. *Bland* [1993] AC 789; *Re A* [1992] 3 Med LR 303), they seem to accept the definition approved by medics. In England and Wales that means that brain death is adopted as the definition of death. The Department of Health has produced *A Code of Practice for the Diagnosis of Brain Stem Death* (1988), which sets out the criteria which doctors should use in determining whether the patient is brain dead. That is explained by the NHS (2010: 3) in this way:

> Brain death occurs when a person in an intensive care unit no longer has any activity in their brain stem, even though a ventilator is keeping their heart beating and oxygen circulating through their blood. . . . The brain stem is the lower part of the brain that is connected to the spinal cord (a column of nervous tissue located in the spinal column). The brain stem is responsible for regulating most of the automatic functions of the body that are essential for life. These are:
>
> • breathing
> • heartbeat
> • blood pressure
> • swallowing
>
> The brain stem also relays all information to and from the brain to the rest of the body, so it plays a vital role in the body's core functions, such as consciousness, awareness and movement.

9.3 There are those who are unhappy with the law's approach to death. They (e.g. Glannon 2009) argue that brain stem death elevates the brain to being the sole organ of significance for life. We are more than our brains: we are our bodies, too. Consider people with severe mental disorder. They may be capable of little thought, but they are still very much people. These critics support a definition of death which involves considering the body as well as the brain. Others (e.g. Chau and Herring 2007) have argued that we should accept death as a process. This might mean that death will have a different meaning for different purposes. So we might have one meaning of death for deciding whether organ donation is permitted and another to determine when a body may be disposed of. Nevertheless, for lawyers, the current law is based on brain stem death.

The criminal law

Murder

9.4 A medical professional can be guilty of murder if he or she kills a patient. A person is guilty of murder if

- she has caused the death of the patient; and
- she intended to cause death or grievous bodily harm.

This means that if a patient asks a nurse to kill her and the nurse smothers the patient with a pillow, that would be murder. However, a doctor who gives pain-relieving drugs, foreseeing, but not intending, that they would cause death, would not be guilty of murder. This is because, according to *Woollin* [1998] 4 All ER 103, a jury does not have to find intention in a case where the result is not the purpose of the defendant, but is foreseen as virtually certain.

> *Adams* **[1957] Crim LR 365** Dr Adams was charged with murder. Devlin J, summing up to the jury, confirmed that if a doctor intentionally killed a patient that could be murder. This was true even though the doctor may only have shortened a patient's life by a matter of weeks. However, he also explained that if a doctor's primary intention when injecting drugs was to relieve pain, then he would not be guilty of murder, even though the doctor realized that the drugs would cause the death. As a result of this direction, Dr Adams was acquitted.

It would be possible for a doctor to be charged with murder for failing to treat a patient, intending that a patient would die. So, if a doctor saw his enemy wheeled into the hospital and deliberately left him alone, hoping he will die, that could plausibly lead to a charge of murder. More likely, however, such a case would be charged as gross negligence manslaughter (see 9.8 below).

Defences

9.5 Section 2 of the Homicide Act 1957 (as amended by the Coroners and Justice Act 2009) sets out the circumstances in which a person has a defence of diminished responsibility to a charge of murder:

> A person ('D') who kills or is a party to the killing of another is not to be convicted of murder if D was suffering from an abnormality of mental functioning which—

    (*a*) arose from a recognised medical condition,

    (*b*) substantially impaired D's ability to do one or more of the things mentioned in subsection (1A), and

    (*c*) provides an explanation for D's acts and omissions in doing or being a party to the killing.

  (1A) those things are—

      (*a*) to understand the nature of D's conduct;

      (*b*) to form a rational judgment;

      (*c*) to exercise self-control.

  (1B) for the purposes of subsection (1)(c), an abnormality of mental functioning provides an explanation for D's conduct if it causes, or is a significant contributory factor in causing, D to carry out that conduct.

It is unlikely that this defence will apply to a medical professional, but it could be relied upon if a relative kills a terminally ill person. The defendant would need to show that he or she suffered from an abnormality of mental functioning. The courts have been willing to use this defence in cases where exhausted carers have killed the terminally ill relative they have been looking after (see Biggs 2007).

Loss of control

9.6 This defence also seems only likely to apply to a relative who kills. In *Cocker* [1989] Crim LR 740, a husband smothered his terminally ill wife after her repeated requests to be killed. He sought unsuccessfully to rely on provocation (as the defence of loss of control was known until the 2009 reforms). The Court of Appeal explained that he had not lost his control, but quite the opposite he acted in a cool, deliberate way. Following this decision, it is difficult for a carer to rely on loss of control, unless they killed in a fit of rage.

Necessity

9.7 The criminal courts have generally been very reluctant to rely on 'the lesser of two evils' defence. It is easy to see why. Consider a doctor who has four patients who need organ transplants within 24 hours. Could she kill a nurse and use her organs to transplant into the four? A doctor might argue that it would be the lesser of two evils to kill the one in order to save the four. To allow a doctor to kill in such a case would fail to respect people's right to life. However, in the following controversial case the courts did allow the defence.

> ***Re A (Conjoined Twins)* [2001] Fam 147 (CA)** Jodie and Mary were born as conjoined twins. They were joined together at the pelvis. Mary's heart and lungs did not function and she was only able to live because she was joined to Jodie. In effect, Jodie's heart was pumping for both of them. The expert evidence was that if the twins were not separated they would both die within a few months. If they were separated, Jodie was likely to live a relatively normal life, but Mary would die immediately. The parents objected to carrying out the operation, but the doctors wanted to go ahead. The doctors sought the guidance of the court.
>
> The Court of Appeal declared that the operation would be lawful. The start of the analysis was that performing the operation would not be a criminal offence. It would cause Mary's death. Lord Justices Ward and Brooke held that the doctors would intend to kill Mary (although in Lord Justice Walker's analysis there was no such intention). All three of their Lordships held, nevertheless, there would be no crime because the defence of necessity was available. The operation would save Jodie's life, while not performing the operation would cause the death of both girls. The Court of Appeal emphasized that the case was highly unusual and they were not setting a precedent that could apply to other cases.
>
> Not only was there no criminal offence, but the court also decided that the operation would be in the best interests of the children. It was necessary to consider the best interests of both. There were benefits to Mary in that even though it would lead to her death, it would promote her bodily integrity and her right to keep her body whole and intact. Without the operation, her life would be one of pain and discomfort. Balancing the interests, it was overall in their best interests for the operation to proceed.

Manslaughter

9.8 A medical professional could also be guilty of manslaughter. This requires proof of the following:

- The defendant owed the victim a duty of care.
- The defendant breached the duty of care.
- The breach caused the death of the victim.
- The breach was so gross as to justify a criminal conviction.

Notice that this offence does not require proof that the defendant intended to kill the patient. The offence is typically used where the defendant has killed the victim as a result of a significant error.

> *R v. Adomako* **[1995] 1 AC 171** An anaesthetist was overseeing an operation. During the operation, the tube from the ventilator which supplied oxygen to the patient became disconnected. An alarm sounded. A reasonable anaesthetist would have spotted the problem very quickly, but it took Dr Adomako over six minutes to spot the error, by which time the patient suffered a cardiac arrest. The House of Lords dismissed the appeal against the conviction. They confirmed that a defendant could be guilty of gross negligence manslaughter if he or she negligently caused the death of the victim, and the conduct of the defendant was so bad that it justifies a criminal conviction.

9.9 There has been much debate over whether doctors who make mistakes should face criminal sanction. After all, doctors have to do a difficult job, saving many lives. A small error can lead to death and we should be sympathetic to the difficulties doctors face (see, e.g. Quick 2010). However, many defendants could make such a claim (e.g. train drivers). It is important, however, that juries are sensitive to the difficult and pressurized situations that doctors have to work in when deciding whether the breach was sufficiently serious to justify a criminal conviction.

Suicide

9.10 The law on suicide is set out in the Suicide Act 1961. The Act states that neither suicide nor attempted suicide are criminal offences. However, it is an offence to aid and abet someone else to commit suicide. Section 2 states:

> (1) A person ('D') commits an offence if—
>
>> (a) D does an act capable of encouraging or assisting the suicide or attempted suicide of another person, and
>>
>> (b) D's act was intended to encourage or assist suicide or an attempt at suicide.
>
> (1A) The person referred to in subsection (1)(a) need not be a specific person (or class of persons) known to, or identified by, D.
>
> (1B) D may commit an offence under this section whether or not a suicide, or an attempt at suicide, occurs.

Notice that the offence is committed whether or not the person assisted or encouraged commits suicide. Notice also that the defendant must intend to encourage the suicide, so that a man breaking up with his girlfriend, foreseeing that as a result she might commit suicide, will not be guilty of this offence.

9.11 At first, it seems odd that it is a crime to help someone do something (suicide) of which the person commits no offence if they do it themselves. The reason is this. The government decided that it was not beneficial to bring criminal proceedings against a person who had committed suicide. They need help, not prosecution. The fact that suicide or attempting suicide is not a crime does not indicate that the law thinks it is a good thing, but simply that prosecuting it is unlikely to be beneficial.

9.12 Aiding and abetting suicide is, therefore, an offence. That means that someone who urges another person to commit suicide or gives them advice on how to, will be committing an offence. However, a person who simply writes a book on ways of committing suicide would not be guilty of the offence (*Able* v. *AG* [1984] QB 795), because the assistance would be too remote from the killing. However, the offence is subject to an important caveat. That is that in section 2(4) of the 1961 Act, prosecutions can only be brought with the agreement of the Director of Public Prosecutions (DPP). That has led to some controversial litigation:

> *R (Purdy)* v. *DPP* [2009] UKHL 45 Debbie Purdy was suffering from multiple sclerosis. The disease had been progressing for several years and she wished to travel to Switzerland in order to commit suicide. In Switzerland assisted suicide is lawful. To do so she needed the assistance of her husband, but she was worried that he might be prosecuted for assisted suicide. Her application to court was based on the argument that the DPP had failed to provide clear guidance as to when he would or would not prosecute for assisted suicide.
>
> The House of Lords agreed that the decision to commit suicide, was a decision affecting someone's private life and so was covered by Article 8(1) of the European Convention on Human Rights (ECHR). So, too, were the actions of someone assisting suicide. However, under Article 8(2), an interference in that right could be justified if it could be shown to be in accordance with the law and necessary to (*inter alia*) protect the interests of others. Their Lordships found that to be 'in accordance with law', any interference had to be clearly defined. This was especially important in this area, given that assisted suicide was a sensitive and controversial subject. Although the DPP had issued some guidance about when he would prosecute, it was too vague to amount to law. The DPP was ordered to produce clearer guidance.

9.13 This decision does not say that assisted suicide is lawful. It says that the DPP had to produce guidelines which would make clear his policy on prosecutions. And so he did. This has taken the form of listing those factors which would favour prosecution and those which would not. The 16 factors that would favour prosecution are that:

- the victim was under 18 years of age;
- the victim did not have the capacity (as defined by the Mental Capacity Act 2005) to reach an informed decision to commit suicide;
- the victim had not reached a voluntary, clear, settled, and informed decision to commit suicide;
- the victim had not clearly and unequivocally communicated his or her decision to commit suicide to the suspect;
- the victim did not seek the encouragement or assistance of the suspect personally or on his or her own initiative;
- the suspect was not wholly motivated by compassion; for example, the suspect was motivated by the prospect that he or she or a person closely connected to him or her stood to gain in some way from the death of the victim;
- the suspect pressured the victim to commit suicide;
- the suspect did not take reasonable steps to ensure that any other person had not pressured the victim to commit suicide;
- the suspect had a history of violence or abuse against the victim;
- the victim was physically able to undertake the act that constituted the assistance him or herself;
- the suspect was unknown to the victim and encouraged or assisted the victim to commit or attempt to commit suicide by providing specific information via, for example, a website or publication;
- the suspect gave encouragement or assistance to more than one victim who were not known to each other;
- the suspect was paid by the victim or those close to the victim for his or her encouragement or assistance;
- the suspect was acting in his or her capacity as a medical doctor, nurse, other health care professional, a professional carer (whether for payment or

not), or as a person in authority, such as a prison officer, and the victim was in his or her care;

- the suspect was aware that the victim intended to commit suicide in a public place where it was reasonable to think that members of the public may be present;

- the suspect was acting in his or her capacity as a person involved in the management or as an employee (whether for payment or not) of an organization or group, a purpose of which is to provide a physical environment (whether for payment or not) in which to allow another to commit suicide.

9.14 The six factors that would count against prosecution would be that:

- the victim had reached a voluntary, clear, settled, and informed decision to commit suicide;

- the suspect was wholly motivated by compassion;

- the actions of the suspect, although sufficient to come within the definition of the crime, were of only minor encouragement or assistance;

- the suspect had sought to dissuade the victim from taking the course of action which resulted in his or her suicide;

- the actions of the suspect may be characterized as reluctant encouragement or assistance in the face of a determined wish on the part of the victim to commit suicide;

- the suspect reported the victim's suicide to the police and fully assisted them in their enquiries into the circumstances of the suicide or the attempt and his or her part in providing encouragement or assistance.

The full document is at http://www.cps.gov.uk/publications/prosecution/assisted_suicide_policy.html.

9.15 It is important to understand the position that we have now reached. It is still an offence to aid or abet assisted suicide. The guidance makes clear that there will be some cases where it will not be appropriate to prosecute. To talk, therefore, of the decision as de-criminalizing assisted suicide would not be correct. The importance of the *Purdy* decision, however, lies not so much in the end result but in the way that the decision was analysed in terms of human rights. Their Lordships held that decisions about how and when to die were covered by Article 8(1) of the ECHR, which protects the right to respect for private life.

Indeed, Lord Brown suggested that there could be cases where the aider and abetter should be seen as 'altruistic rather than criminal' and whose conduct respected the intending suicide's rights under Article 8.

9.16 So, for the first time we have a very limited acknowledgement of 'a right to die' (Du Bois-Pedain 2007; Hale 2003). I say limited for three reasons. First, and obviously, the right only applies to those who are competent. Some (maybe most) of those who try to commit suicide are suffering mental illness and are not competent to decide to die. The right only applies to those who have the capacity to make the decision and have thought through the issues. Second, their Lordships seem to see the issue in negative terms. In other words, Article 8 protects you from state intervention preventing you from committing suicide. Their Lordships are not claiming a right to die; but rather a right not to be prevented from committing suicide. Experts in jurisprudence sometimes draw the distinction between a right you can demand from someone and a liberty, a right to be left alone (see Hohfeld 1917). Using that terminology this is a liberty rather than a right.

9.17 Third, their Lordships are clear that the law must protect people from being manipulated or coerced into suicide. Indeed, under Article 2 of the ECHR, the state has an obligation to protect the right to life. So the law on assisted suicide needs to strike a balance between protecting the rights of those who wish to commit suicide and protecting the rights of people who lack capacity. As Baroness Hale put it:

> Clearly the prime object [of the law on assisted suicide] must be to protect people who are vulnerable to all sorts of pressures, both subtle and not so subtle, to consider their own lives a worthless burden to others ... But at the same time, the object must be to protect the right to exercise a genuinely autonomous choice. (para. 65)

9.18 The following cases show how in some circumstances the state has an obligation to prevent someone from committing suicide.

> **Savage v. South Essex [2010] EWHC 865 (QB); [2008] UKHL 74** Ms Savage claimed that the South Essex NHS Trust had violated its obligations under Article 2 of the ECHR, in respect of her mother. The mother had a long history of mental illness. She had been detained under section 3 of the Mental Health Act 1983. She had expressed suicidal thoughts and had been previously assessed as a suicide risk. The staff had failed to follow the Trust's policy in continually assessing her and

keeping the degree of observation under review. The mother in fact was kept on the lowest level of observation. She absconded from the hospital and committed suicide.

The House of Lords had determined that the Trust had an obligation to protect the life of those in their care who were detained under the Act. However, a breach could only be found if the Trust had actual or constructive knowledge of a real and imminent risk to the mother of self-harm and had failed to do all that it reasonably could be expected to do to avoid the risk.

On a rehearing it was held that the staff knew, or ought to have known that there was a real and imminent risk to M's life because M had previously been assessed as a suicide risk and had made a significant attempt to kill herself. There was a real and immediate risk of suicide and had a higher level of observation been undertaken, her suicide would not have occurred. As a symbolic acknowledgement of Ms Savage's loss, £10,000 was awarded.

***Rabone* v. *Pennine Care NHS Trust* [2009] EWHC 1827 (QB)** M (Ms Rabone's daughter) suffered from depression and had made attempts to commit suicide. M agreed to her daughter being voluntarily detained, but it was agreed that if M attempted to leave she would be forcibly detained under the Mental Health Act 1983. On admission to the hospital, M was found to be a moderate to high suicide risk. A few days later, it seemed that M was feeling better and she asked a consultant psychiatrist to be allowed to leave for two days. Leave was granted and the next day she committed suicide. It was accepted that the decision was negligent. The legal issue was whether the Trust had a positive obligation under Article 2 of the ECHR to protect the life of M. While such an obligation had previously been found to exist in cases where a patient was compulsorily detained under the 1983 Act, it had not been found in cases where the patient was involuntarily detained.

It was held that the positive obligation under Article 2 to protect life by taking preventative measures only applied to patients detained under the Mental Health Act. Voluntary patients were entitled to leave when they wished. She was not subject to complete or effective control over her movements. Therefore her Article 2 rights were not violated. In any event, it could not be said that there was a real and immediate risk to her life. Even though the consultant had acted negligently, that would not have meant that there would have been a breach of Article 2, even if it had applied.

***Re Z (Local Authority: Duty)* [2004] EWHC 2817 (Fam)** A local authority discovered that in its area there was a person (Mrs Z), who was planning to commit suicide in Switzerland. She suffered from a terminal illness. Mr Z was planning to help her to go there. The local authority sought guidance on their duties in such a case. Hedley J emphasized that she had capacity and that suicide was no longer a crime. It was accepted that Mrs Z was a vulnerable adult who was owed duties by the local authority. Hedley J held they were the following:

(i)   to investigate the position of a vulnerable adult to consider what was her true position and intention;

(ii)   to consider whether she was legally competent to make and carry out her decision and intention;

(iii)   to consider whether any other (and if so, what) influence may be operating on her position and intention and to ensure that she has all relevant information and knows all available options;

(iv)   to consider whether she was legally competent to make and carry out her decision and intention;

(v)   to consider whether to invoke the inherent jurisdiction of the High Court so that the question of competence could be judicially investigated and determined;

(vi)   in the event of the adult not being competent, to provide all such assistance as may be reasonably required both to determine and give effect to her best interests;

(vii)   in the event of the adult being competent to allow her in any lawful way to give effect to her decision although that should not preclude the giving of advice or assistance in accordance with what are perceived to be her best interests;

(viii)   where there are reasonable grounds to suspect that the commission of a criminal offence may be involved, to draw that to the attention of the police;

(ix)   in very exceptional circumstances, to invoke the jurisdiction of the court under s. 222 of the Local Government Act 1972.

My view is that its duties do not extend beyond that.

Hedley J emphasized that the case would be different had Mrs Z lacked capacity, in which case an assessment of her best interests would have to be made. Applying the approach to the case at hand, the local authority were not required to intervene.

Refusal of treatment

9.19 The law on refusal of treatment is refreshingly straightforward after the complexities of the law on assisted suicide and euthanasia (McGee 2005). A single statement says it all:

> A competent patient has the absolute right to refuse treatment, even if without it she will die.

That is in line with the normal law on consent to treatment (see Chapter 4).

> **Re B (Adult: Refusal of Treatment) [2002] EWHC 429 (Fam)** Ms B, aged 41, was paralyzed from the neck down and dependant on a ventilator. She made it clear that she wanted the ventilator to be switched off. The medical team tried hard to persuade her to keep it on. However, she was clear that she wanted it switched off. Butler Sloss P (who visited Ms B herself) confirmed that Ms B understood the relevant issues and had capacity to make the decision. She, therefore, had the right to refuse treatment and it was unlawful for the hospital to keep her on the ventilator. This was so even if the medical team did not agree with her decision.

Remember, too, the decision in *S* v. *St George's Healthcare NHS Trust* [1998] 3 WLR 936, where the Court of Appeal confirmed that a competent woman in labour could refuse treatment, even where without it she and the fetus would die.

9.20 The law is straightforward, but don't forget that the patient must be competent. A patient who has just discovered that they are paralyzed may lack the capacity to decide to die and a medical team will need to be sure there is capacity. The following case shows that where it is clear a patient is competent and wishes to die, there is no obligation on relatives or carers to summon help.

> **R (Jenkins) v. HM Coroner for Portsmouth and South East Hampshire and Cameron and Finn [2009] EWHC 3229 (Admin)** Mr Jenkins had developed an infection in his foot. He wished to treat it with alternative remedies. Despite requests from several friends, he refused to seek medical help. His medical condition worsened and his companion, Ms Cameron, did not summon help because he refused to agree to her doing this. Mr Jenkins died. The Coroner refused to find there was a case for unlawful killing as a result of Ms Cameron not seeking medical help. The family appealed.
>
> Pritchard J held that Mr Jenkins had the capacity to refuse treatment. As he did not want medical treatment there could be no obligation on those caring for him

to demand it. When he became unconscious and so unable to make decisions, Ms Cameron should have acted in his best interests, but by that stage it was too late to save his life. The Coroner was, therefore, right to find this was not a case of unlawful killing.

The Human Rights Act 1998

9.21 The leading cases and much of the academic debate now centres on the relevance of the Human Rights Act 1998 (HRA) and it will be useful to discuss each of the relevant Articles of the ECHR.

9.22 *Article 2*: Protects the right to life. This requires the state not to kill citizens. More importantly, it requires the state to have in place laws which protect citizens from being killed at the hands of others. In *R (Purdy)* v. *DPP* [2009] UKHL 45, the House of Lords relied on Article 2 to state that laws against assisting suicide were needed to ensure that vulnerable people were not pressurized or forced into committing suicide (see further House of Lords Select Committee 2005).

The right to life in Article 2 does not include the right to die. This was confirmed by the House of Lords and European Court of Human Rights (ECtHR) in *R (Pretty)* v. *DPP* [2002] 1 AC 800 and *Pretty* v. *UK* [2002] FCR 976, which stated that to read in a right to die into the right to life would be to stretch the words too far.

9.23 *Article 3*: The right not to suffer torture or inhuman or degrading treatment. This has been defined to include not only physical suffering, but also mental anguish. Ms Pretty argued in her case that not being able to have assistance in suicide amounted to inhuman or degrading treatment. The ECtHR was not sympathetic to this argument, holding that Article 3 had to be read with Article 2 in mind, so killing someone in breach of Article 2 could not be justified by reference to Article 3. However, the issue is not closed. In *R (Burke)* v. *GMC* [2005] 3 FCR 169, it was held that Article 3 could be used to protect a patient from receiving treatment which would result in dying in degrading or distressing circumstances. It may be that this holding is limited to cases where a patient is refusing to consent to treatment or the issue concerns withdrawal of treatment. It might, however, be expanded to cover cases where a patient wishes to receive treatment which will end their life, but avoid an undignified death.

The reconciliation with Article 2 may be that although one cannot choose to end one's life, one can use Article 3 to seek a right to control the exact method of death. So, if life is shorted by just a few hours or perhaps days, Article 3 can be used, but not if otherwise.

9.24 *Article 8*: In *R (Purdy)* v. *DPP* [2009] UKHL 45, the House of Lords accepted that the right to respect for private life included the right to make decisions about one's death. They relied on this statement in *Pretty* v. *UK*, where the ECtHR held:

> The very essence of the Convention is respect for human dignity and human free-dom. Without in any way negating the principle of sanctity of life protected under the Convention, the Court considers that it is under Article 8 that notions of the quality of life take on significance. In an era of growing medical sophistication combined with longer life expectancies, many people are concerned that they should not be forced to linger on in old age or in states of advanced physical or mental decrepitude which conflict with strongly held ideas of self and personal identity. (para. 65)

Lord Brown put the tension this way:

> Of course it is wrong—often terribly wrong—to assist in the suicide of someone who is not mentally competent or not clearly fixed in their intention or who may feel under pressure to end their life for the benefit of others or whose condition may not be extreme or may perhaps be curable rather than deteriorating. Assistance in those kind of situations is clearly to be condemned. But suppose, say, a loved one, in desperate and deteriorating circumstances, who regards the future with dread and has made a fully informed, voluntary and fixed decision to die, needing another's compassion-ate help and support to accomplish that end (or at any rate to achieve it in the least distressing way), is assistance in *those* circumstances necessarily to be deprecated? Are there not cases in which (although no actual defence of necessity could ever arise) many might regard such conduct as if anything to be commended rather than condemned? In short, as it seems to me, there will on occasion be situations where, contrary to the assumptions underlying the Code, it would be possible to regard the conduct of the aider and abettor as altruistic rather than criminal, conduct rather to be understood out of respect for an intending suicide's rights under Article 8 than discouraged so as to safeguard the right to life of others under Article 2. (para. 83)

Lord Brown's statement is interesting, but it seems to suggest that not only is the assister not to be seen as criminal, but rather as acting in order to respect the individual's rights. It is a small step from this to suggest that a person has a right to assistance in dying. Consider, for example, a case where a person wants assistance in dying, but there are no friends they can rely on. Can they request or even demand that the state provide someone who can assist them? Lord Brown certainly does not go that far, but it would not be a large step from what he is saying to reach that position.

9.25 *Article 9*: this was raised in the *Pretty* v. *UK* (2002) 35 EHRR 1 decision. It was argued that not allowing assisted suicide interfered with her right to freedom of thought, conscience, and religion protected by Article 9. However, the court held that even if she had a particular opinion about end of life issues, the law prohibiting assisted suicide did not prevent her from holding her belief, nor from informing others about it. Article 9 was therefore not breached by a law prohibiting assisted suicide.

9.26 *Article 14*: of great significance is Article 14 which prohibits discrimination in the exercise of rights. The relevance to the debate is this. An able-bodied person is able to commit suicide. If a disabled person cannot do this, and wants to die, is denying them the assistance of another person a form of discrimination? The ECtHR in *Pretty* v. *UK* held not, but there was relatively little analysis of the issue, because they held that any discrimination that might exist would be justified by the need to leave in place laws which protected the vulnerable.

9.27 To recap. It is easy to lose sight of the fact that HRA arguments pull in both ways. On the one hand, there are the obligations under the ECHR to protect vulnerable people from committing suicide or dying. On the other hand, there is a recognition of the right to commit suicide. The law must seek to strike an appropriate balance between both rights. Indeed, in the following case, the HRA was relied upon in a claim that the patient had the right to be kept alive:

> ***R (Burke)* v. *GMC* [2005] 3 FCR 169** Leslie Burke suffered from a serious degenerative disease. It was highly likely that in the future he would require artificial nutrition and hydration (ANH) to keep him alive. He was concerned that his medical team might decide not to offer him this and to let him die. Therefore, unlike other cases where patients have sought the right to die, he was claiming the right to be kept alive. He wanted the court to declare that withdrawing ANH would amount to interferences under Articles 2, 3, and 8 of the ECHR. The Court of Appeal refused to make such a declaration. The court felt it inappropriate to make an order based on a hypothetical situation. In any event, they confirmed that a patient has no right

to demand treatment. It is for the medical professional to decide what treatment to offer and the patient can then select from the options. If a patient requests a procedure, then the doctor must determine whether or not the procedure will be in the person's interests, but the doctor is not required to provide it. The Court of Appeal explained:

> Autonomy and the right of self-determination do not entitle the patient to insist on receiving a particular medical treatment regardless of the nature of the treatment. Insofar as a doctor has a legal obligation to provide treatment this cannot be founded simply upon the fact that the patient demands it. The source of the duty lies elsewhere. (para. 31)

9.28 While the court accepted that a patient with capacity had the right to refuse treatment, it did not follow that they had a right to demand treatment. Mr Burke took his case to the ECtHR (Application No. 19807/06, 11 July 2006), who held that if a patient lost capacity

> a doctor would be obliged to take account of the applicant's previously expressed wishes and those of the persons close to him, as well as the opinions of other medical personnel and, if there was any conflict or doubt as to the applicant's best interests, then to approach a court. This does not, in the Court's view, disclose any lack of respect for the crucial rights invoked by the applicant. (para. 56)

Persistent vegetative state (PVS)

9.29 Patients can fall into a serious coma. Some suffer from persistent vegetative state (PVS). Such patients are unable to move, but can retain some reflexes and some can respond to stimuli. Patients suffering PVS have, however, very limited awareness of their condition and ability to control movement. Such a patient is not dead, because there is no brain stem death. So, is it permissible to switch off the life support machine? The leading case is the following:

> ***Airedale NHS Trust v. Bland* [1993] 1 All ER 821** Tony Bland had been in a coma for over three years and was diagnosed as having PVS. His medical team sought authorization from the courts to switch off the life support machine. His family agreed. The House of Lords started their analysis by confirming that Tony Bland was alive. He was not brain dead. The majority of their Lordships held that switching off the life support would be an omission, rather than an act. That was because they were stopping the treatment they had previously been providing. Tony Bland was being returned to

the medical position he was in when he first entered the hospital. This meant that the overall impact of what the doctors had done was nothing.

The next issue was whether switching off the machine was in breach of the duty that a doctor owed to a patient. The conclusion was that keeping Bland on the life support machine was not positively in his best interests, but there again it did not harm him. In other words, keeping him on the life support machine was neutral in best interests terms. The effect of this was that the doctors were authorized to withdraw the life support, although they would also be permitted to keep him on the life support machine.

9.30 This case still governs the law's approach to those in PVS. Their Lordships, through the crafty device of finding the life support machine to be neither harming nor benefiting the patient, have delegated the decision to doctors. As long as the doctors decide reasonably, they will be acting lawfully whether they decide to switch the machine off, or keep it on. Doctors will be guided by the British Medical Association (BMA) guidance on the treatment of patients with PVS:

The guiding principles underlying any such decision must be to protect the dignity, comfort and rights of the patient; to take into account any known wishes of the patient and the views of people close to patients who lack capacity.

9.31 The issue of PVS patients was considered in the following case:

Frenchay Healthcare NHS Trust v. S [1994] 1 WLR 604 A 24-year-old man had been in PVS since the age of 19, following a drugs overdose. He had been diagnosed as being brain dead. His feeding tube had become disconnected and required reinserting. There was not time to obtain a full set of medical reports, given the urgency of the application. While normally the court would only consider applications to withdraw medical support from a PVS patient with detailed reports, in this case it was legitimate to rely on the facts of the case and the existing medical reports. It was therefore permissible not to insert the feeding tube and let the patient die.

9.32 There was a challenge in *A Hospital* v. *SW* [2007] EWHC 425 (Fam) to *Bland*, suggesting that the decision would be different after the HRA. The argument that the withdrawal of hydration from a patient would infringe their Article 3 rights was firmly rejected by Sir Mark Potter. In *D* v. *An NHS Trust Hospital* [2005] EWHC 2439, *Bland* was applied even in a case where the parents objected to the withdrawal of the treatment. It was held that it was for the courts, not the family, to determine what was in a patient's best interests.

9.33 One case which stands out against the general trend of the case law is *NHS Trust v. J* [2006] EWHC 3152 (Fam), where Sir Mark Potter accepted evidence that there was an outside chance that a new drug would offer a chance of recovery, albeit a slim one. He refused to allow the medical team to turn off the machine until the experimental drug had been tried. Later it transpired that the drug had not succeeded and so permission was given to switch off the machine.

Other adults

9.34 Can the reasoning in *Bland* apply to those who are not suffering PVS, but are severely disabled? Assuming that such a person lacks capacity, the issue will be determined by the best interests test under the Mental Capacity Act 2005. The courts have confirmed that there are cases where giving a patient treatment to keep them alive will not be in that person's best interests. The courts work on a presumption that it is in a person's best interests to be alive, but there are circumstances where this is not so. At one time, the test used by the courts was whether the continued life would be 'intolerable' (*Re R (Adult: Medical Treatment)* (1996) 31 BMLR 127). However, in more recent cases, the courts have preferred an approach based simply on best interests (*Re G (Adult Incompetent: Withdrawal of Treatment)* (2001) 65 BMLR 6). The law is not therefore dependent on the severity of the disease, but rather the condition of the patient. Just to emphasize, however, the medical team are never permitted to act to end intentionally a person's life, we are discussing here only withdrawal of treatment.

Children

9.35 There have been more cases concerning the withdrawal of treatment for children. You will be familiar with the basic principles at play. Doing an act intending to kill the child would not be permitted. However, treatment can be withdrawn if that treatment is not in the child's best interests. The courts have taken a fairly strict line on this. Lord Justice Taylor made an important point in *Re J (A Minor) (Wardship: Medical Treatment)* [1990] 3 All ER 930:

> Even severely handicapped people find a quality of life rewarding which to the unhandicapped may seem manifestly intolerable.

9.36 This emphasizes the point that the assessment of whether the treatment is benefiting the patient must be made from the point of view of the patient and not from a view outside. He suggested that the question be asked whether the child's life was intolerable, for that child. As already mentioned, in more recent cases the courts have preferred to ask simply whether or not the treatment benefited the child. Still, the issue raises some complex issues.

The views of parents

9.37 At the end of the day, it is for the courts to decide what is in the child's best interests, not the parents. So where the court concludes that the treatment is not benefiting the child, the court will approve of its removal, even where the parents object (*Re C* [1998] LL Rep Med 1). However, the wishes of the parents will be taken into account. And, particularly in cases where the issue is very finely balanced, the wishes of the parents may prove decisive.

> ***Charlotte Wyatt Litigation* [2005] EWCA Civ 1181** The care of Charlotte Wyatt has been the subject of extensive litigation. She was born prematurely and has a complex array of medical difficulties. The medical team and her parents had not found agreement over her care, and particularly over what efforts should be made to keep her alive if she were to acquire an infection which requires extensive treatment. The courts made the following point: they emphasized that the key question is best interests. The 'intolerability' test could be considered, but ultimately the question is simply one of what is in the best interests of the child, looked at from the point of view of the child. The presumption is that being kept alive will be in the child's best interests, but that is a rebuttable presumption. When ascertaining the welfare of the child, all relevant factors are to be weighed up, including medical but also emotional issues. The views of the parents will be taken into account but will not determine the issue.

> ***Glass* v. *UK* [2004] 1 FCR 553 (ECtHR)** Mr and Mrs Glass disagreed with the medical team over the treatment of their seriously ill son, David. The medical team wished to administer a lethal dose of a pain-relieving drug, believing that he had only a short time to live and that the remaining time would be painful. The medical team sought to give David the medication but the Glasses managed to fight them off.

> Before the ECtHR, the Glasses argued that the failure of the doctors to seek court authorization to remove the life support breached their and the child's rights under Article 8, the right to respect for private and family life. The decision of the doctors to treat David Glass without his mother's consent and without court authorization infringed his rights under Article 8. As the situation was not an emergency, the decision to try to administer the drug without seeking court approval was a breach of David's Article 8 rights. The court also noted that the fact that David was still alive

showed that sometimes a mother's intuition can be more accurate than the views of an expert.

9.38 Sometimes, it is the parents who seek the withdrawal of treatment. Typical of such a case is the following:

> *Re B* **[1990] 3 All ER 927** A baby was born with Down's syndrome and had an intestinal blockage. This could easily be removed by an operation. The parents refused to consent to the operation, believing that it would be better for her to die. The Court of Appeal had no difficulty in authorizing the procedure. That would be in the best interests of the girl. It could not be said that her life would be one of suffering and pain. The court made the important point that the parents would not be forced to care for the child. If they did not feel able to raise her, the local authority could provide alternative care.

9.39 But there are cases where the parents have won out over the views of medical professionals.

> *Re T* **[1997] 2 FCR 363** A young boy suffered from a number of medical conditions and had been receiving medical treatment for much of his life. His liver had failed and he needed a liver transplant, without which he would die. The doctors wanted to arrange the liver transplant, but the parents objected. They were health care professionals and had recently moved overseas to take up new jobs. Their argument was that the boy had already received extensive medical care and there was no guarantee that the procedure would work. The Court of Appeal did not authorize the procedure. Controversially, Butler Sloss LJ remarked that the mother and child 'were one' for the purposes of the application. She emphasized that the doctors had stated that only if the parents were fully involved in the rehabilitation process would it have a reasonable chance of success.

9.40 The decision has certainly had its critics, with Andrew Bainham (1997) commenting that if the parents did not wish to provide care for the child, alternative carers could be found. An interesting aspect of the decision is that the objections from the parents in this case were not based on religion (as they are in most cases), but from their views as health care professionals. Maybe that meant that they were given more weight than in other cases.

9.41 Another case where the parents won was *NHS Trust* v. *MB* [2006] EWHC 507 (Fam), where although the medical prognosis for the child was grim, the parents gave evidence that the child was able to communicate with them and received pleasure in seeing them. The judge refused to side with the medical team and authorize the removal of the ventilation, emphasizing that the child still enjoyed a relationship with his parents and that was 'the single most important source of pleasure and emotion to a small child'. The point to emphasize here is that when considering best interests it is not just a case of considering the medical issues, but that the family and emotional welfare can also be taken into account.

The ethical issues

9.42 To present the ethical issues, I will imagine four speakers representing some of the different points of view on these controversial issues:

Speaker 1 (the sanctity of life view)

9.43 At the heart of these end of life principles should be one simple principle: the principle of the sanctity of life. In short, this states that it is impermissible to kill intentionally an innocent person (see for further discussion McMahan 2002). That is an absolute principle. A breach of it cannot be justified. It may be argued that by killing an innocent person a great good will arise but once we accept that, we start down a slippery slope. Soon, we will be justifying killing someone so that we could use their organs to save the lives of others.

9.44 The reason why the principle of sanctity of life is important is that it recognizes that each life is precious. It has inherent value, which transcends the current experiences of an individual. This is important because we must recognize each life as precious: be it the life of a person suffering with severe mental disorder or the life of baby. Once we start to value life by what a person feels or how much pain they are in, we are in danger of failing to protect the most vulnerable in society. Many of the most evil regimes in history were based on the principle that some people's lives were worth less than others.

9.45 So, how does this principle apply to the end of life issue? It provides a clear set of guidelines. It is never permissible intentionally to kill someone, i.e. to commit euthanasia. Nor is it permissible to refrain from acting with the intention of causing someone's death. The division between an act and an omission is too fine to carry any moral weight (Price 2009). Nor is it permissible to assist a person to commit suicide. What, however, is permissible is to kill or let die, where causing death is not the primary purpose. This is permitted under the doctrine of double effect, which has been neatly summarized by John Keown (2002) to require proof of four things:

1 The act one is engaged in is not itself bad.

2 The bad consequence is not a means to the good consequences.

3 The bad consequence is foreseen but not intended.

4 There is sufficiently serious reason for allowing the bad consequence to occur.

This means that a medical professional could give pain-relieving medication, realizing that it will shorten the life of the patient, as long as that was neither the aim nor the purpose of giving the medication and the pain was sufficiently bad to require that medication. This is permitted because it does not involve the intentional taking of a life, and so does not violate the principle of sanctity of life (see Williams 2007).

9.46 I would also add that it is permissible to withdraw life-sustaining treatment from a patient, with two caveats. The first, as you will have guessed, is that there is no intention to kill the patient by the withdrawal. The second, is that the decision is made based on whether the treatment is beneficial, rather than whether or not the patient's life is futile. This is an important point. We are entitled to decide on the worthwhileness of medical treatment, but it is impermissible to start making assessments about the worth of a person's life.

9.47 That last point is worth exploring further. Those who espouse euthanasia do not suggest that everyone should have access to it. A teenager whose girlfriend or boyfriend has just left him or her should not be permitted to be killed, only those who are suffering terribly. So, despite the claim that we are respecting people's choices, euthanasia supporters only actually respect some people's choices. This shows that supporters of euthanasia make an implicit assumption about whether or not their decision is a good one. They are, therefore, making a judgement about who deserves to die and who does not.

9.48 I must also address the argument of supporters of assisted suicide and euthanasia that they are justified by the principle of autonomy. This is misguided. First, it assumes that autonomy is the only principle in town. It clearly is not. We do not allow people to do anything they want. We restrict people's autonomy for the good of others, themselves, or society in a wide range of situations (from the requirement of the wearing of seatbelts, to the requirements of the criminal law). In this case, we are justified in restricting autonomy in order to uphold the principle of sanctity of life which forms the moral bedrock of our society (see Sommerville 2001). Second, the argument assumes that those who wish to kill themselves are acting autonomously. In fact, most of those who try and commit suicide are suffering from mental disorder or severe disturbance and we cannot assume that they are acting autonomously. Finally, we must remember that if we allow euthanasia or assisted suicide, this is likely to lead to the death of people who have not autonomously made a choice to die. That will profoundly impact on their autonomy. Thinking about autonomy a little more, it might be questionable whether or not anyone can make an autonomous decision to die. None of us know what death will be like. We cannot really know how effective are palliative care or rehabilitative care. We should recall, too, that autonomy is necessarily good in and of itself, what it leads to is enabling us to develop our own lives which enables us to experience the good of life.

Speaker 2 (the autonomy view)

9.49 In 1972, Alan Clark wrote a play entitled 'Who's life is it anyway?' That captures my argument well. We should be in control of our lives, not only that but our deaths, too (Dworkin 1993; Warnock and MacDonald 2008). It is a fundamental principle of our society that other people cannot control how we live our lives, unless we are wanting to do something that will harm other people. It is known as the principle of autonomy. Other people may find our decisions foolish or believe them to be immoral, but that does not entitle them to use the law to require us to act in what they regard as a sensible or moral way. For some, being alive in a state of severe infirmity or incapacity is deeply degrading. Respect for autonomy and dignity requires that for those people who find themselves in such a condition there should be the option of escape through assisted suicide or euthanasia (Biggs 2001). It is undignified to leave a patient alive, when they want to die. We don't allow animals to die painful deaths, we kill them and put them out of their misery. We should do the same to people.

9.50 This autonomy principle applies to end of life decisions as it does to other decisions. If I am seriously ill and in great pain, I should be able to make the decision that I want my life to end and to implement that decision. There may be those who think that I am making a mistake or whose religious beliefs indicate that that infringes the sanctity of life or some such religious doctrine, but that does not give them the right to interfere in my autonomous choice. If someone else wants to live their lives in accordance with the principle of sanctity of life, that is fine by me. Just don't impose that principle on other people. The manner of our death is the important final chapter in our lives and it is important we have control over it. It may be that we simply wish to commit suicide, we may need help in doing that, or we may prefer someone else to kill us. In any event, the law should allow us to decide how we wish to die. As the *Purdy* case recognized, our decision to die is an important part of our right for respect for our private lives. The law should therefore make euthanasia and assisted suicide legal. I hope it goes without saying that I am talking here about voluntary euthanasia. The killing of someone without their consent is murder and is something completely different.

9.51 I appreciate that there are concerns that some people may say they want to die, but not really want to. We will need to make sure that there is in place a proper set of procedures to ensure that only those who genuinely want to die are allowed to have assistance in suicide or euthanasia. Maybe a panel of experts could be created who would ensure that those seeking suicide or euthanasia have the mental capacity to make the choice. There is no reason to think that with appropriate safeguards in place, we cannot protect vulnerable people. Looking at the Netherlands and Oregon, there is no evidence that people are forced into euthanasia without their consent (Lewis 2007; Smith 2005; but for a contrary view see Keown 2006).

Speaker 3 (the slippery slope view)

9.52 I agree with Speaker 2 on the moral issue. It seems a straightforward moral issue that autonomy should be the principle but I am very worried about how this would work in practice. In particular, I have concerns about whether there would be adequate protection for vulnerable people. We have a choice to respect people's autonomy in choosing when to die, but then cause an interference in the autonomy of those who wish not to die; *OR* to interfere in the autonomy of those who want to die by outlawing euthanasia and assisted suicide, but thereby protecting the autonomy of vulnerable people who would otherwise die without proper consent. Between these two, all true supporters of autonomy should prefer the latter option of outlawing assisted suicide or euthanasia. To me, having someone killed who didn't wish to die is far worse than not being allowed to die when you want to. So we should err on the side of caution and not permit euthanasia and assisted suicide. It should also be remembered that advances in palliative care and the hospice movement have meant that people are not nowadays left in a lingering painful death. Those who claim that death is undignified are usually unaware of the effectiveness of modern pain relief and palliative care.

9.53 Some of the studies on the issue give weight to my concerns. First, Katrina George's study found that women were more likely than men to request assistance in dying and to feel pressure to do so (George 2007). That concerns me. Second, the studies showing the prevalence of depression among those seeking death (Royal College of Psychiatrists 2006). Again, it may be that people wishing to die need counselling and support, rather than death. Third, studies support claims that there is a fluctuation in the views of those wishing to commit suicide. They may want to die one day and not the next. It is not as straightforward as saying that euthanasia enables us to respect people's autonomy.

9.54 These studies are backed up by reference to the lessons from the Netherlands and Oregon, where forms of euthanasia or assisted suicide are permitted. The Netherlands has permitted assisted suicide and around 3,800 people have died relying on assisted suicide or death, some 2.5 per cent of all deaths. There are grounds for concern: there is evidence that doctors are not ensuring that the formal guidelines or paperwork is complied with. John Finnis claims that there is extensive termination of life without consent, although that is disputed. Doctors who do not comply with the guidelines are not punished. In Oregon, a quarter of those using physician-assisted suicide suffered from depression. I admit that there is considerable debate over how the figures in these jurisdictions should be interpreted, but there is enough to be worried about in my view that it is not safe to assume that we can proceed.

Speaker 4 (the practical view)

9.55 All of this talk of high-sounding principles such as autonomy and sanctity of life is all very well. I am sure it leads to fascinating debates among those of a philosophical bent. But for lawyers we have to be a little more practical, the law cannot always reflect the niceties of ethical analysis. We need rules which work: rules which are able to guide people who are expected to follow them and are sufficiently clear to determine whether or not a person has broken the rules.

9.56 Some of the current law works well in this regard. The distinction the law plays with between intention and foresight is hopeless. If a patient is in great pain and needs life-shortening pain medication, a doctor can give it as long as it is not her intention to kill the patient. But how are we to know what her intention was and how can a doctor ensure she does not (or does not appear) to have that intention. The distinction is hopeless as a guide for conduct or as a rule for assessment. The act/omission distinction, on the other hand, is helpful. Many philosophers don't like it (e.g. Rachels 1975), but in most cases it provides a clear guideline for doctors: you can't kill a patient, but you can let him die. It also has the practical benefits of 'letting doctors sleep at night'. What I mean is that it helps doctors live with what they are doing if they see themselves as letting patients die, rather than killing patients. This distinction helps them to do their job. As I have said, the philosophically pure might not like it, but it works.

9.57 What a lot of the debate over euthanasia misses is the fact that doctors are making decisions about life and death. Indeed, many deaths are a result of a decision of a doctor, be that a decision to remove treatment or do something that would end life. Seale (2009) found that 21.8 per cent of court cases followed end of life decisions. So this is where I am unconvinced by the arguments of Speaker 3. Even if we did not allow euthanasia explicitly, doctors would still be making end of life decisions and all the concerns raised by Speaker 3 would apply to those decisions just as much. So we cannot avoid the concerns about the vulnerable. Indeed, if we adopted the approach suggested by Speaker 2, we might in fact better protect vulnerable people.

9.58 But, we need to be careful. The distinction between killing and not killing is one that, as I mentioned earlier, provides great comfort to doctors. I suspect that it is also a comfort to patients, too. We know that our doctors will not kill us, but not necessarily strive to keep us alive for as long as possible. That is a fair basis for a doctor–patient relationship. So, I think that the current law works reasonably well. It is not doctrinally neat, but generally it works. Perhaps the one issue which could be clarified is that when a doctor gives appropriate pain-relieving drugs which will shorten life that should not be an offence, regardless of their intention. Maybe you can think of a law which would be better, then that is all right, but I would urge that we seek a law which works and is practical, rather than one which is idealistic.

CONCLUSION

At the end of the day, many of the debates over end of life issues go back to whether one takes a utilitarian or deontological approach to ethics: see Chapter 1. For deontologists, the key principle is that of the sanctity of life: an innocent life must never be taken. For consequentialists, the key question is whether the end of life will produce greater good. Consequentialist supporters will say that sometimes it will.

The law's approach to end of life issues is gradually changing. Traditionally, the law was based on the criminal law with the focus being on the definition of murder. However, in recent times human rights have begun to play an important part in the development of the law. We are moving towards accepting some kind of right to die, or at least liberty to commit suicide. However, there is also an acceptance of the need to protect people from being forced into euthanasia or committing suicide involuntarily. Quite how these will be balanced remains to be seen.

FURTHER READING

Bainham, A. (1997) 'Do Babies Have Rights?', *Cambridge Law Journal* 56: 48–51.

Battin, M. (2005) *Ending Life* (Oxford: Oxford University Press).

Biggs, H. (2001) *Euthanasia* (Oxford: Hart).

Biggs, H. (2007) 'Criminalising Carers: Death Desires and Assisted Dying Outlaws', in B. Brooks-Gordon, F. Ebtehaj, J. Herring, M. Johnson, and M. Richards (eds), *Death Rites and Rights* (Oxford: Hart), pp. 57–74.

Chau, P.-L., and Herring, J. (2007) 'The Meaning of Death', in B. Brooks-Gordon, F. Ebtehaj, J. Herring, M. Johnson, and M. Richards (eds), *Death Rites and Rights* (Oxford: Hart), pp. 13–36.

Coggon, J. (2006) 'Could the Right to Die with Dignity Represent a New Right to Die in English Law?', *Medical Law Review* 14: 219–37.

Dworkin, R. (1993) *Life's Dominion* (London: Harper Collins).

Du Bois-Pedain, A. (2007) 'Is There a Human Right to Die?', in B. Brooks-Gordon, F. Ebtehaj, J. Herring, M. Johnson, and M. Richards (eds), *Death Rites and Rights* (Oxford: Hart), pp. 75–92.

George, K. (2007) 'A Woman's Choice? The Gendered Risks of Voluntary Euthanasia and Physician-assisted Suicide', *Medical Law Review* 15: 1–33.

Glannon, W. (2009) 'Our Brains are Not Us', *Bioethics* 23: 321–9.

Hale, B. (2003) 'A Pretty Pass: When is There a Right to Die?', *Common Law World Review* 32: 1–14.

Hohfeld, W. (1917) 'Fundamental Legal Conceptions as Applied in Judicial Reasoning', *Yale Law Journal* 26: 710–70.

House of Lords Select Committee (2005) *On the Assisted Dying for the Terminally Ill Bill* (London: The Stationery Office).

Huxtable, R. (2007) *Euthanasia, Ethics and the Law* (Abingdon: Routledge).

Keown, J. (2002) *Euthanasia, Ethics and Public Policy* (Cambridge: Cambridge University Press).

Keown, J. (2006) *Considering Physician-Assisted Suicide* (London: Care Not Killing).

Lewis, P. (2007) *Assisted Dying and Legal Change* (Oxford: Oxford University Press).

McGee, A. (2005) 'Finding a Way through the Ethical and Legal Maze: Withdrawal of Medical Treatment and Euthanasia', *Medical Law Review* 3: 357–85.

McMahan, J. (2002) *The Ethics of Killing* (Oxford: Oxford University Press).

National Health Service (NHS) (2010) *Brain Death* (London: NHS).

Price, D. (2009) 'What Shape to Euthanasia after *Bland*? Historical, Contemporary and Futuristic Paradigms', *Law Quarterly Review* 125: 142–74.

Quick, O. (2010) 'Medicine, Mistakes and Manslaughter: A Criminal Combination?', *Cambridge Law Journal* 69: 186–203.

Rachels, J. (1975) 'Active and Passive Euthanasia', *New England Journal of Medicine* 292: 78–80.

Royal College of Psychiatrists (RCP) (2006) *Assisted Dying for the Terminally Ill Bill—Statement from the Royal College of Psychiatrists on Physician Assisted Suicide* (London: RCP).

Seale, C. (2009) 'End-of-life Decisions in the UK Involving Medical Practitioners', *Palliative Medicine* 23: 198–203.

Smith, S. (2005) 'Evidence for the Practical Slippery Slope in the Debate on Physician-Assisted Suicide and Euthanasia', *Medical Law Review* 13: 17–44.

Sommerville, M. (2001) *Death Talk* (Montreal: McGill-Queen's University Press).

Warnock, M., and MacDonald, E. (2008) *Easeful Death* (Oxford: Oxford University Press).

Williams, G. (2007) *Intention and Causation in Medical Non-Killing* (Abingdon: Routledge).

SELF-TEST QUESTIONS

1 Is there a right to die? What does it mean to have a right to die?

2 Dr Brown gives a lethal injection in order to kill Susan so as to end her suffering. Dr Smith gives a lethal injection in order to relieve Brian's pain, knowing it will also kill him. Is there any legal or moral difference between these two cases?

3 Are end of life decisions essentially private matters or is there a public interest in them?

4 If there is a risk that legalizing euthanasia will lead to the death of a single person who did not genuinely want to die, is that sufficient reason not to proceed with legalisation?

5 Should the distinction between acts and omissions play such an important role in medical law and ethics?

Mental health

SUMMARY

This chapter will examine the law which permits the detention and treatment of patients with mental health issues, even without their consent. It will set out the legal orders that can be made and the facts that need to be established to justify detention under the Mental Health Act 1983. It will also consider the justifications that have been made for the laws we have in this area. The chapter will also look at the orders that can be made if the patient is to be cared for in the community.

Introduction

10.1 This chapter will consider the special provisions in place to deal with those suffering from mental illness which are found in the Mental Health Act 1983 (MHA). Of course, in many cases, the normal principles of law apply to someone with mental illness. So, for example, a person with a mental illness might be perfectly competent to consent to a medical procedure, in which case there is no need to rely on any special provisions to do that. Similarly, if a patient lacks the capacity to make a decision then decisions can be made on their behalf, based on what is in their best interests, under the Mental Capacity Act 2005 (MCA). The MHA is only needed where the patient is competent to make the decision, but refuses to consent to treatment. Indeed, the Code of Practice produced by the Department of Health makes it clear that the MHA should not be used where treatment can be provided under the MCA or without the consent of the patient.

Admission under the Mental Health Act 1983

10.2 There are three primary orders that can be sought under the MHA:

1 Admission for assessment: section 2.

2 Emergency admission: section 4.

3 Admission for treatment: section 3.

If the state of the patient's mental health is uncertain, then an order under section 2 should be sought. If short-term emergency admission is required, then section 4 should be used. For long-term admissions and treatment, section 3 should be relied upon.

Section 2: admission for assessment

10.3 An application for admission under section 2 can be made by the nearest relative of the patient, or an approved social worker. The application must be supported by two medical practitioners, including one who has a qualification in mental health. The grounds for the application are set out in section 2(2):

An application for admission for assessment may be made in respect of a patient on the grounds that—

(a) he is suffering from mental disorder of a nature or degree which warrants the detention of the patient in a hospital for assessment (or for assessment followed by medical treatment) for at least a limited period; and

(b) he ought to be so detained in the interests of his own health or safety or with a view to the protection of other persons.

10.4 Notice that the application is restricted to a mental disorder, defined broadly in section 1(2) as 'any disorder or disability of the mind'. The Act makes it clear that a learning disability or alcohol or drug dependency are not mental disorders for the purposes of the legislation (section 1(3)). This is, in part, due to the sad history of mental health legislation, where in the past those who were seen as 'immoral' or 'eccentric' were detained.

10.5 In order to obtain a section 2(2) admission, it must be shown that the detention is in the interests of the patient or the protection of other persons. This is a broad provision and would mean that a suicidal patient would be covered.

10.6 Once a patient is admitted under section 2, they can be kept in a hospital for 28 days. If a longer period is needed, than section 3 must be used. At any time during the first 14 days a patient can apply to have their case reviewed by a Mental Health Review Tribunal (MHRT). The nearest relative can discharge the order on three days' notice. However, this is not as dramatic as it appears because the Responsible Medical Officer (the doctor in charge of the patient's case) can veto that. The three days' notice also gives time for section 3 to be invoked.

10.7 The leading case regarding section 2 is the following:

> **MH v. Secretary of State for Health [2005] UKHL 60** M was a mentally ill woman detained under section 2. She did not apply to an MHRT within the first 14 days (due to her health). The hospital sought to receive her into their guardianship. M's mother objected on a number of grounds and various issues were considered by the House of Lords. The mother argued that the section 2 procedure, which does not require court approval, violated Article 5 of the European Convention on Human Rights (ECHR). Their Lordships disagreed. They held that the system which allowed a challenge to the tribunal was sufficient. The difficulty in this case was that M was not in a state to make such a challenge. Their Lordships acknowledged this problem and held that if there was reason to think that the patient wanted to challenge their detention, then every sensible effort should be made by those caring for her to enable her to do so.

Section 4: emergency admission

10.8 Section 4 is for use in emergencies. Dramatically, it allows admission on the recommendation of a single doctor, who does not even have to specialize in mental health issues. However, that doctor must confirm that it is of 'urgent necessity' that the patient be admitted and detained. He or she must also confirm that waiting for a second doctor's opinion in order to rely on section 2 would cause 'undesirable delay'. One can imagine this section being used in the case of a suicidal patient, or a patient in considerable distress, or a patient whose condition is making them violent.

10.9 A person can only be detained under section 4 for 70 hours and then either released, or detained under section 2 or 3. Very importantly, treatment cannot be provided to a patient detained under section 4 without their consent. If the patient refuses to consent and has capacity, then section 3 must be used.

Section 3: admission for treatment

10.10 This section is the most significant ground for admission because it is designed for longer-term detention and treatment can be authorized under it, even without the consent of the patient. An application can be made by either the patient's nearest relative or an approved social worker. The grounds for the order are found in section 3(2):

> An application for admission for treatment may be made in respect of a patient on the grounds that—
>
> (a) he is suffering from mental disorder of a nature or degree which makes it appropriate for him to receive medical treatment in a hospital; and
>
> (b) it is necessary for the health or safety of the patient or for the protection of other persons that he should receive such treatment and it cannot be provided unless he is detained under this section; and
>
> (c) appropriate medical treatment is available to him.

As this section indicates, there are three elements in the grounds for admission under section 3:

1 That the patient is suffering from a mental disorder which makes it appropriate to receive medical treatment in a hospital. Notably, this makes it clear that it is not enough just to show that the patient has a mental disorder. The condition must be such that he or she cannot be treated in the community or as an outpatient, but rather that he or she requires hospital treatment.

2 It must also be shown that it is necessary for the health or safety of the patient or the protection of others that the patient be detained, and that these cannot be provided unless he is detained. This makes it clear that a suicidal patient would be included, as well as a person who posed a risk

to others. Note that it must be shown that he needs to be detained under section 3. That suggests that if the patient is competent and is happy to receive the treatment then this element will not be made out.

3 Finally, and significantly, 'appropriate medical treatment' must be available for the patient. This is a controversial requirement. It means that even if a patient poses a risk to himself or others, he cannot be detained if there is no treatment available to him. A patient may be so ill that no treatment can assist, or there may be no known cause of his condition and so a treatment may not be available. The treatment in issue must be treatment for the disorder 'or one or more if its symptoms or manifestations'. So it cannot be argued that if a patient has an untreatable mental illness he can be detained to deal with other medical issues he may have.

10.11 The significance of this third condition is that a patient cannot be detained under the MHA purely to 'warehouse' him. There must be some benefit to the patient of being detained. A patient cannot be detained simply for the purposes of protecting others.

10.12 Some ambiguity surrounds the word 'treatment' here. In section 145 it is defined as including 'psychological intervention and specialist mental health habilitation, rehabilitation and care'. It is the word 'care' which is key. If 'care' is given a broad meaning, it might be said that anyone could benefit from care. If a broad meaning is taken then it will be rare when the treatability criterion is not made out. If a narrower meaning is given and it must be shown that some kind of specialist care is required then it would be harder to satisfy. It should be added that section 145 makes it clear that treatment can include preventing the deterioration of a condition, as well as improving it.

10.13 Admission under section 3 can last up to six months and can be extended for a second period of six months. It can then be extended a year at a time. In theory, a person could spend the rest of their life detained under section 3. Renewal requires the medical officer to report that the patient satisfies the section 3 criteria and that the treatment will alleviate or prevent deterioration of the condition or that if the patient is suffering a severe mental impairment the patient would not be able to care form themselves or would be liable to serious exploitation; and that detention is necessary for the health and safety of the patient or others. Detention can be challenged by an application to an MHRT.

Treatment

10.14 A patient detained under the MHA can consent to treatment if competent. If not competent, she or he must be treated in the way which promotes her or his best interests. If competent and refusing then they cannot have treatment imposed upon them, except under Part IV of the MHA. However, section 63 only permits treatment for mental disorders and does not authorize treatment for physical conditions unrelated to the mental disorder.

10.15 This means that the distinction between treatment for mental disorder and treatment for other conditions is key to the operation of the Act. The case law provides some guidance on the issue:

> *Re KB* **(Adult) (Mental Patient: Medical Treatment) (1994) 19 BMLR 144** It was held that forced feeding could be regarded as medical treatment. The argument that this was not treatment of the patient's mental condition was rejected because it was held that treating the symptoms was part of treating the disorder (anorexia nervosa).

> *B* **v. *Croydon Health Authority* [1995] Fam 13** It was held permissible under section 63 to provide forced feeding for a patient suffering 'borderline personality disorder'. The Court of Appeal held that treatments designed to alleviate the consequences of the disorder could be regarded as treatment of the disorder.

> *Tameside and Glossop Acute Services Trust* **v. *CH* [1996] 1 FCR 753** A schizophrenic patient was 38 weeks pregnant. There were concerns that she would refuse to consent to a Caesarean section. The court found that the Caesarean section would be treatment and if necessary restraint could be used to carry it out. The argument for this was that an ancillary aim of the Caesarean section was to prevent deterioration of the mother's mental health. This extends further the notion of treatment for a mental disorder to treatment designed to deal with physical matters which if untreated would worsen the mental condition of the patient.

> *R (B)* **v. *Ashworth Hospital Authority* [2005] 2 All ER 289** The House of Lords held that it was permissible to provide treatment for any mental disorder from which the individual was suffering, even if it was not the one for which he had been originally detained under the MHA.

> *Norfolk and Norwich Healthcare (NHS) Trust* **v. *W* [1996] 2 FLR 613** A reasonable degree of force can be used to require a patient to undergo treatment which is permitted under section 63.

10.16 As can be seen, the courts have been fairly flexible about what can count as treatment for a mental disability. An argument that may need to be considered further in the future is that treating a patient without their consent infringes the protection in Article 3 of the ECHR, which prohibits torture and inhuman and degrading treatment. This was considered in *Herczegfalvy* v. *Austria* (1993) 15 EHRR 437 and *R (B)* v. *SS* [2005] EWHC 86 (Admin). There it was held that compulsory treatment for a mental disorder would interfere with Article 3 rights. However, the ECHR angle suggests that the interpretation of 'treatment' should be kept as narrow as possible. In *R (N)* v. *Dr M* [2003] 1 WLR 562, the Court of Appeal held the following factors to be relevant:

> The answer to that question [whether the treatment is justifiable in the light of Article 3] will depend on a number of factors, including (a) how certain is it that the patient does suffer from a treatable mental disorder, (b) how serious a disorder it is, (c) how serious a risk is presented to others, (d) how likely is it that, if the patient does suffer from such a disorder, the proposed treatment will alleviate the condition, (e) how much alleviation is there likely to be, (f) how likely is it that the treatment will have adverse consequences for the patient and (g) how severe may they be? (para. 19)

The potential impact of the decision was lessened with the court's comment that as long as the treatment complied with a respectable body of opinion, it would be compliant with Article 3. That is a controversial approach to take. Whether treatment is torture or inhuman or degrading should not depend on professional opinion, but should be set at a consistent level.

10.17 Where treatment is being given against the wishes of a competent patient, then a second opinion must be obtained from a registered medical practitioner appointed by the Secretary of State (known as an SOAD (a second opinion appointed doctor)), who must consult two persons concerned with the patient's treatment who are not themselves doctors. The patient has the option of taking the matter to a court if she or he disagrees with the decision reached by the doctor. However, only rarely will a judge overrule a doctor on such an issue (*R (B)* v. *Haddock* [2006] EWCA 961).

Codes of practice

10.18 The MHA, s. 118 allows the Secretary of State to issue codes of practice governing how patients being detained under the Act should be treated. The legal position of these codes was considered in the following decision:

> *R (Munjaz)* **v. *Ashworth Hospital Authority* [2005] UKHL 58** Mr Munjaz was being detained under the MHA in a high security mental hospital. He had been placed in seclusion for periods of more than four days, which was in breach of the code of practice issued by the Secretary of State for Health. It was argued that the hospital's use of exclusion was unlawful under UK law and breached Articles 3, 5, and 8 of the ECHR.
>
> Their Lordships divided three to two. The majority held that the code of practice amounted to guidance and not instruction. The code could be departed from, but only with great care and where the hospital had cogent reasons for doing so. Here the Trust, in departing from the code, had taken into account three key issues:
>
> (i) The code had been written with mental hospitals generally in mind and not with the special problems facing high security hospitals.
>
> (ii) The code had not recognized that there were patients for whom exclusion for longer than four days would be appropriate.
>
> (iii) The code had made it clear that the Secretary of State's code was guidance and that the final decision of the treatment of patients rested with those with practical care for them.
>
> Lord Bingham, writing for the majority, accepted that the practice of the hospital was to use exclusion only as a last resort and where necessary to protect other patients. The hospital's policy included sufficient protections to ensure that a patient secluded for more than seven days would not have her or his Article 3 rights infringed. He was observed by a nurse every 15 minutes and his condition was regularly reviewed. The policy was an infringement of a patient's Article 8(1) rights, but the infringement was justified under Article 8(2) as necessary to prevent disorder or crime, for the protection of health or morals, or for the protection of the rights and freedoms of others. The policy was sufficiently precise and accessible to that mean the infringement of the Article 8(1) rights was in accordance with the law.
>
> Lord Steyn, dissenting, regarded the code as setting down 'minimum centrally imposed safeguards' for vulnerable patients (para. 46). For him, the judgment of the majority

permits a lowering of the protection offered by the law to mentally disordered patients. If that is the law, so be it. How society treats mentally disordered people detained in high security hospitals is, however, a measure of how far we have come since the dreadful ways in which such persons were treated in earlier times. For my part, the decision today is a set-back for a modern and just mental health law. (para. 48)

10.19 The Code of Practice produced in 2008 (Department of Health 2008) states the following guiding principles:

Purpose principle

1.2 Decisions under the Act must be taken with a view to minimising the undesirable effects of mental disorder, by maximising the safety and wellbeing (mental and physical) of patients, promoting their recovery and protecting other people from harm.

Least restriction principle

1.3 People taking action without a patient's consent must attempt to keep to a minimum the restrictions they impose on the patient's liberty, having regard to the purpose for which the restrictions are imposed.

Respect principle

1.4 People taking decisions under the Act must recognise and respect the diverse needs, values and circumstances of each patient, including their race, religion, culture, gender, age, sexual orientation and any disability. They must consider the patient's views, wishes and feelings (whether expressed at the time or in advance), so far as they are reasonably ascertainable, and follow those wishes wherever practicable and consistent with the purpose of the decision. There must be no unlawful discrimination.

Participation principle

1.5 Patients must be given the opportunity to be involved, as far as is practicable in the circumstances, in planning, developing and reviewing their own treatment and care to help ensure that it is delivered in a way that is as appropriate and effective for them as possible. The involvement of carers, family members and other people who have an interest in the patient's welfare should be encouraged (unless there are particular reasons to the contrary) and their views taken seriously.

Effectiveness, efficiency and equity principle

1.6 People taking decisions under the Act must seek to use the resources available to them and to patients in the most effective, efficient and equitable way, to meet the needs of patients and achieve the purpose for which the decision was taken.

Special regulation for brain surgery and electro-convulsive therapy

10.20 Under the MHA, some kinds of treatment can only be provided if certain special procedures are undertaken: some brain surgery and ECT (electro-convulsive therapy). Surgical operations that destroy brain tissue or interfere with the brain's function, and hormone implants designed to reduce the male sex drive (section 57(1)) are the kinds of brain surgery covered. Such treatment can only be given when the patient consents and a second opinion provided by a panel appointed by the Secretary of State (section 57(2)) agrees. The panel can only authorize the treatment if the doctor on the panel certifies that the treatment should be given. That doctor should consult two people, one a nurse and the other neither a nurse nor a doctor, who have been concerned with the patient's treatment.

10.21 ECT is governed by sections 58 and 58A. It can be given if either the patient consents or the patient is found to be incompetent. Where a second opinion is relied upon, it must be the opinion of a doctor appointed for the purpose; she or he must certify that the treatment is appropriate, bearing in mind the likelihood that it will alleviate or prevent the deterioration of the patient's condition. The fact that ECT can be given against the wishes of a competent patient is highly controversial because the benefits and disadvantages of ECT are hotly debated amongst specialists in the field (see Ottosson 2004).

Discharge under the MHA

10.22 Detained patients can be discharged if the responsible medical officer believes that it is no longer necessary to detain the patient. Where appropriate, a community treatment order can be made (see below, para. 10.24). A patient believing she or he has been improperly detained can bring an action for habeas corpus; if this is established then the court will order her or his release. The action is appropriate when there was no legal power to detain the patient. It is not appropriate where there was a legal power to detain the patient but it is claimed that there was an improper exercise of discretion in deciding whether or not to detain the patient; in the latter claim an application for judicial review could be brought.

10.23　More commonly, an application is made to an MHRT. Patients have the right to appeal to a tribunal once for each period of time during which their detention is authorized. The following decision considers further the significance of being discharged by an MHRT:

> *R (von Brandenburg)* v. *East London and the City Mental Health NHS Trust* **[2004] 2 AC 280** The appellant had been detained in a hospital under MHA, s. 2. He successfully applied to an MHRT for a review of his decision. The tribunal ordered his discharge within eight days, having concluded that he did not suffer from a mental illness. The eight days was to give time for a care plan to be prepared. Before the eight days expired and before the appellant had been discharged, he was readmitted under section 3. The approved social worker argued that the appellant had failed to take his medication and so his mental condition had deteriorated. The appellant challenged his readmission under section 3. The key question for the House of Lords was whether it was lawful to readmit a patient under section 3 when an MHRT had ordered his discharge and there was no relevant change of circumstances.
>
> The House of Lords held that
>
> > an ASW [approved social worker] may not lawfully apply for the admission of a patient whose discharge has been ordered by the decision of a Mental Health Review Tribunal of which the ASW is aware unless the ASW has formed the reasonable and bona fide opinion that he has information not known to the tribunal which puts a significantly different complexion on the case as compared with that which was before the tribunal. (para. 10, Lord Bingham)
>
> Where a patient was readmitted it would be helpful if the medical recommendation in support of that identified the new information upon which it was based. There was a limited duty on an ASW to give reasons why there should be readmission. The duty was limited because the disclosure of reasons could be harmful to the patient and so the reasons might have to be given in very general terms.
>
> On the facts, their Lordships thought that the ASW had reasonably and in bona fides concluded that there was further evidence which was not available to the tribunal. The readmission was, therefore, lawful.

Community treatment order

10.24 When a patient is discharged, having been detained under the MHA, the clinician can impose a community treatment order under section 17A of the MHA. This order was introduced in the Mental Health Act 2007. It means that release will be conditional. The order can be made if a clinician and a mental health professional agree that it is appropriate to make an order and that the following conditions in section 17A(5) are made out:

 (a) the patient is suffering from mental disorder of a nature or degree which makes it appropriate for him to receive medical treatment;

 (b) it is necessary for his health or safety or for the protection of other persons that he should receive such treatment;

 (c) subject to his being liable to be recalled as mentioned in paragraph (d) below, such treatment can be provided without his continuing to be detained in a hospital;

 (d) it is necessary that the responsible clinician should be able to exercise the power under section 17E(1) below to recall the patient to hospital; and

 (e) appropriate medical treatment is available for him.

10.25 If any conditions are placed on the release they must be for the following purposes (section 17B(2)):

 (a) ensuring that the patient receives medical treatment;

 (b) preventing risk of harm to the patient's health or safety;

 (c) protecting other persons.

The conditions can be suspended or varied by the responsible clinician.

10.26 The responsible clinician can recall a patient subject to a community treatment patient order as set out under section 17E:

 (1) The responsible clinician may recall a community patient to hospital if in his opinion—

 (a) the patient requires medical treatment in hospital for his mental disorder; and

 (b) there would be a risk of harm to the health or safety of the patient or to other persons if the patient were not recalled to hospital for that purpose.

(2) The responsible clinician may also recall a community patient to hospital if the patient fails to comply with a condition specified under section 17B(3) above.

Guardianship

10.27 An approved social worker or nearest relative can apply for guardianship (MHA, s. 8). This lasts for up to six months, but can be renewed. Two doctors must confirm that the patient is suffering from mental illness, severe mental impairment, psychotic disorder, or mental impairment of a degree that warrants guardianship and that the guardianship is in the interests of the patient's welfare or for the protection of others. The guardian must be a local social services authority or a person approved by them. Under section 8, the guardian can require the patient to live at a particular place; attend places for the purposes of occupation, training, or medical treatment; or permit a doctor, social worker, or other person specified by the guardian to see the patient. What a guardian cannot do is force the patient to undergo treatment. Guardianship can be discharged by the registered medical officer, the local social service authority, or the nearest relative. The patient can also apply to the MHRT for discharge (Richardson 2002).

Informal treatment

10.28 Many patients with serious mental disorders are looked after in care homes, without any order being made. Where they lack capacity, their care may be justified under the MCA. However, there are a large group of patients who lack capacity, but are compliant in their care. In other words, they are not positively consenting to receiving treatment, but on the other hand they are not objecting either. One of the issues which has bedevilled mental health law in recent years is whether it is permissible to treat such a person without capacity under the principle of necessity, rather than using the MHA (Fennell 2005).

> ***R v. Bournewood and Mental Health NHS Trust ex p L* [1998] 3 All ER 289;**
> ***HL v. UK* [2005] 81 BMLR 131** A profoundly autistic young man was admitted for in-patient treatment after self-harming and disturbed behaviour. He did not resist admission and so was not detained under the MHA. Relations between the man's carers and the hospital broke down and they brought an action claiming damages

for unlawful detention. The Court of Appeal awarded damages but the House of Lords overturned this. They received evidence that many people were detained in this way and treated under the principle of necessity. To find this illegal would put a huge burden on the system of care for those with mental health issues. They held that if a patient was compliant and incapable of consenting, they could be treated on the basis of necessity. The issue was referred to the European Court of Human Rights (ECtHR) which held that keeping people in hospital on the basis of necessity amounted to detaining them and that interfered with their rights under Article 5 of the ECHR. This could be justified under Article 5(4) in the case of those with mental disorder, but only if they had the opportunity to have their case heard speedily by the court and if the detention was approved in the law. Neither of these was true with detention relying on the defence of necessity.

10.29 The Government responded in two ways. First, a new section 64 was inserted into the MHA by the 2007 Mental Health Act. This deals with patients who are not being formally detained under the Act but are not resistant to receiving treatment for mental disorder. The treatment can certainly be given if the patient has capacity and consents. However, if the patient lacks capacity then if the five conditions in section 64D are met, a person can provide treatment to them:

(2) The first condition is that, before giving the treatment, the person takes reasonable steps to establish whether the patient lacks capacity to consent to the treatment.

(3) The second condition is that, when giving the treatment, he reasonably believes that the patient lacks capacity to consent to it.

(4) The third condition is that—

(a) he has no reason to believe that the patient objects to being given the treatment; or

(b) he does have reason to believe that the patient so objects, but it is not necessary to use force against the patient in order to give the treatment.

(5) The fourth condition is that—

(a) he is the person in charge of the treatment and an approved clinician; or

(b) the treatment is given under the direction of that clinician.

(6) The fifth condition is that giving the treatment does not conflict with—

(a) an advance decision which he is satisfied is valid and applicable; or

(b) a decision made by a donee or deputy or the Court of Protection.

It should be noted that this provision does not authorize the use of force. If force needs to be used then detention under MHA, s. 4 must be authorized.

10.30 The second response was to insert a new Schedule A1 into the MCA. This Schedule deals with those cases which meet three conditions set out in paragraph 1 as follows:

(2) The first condition is that a person ('P') is detained in a hospital or care home—for the purpose of being given care or treatment—in circumstances which amount to deprivation of the person's liberty.

(3) The second condition is that a standard or urgent authorisation is in force.

(4) The third condition is that the standard or urgent authorisation relates—

(a) to P, and

(b) to the hospital or care home in which P is detained.

In such cases, a person may be detained if they satisfy six conditions (para. 12(1)):

(a) the age requirement;

(b) the mental health requirement;

(c) the mental capacity requirement;

(d) the best interests requirement;

(e) the eligibility requirement;

(f) the no refusals requirement.

10.31 The age requirement is that they are over 18. The mental health requirement is that they suffer from a mental disorder as understood in the MHA. The mental capacity requirement is that they lack capacity to determine whether they should be detained in the hospital. The best interests requirement requires that it is in the person's best interests that they be detained so that they can be protected from harm to themselves and that the detention is a proportionate response to that harm. The eligibility requirement is that he or she is a person who is eligible for treatment under the mental capacity requirement. The no refusals requirement is that there is no advance directive which refuses the treatment at issue or no decision from a deputy or donee. The detention must be authorized by a supervisory body which may be the Primary Care Trust or the local authority.

Dangerousness

10.32 Turning now to some of the ethical issues. One key theme justifying the provisions over the mentally ill is that they are dangerous and that this justifies treatment, without their consent. That claim has been challenged by many academics (Large et al. 2008).

10.33 Newspapers regularly portray the mentally disordered as a violent and dangerous group who could attack at any time. But in fact the majority of those with psychiatric problems are not dangerous. When there is an attack by a mentally ill person, the media gives the case extensive coverage and this creates an exaggerated perception of the issue. As Eldergill (2003: 333) states:

> People are more likely to win the National Lottery jackpot than they are to die at the hand of a stranger with a mental illness.

He goes on to point out that

> people suffering from schizophrenia are one hundred times more likely to kill themselves than someone else, and those with a mood disorder are one thousand times more likely. (p. 333)

10.34 Perhaps the argument is better made that it is not that the mentally ill as a group are dangerous, but that some of them are dangerous (Peay 2003). Where we are aware of a risk, the state is entitled forcibly to give them treatment. The problem with that argument is that even experts are notoriously bad at predicting who is dangerous (Large et al. 2008). Even the most successful predictors have a significant rate of 'false positives' (those predicted to be dangerous, but who in fact were not). In one leading study (Monahan 2001), 25 per cent of those predicted as dangerous proved not to be. That is one of the best results achieved in studies of this kind, but it shows that for every four people detained for being dangerous, one would not be dangerous. To many, that is an unacceptable percentage of unjustly detained people.

10.35 On the assumption that it is possible to identify a mentally ill individual as dangerous, does this justify detaining her or him? To some it does. The state has an obligation to protect its citizens from death. Indeed, this might be regarded as one of the primary duties of the state and required under Article 2 of the ECHR. Any interference in the rights of the person detained is justified because the state is acting to protect the even greater rights of citizens not to suffer death or serious injury. Opponents argue that we do not normally detain people who are not mentally ill, even if they have been classified as dangerous. Having a propensity to commit a crime is very different from committing it. Until a person has committed a criminal act, predictions as to dangerousness do not normally justify detention. And why should we regard the mentally ill in any way differently from those with no mental disorder? To do so would be discriminatory. Car drivers are a dangerous lot and are responsible for many deaths, as are those who drink alcohol. Should we detain dangerous drinkers and drivers?

10.36 There is another issue here. If the dangerously mentally ill are to be detained for the purpose of prevention: where, how, and by whom is this to be done? Doctors are unlikely to be willing simply to oversee people who are not being detained for treatment but for prevention, but non-medically qualified 'guards' may lack the experience and skills to care for those detained. Bartlett (2003) argues that hospitals are willing to care for the physically disabled even where nothing can be done for them, and the same attitude could be taken towards the mentally ill who have to be detained.

Paternalism

10.37 If we reject dangerousness as a ground to justify detention under the MHA, it could be argued that paternalism justifies the detention (Fennell 2008; contrast Gurnham 2008). We could simply say that treatment for mental illness is justified because that is best for the patient. This would especially be so where an effective treatment would be available. However, this is generally regarded as a justification in cases where the patient is incompetent: where the patient is competent and refuses treatment it is not. We do not allow treatment for physical conditions to be given to competent patients on the basis of paternalism, why should it be any different if the illness is mental?

Rejecting the justifications for the Mental Health Acts

10.38 Many commentators working in this area have concluded that it is not possible to justify detention under the Mental Health Acts (see the discussion in Bartlett and Sandland 2007; Prinsen and Van Delden 2009). Some argue that the test of treatment and detention should be based on capacity alone. Treatment and detention is only permissible on competent patients if they consent to treatment. If she or he is incompetent, then treatment and detention can be given if that is in the patient's best interests. To treat mentally ill competent people differently from non-mentally ill competent people is to discriminate on the grounds of mental illness. Bartlett (2003: 327) emphasizes the wrong that is done to a competent person who receives mental health treatment against their wishes in this way:

> The violation of autonomy consequent on enforced treatment of a person with capacity is considerable. The introduction of psychiatric medication into an individual's body results in fundamental and substantial changes to the person's self. These changes are, of course, the objective of the treatment, and have social benefits. Many patients will also willingly consent to them, as they are perceived to have benefits to them too. That in no way alters the extraordinary nature of the intervention, however, and it is difficult to see that it should be provided to a patient with capacity who refuses it.

While the repeal of the Mental Health Acts might receive some support in academic circles, it is probably politically unacceptable. One can imagine the media outcry if a doctor, aware that a patient was dangerous, released him into the community, and he went on to kill a child.

The debates over the future of mental health care

Speaker 1 (pro-mental health law)

10.39 It is very easy in the debates over this area of the law to get caught up in the theoretical arguments and the discussion of human rights. We need, however, to be realistic. Those who work with people with mental disorder are aware of the distress that untreated mental disorder can cause. We are discussing people whom, while competent, are impacted in the way they process their thoughts and develop their plans by their condition. Anorexia nervosa is a good example of a condition which, while not necessarily destroying a person's capacity, means that their ability to make decisions for themselves is severely impeded. Allowing someone with anorexia nervosa to starve themselves to death is putting autonomy on an absurdly high pedestal and fails to recognize that the so-called 'autonomous wishes' of the individual are in fact a product of their illness.

10.40 We therefore need a greater appreciation of the impact and harm caused by mental illness to address this issue. If anything, I think that the MHA does not go far enough. We need to protect people with mental health issues from the impact of their conditions.

Speaker 2 (anti-mental health law)

10.41 The current law on mental health is nothing short of blatant discrimination. The United Nations High Commissioner for Human Rights (2009) recently issued an important report emphasizing the significance of the United Nations Convention on the Rights of Persons with Disabilities. The Convention

> forbid[s] deprivation of liberty based on the existence of any disability, including mental or intellectual, as discriminatory. Article 14, paragraph 1(b), of the Convention unambiguously states that 'the existence of a disability shall in no case justify a depriving of liberty'. (United Nations High Commissioner for Human Rights 2009: 12)

Critics of mental health

10.42 Criticism of the very concept of mental health can be found among those working in psychiatry. The concept of mental health is highly problematic. Society's understanding of mental illness is fluid. Tony Hope (2005: 75) refers to a condition diagnosed by Dr Samuel Cartwright in 1851 called 'drapetomania', which was described as the tendency of Negro slaves to run away from their masters. Until recently, homosexuality was considered a psychological disorder. As these examples show, today's mental illness may be tomorrow's normality.

10.43 Observations of this kind have led to a school of thought known as 'anti-psychiatry' (Double 2006). Although there are relatively few commentators who accept the extreme tendencies of its leading proponents, their arguments are important because at the very least they reveal how the concept of mental illness is contestable. The leading proponent of anti-psychiatry is Thomas Szasz (2001; 2002; 2005). He argues that psychiatric disorders are not illnesses, but rather a description of behaviour which offends or annoys people. We have an image of how people 'ought' to behave and if they do not behave in that way, we label them as suffering from a mental illness. Psychiatry is therefore a means of exercising social control over the 'different' and Szasz has even claimed psychiatry is analogous to slavery. Richard Bentall (2004), sympathetic to such claims, suggests that hallucinations and delusions are exaggerated forms of mental foibles which we all experience.

10.44 A rather different critique of psychiatry is to claim that mental health problems are (or nearly always are) the reaction of normal people to abnormal social pressures or oppressive family institutions. For example, when a women who has suffered years of abuse kills her partner in desperation, some psychiatrists might claim that she suffered from 'battered women's syndrome', whilst others will classify it as an understandable and reasonable reaction to an extreme situation, and not indicative of mental disorder (Kaganas 2003).

10.45 Those who disagree with the anti-psychiatrists accept that, in the past, the concept of mental health was misused, and perhaps there are conditions currently regarded as being a manifestation of mental ill-health which will not be so regarded in the future; however, they maintain that we should not throw out the baby with the bathwater (Adshead 2003). There are people who are genuinely suffering and for whom mental health services offer real help for which they are extremely grateful. To follow Szasz's line and not recognize their illness and to leave them without treatment would be cruel.

Mental health and criminal liability

10.46 A key principle of criminal law is that a person should not be convicted of a crime if they are not responsible for their actions. This means that there are special defences that can be used for those charged with crimes which they have committed, while suffering from a mental disorder. The plea of insanity can be entered in cases where the defendant was suffering from a defect of reason caused by a disease of the mind which meant that either

(1) he did not know the nature or quality of his actions; or

(2) he did not know that what he was doing was wrong. (*M'Naghten's Case* [1843–60] All ER Rep 229).

10.47 There is also a partial defence of diminished responsibility which can be found in section 2 of the Homicide Act 1957:

(1) A person ('D') who kills or is a party to the killing of another is not to be convicted of murder if D was suffering from an abnormality of mental functioning which—

(a) arose from a recognised medical condition,

(b) substantially impaired D's ability to do one or more of the things mentioned in subsection (1A), and

(c) provides an explanation for D's acts and omissions in doing or being a party to the killing.

(1A) Those things are—

(a) to understand the nature of D's conduct;

(b) to form a rational judgment;

(c) to exercise self-control.

(1B) For the purposes of subsection (1)(c), an abnormality of mental functioning provides an explanation for D's conduct if it causes, or is a significant contributory factor in causing, D to carry out that conduct.

10.48 If a defendant is convicted of an offence, then a judge can order hospitalization or guardianship (MHA, s. 37). In the case of hospitalization, the court can add a restriction order. That limits the statutory rights to release or community treatment that are otherwise available to a person subject to a hospital order. To be able to impose a hospital order, it must be shown that a person is suffering from a mental disorder and it is therefore appropriate for them to be detained in a hospital and that treatment will be available.

CONCLUSION

The law relating to those with mental health disorders is striking. It goes against some of the key principles of medical law, not least that a patient may not be treated without their consent. This justifies the severe restriction on how those with capacity, but with a mental disorder, can be compelled to receive treatment.

FURTHER READING

Adshead, G. (2003) 'Commentary on Szasz', *Journal of Medical Ethics* 29: 230–2.

Bartlett, P. (2003) 'The Test of Compulsion in Mental Health Law: Capacity, Therapeutic Benefit and Dangerousness as Possible Criteria', *Medical Law Review* 11: 326–52.

Bartlett, P., and Sandland, R. (2007) *Mental Health Law* (Oxford: Oxford University Press).

Bentall, R. (2004) *Madness Explained* (London: Penguin).

Department of Health (DoH) (2008) *Mental Health Act Code of Practice* (London: DoH).

Double, D. (2006) *Critical Psychiatry* (Basingstoke: Palgrave).

Eldergill, A. (2003) 'Is Anyone Safe? Civil Compulsion under the Draft Mental Health Bill', *Journal of Mental Health Law* 8: 331–59.

Fennell, P. (2005) 'Convention Compliance, Public Safety, and the Social Inclusion of Mentally Disordered People', *Journal of Law and Society* 32: 90–110.

Fennell, P. (2008) 'Best Interests and Treatment for Mental Disorder', *Health Care Analysis* 16: 255–67.

Gurnham, D. (2008) ' "Reader, I Detained Him under the Mental Health Act": A Literary Response to Professor Fennell's Best Interests and Treatment for Mental Disorder', *Health Care Analysis* 16: 268–78.

Hope, T. (2005) *Medical Ethics: A Very Short Introduction* (Oxford: Oxford University Press).

Kaganas, F. (2003) 'Domestic Homicide, Gender and the Expert', in A. Bainham, S. Day Sclater, and M. Richards (eds), *Body Lore and Laws* (Oxford: Hart), pp. 145–61.

Large, M., Ryan, C., Nielssen, O., and Hayes, R. (2008) 'The Danger of Dangerousness: Why We Must Remove the Dangerousness Criterion from Our Mental Health Acts', *Journal of Medical Ethics* 34: 877–82.

Laurance, J. (2003) *Pure Madness* (Abingdon: Routledge).

Monahan, J. (2001) 'Major Mental Disorder and Violence: Epidemiology and Risk Assessment', in G. Pinard and L. Pagani (eds), *Clinical Assessment of Dangerousness: Empirical Contributions* (Cambridge: Cambridge University Press), pp. 89–102.

Ottosson, J.-O. (2004) *Ethics in Electroconvuslive Therapy* (Abingdon: Routledge).

Peay, J. (2003) *Decisions and Dilemmas* (Oxford: Hart).

Prinsen, E., and Van Delden, J. (2009) 'Can We Justify Eliminating Coercive Measures in Psychiatry?', *Journal of Medical Ethics* 35: 69–72.

Richardson, G. (2002) ' "Autonomy, Guardianship and Mental Disorder": One Problem, Two Solutions', *Modern Law Review* 65: 702–3.

Szasz, T. (2001) 'Mental Illness: Psychiatry's Phlogiston', *Journal of Medical Ethics* 27: 297–303.

Szasz, T. (2002) *Liberation by Oppression: A Comparative Study of Slavery and Psychiatry* (New Brunswick, NJ: Transaction).

Szasz, T. (2005) ' "Idiots, Infants, and the Insane": Mental Illness and Legal Incompetence', *Journal of Medical Ethics* 31: 78–82.

United Nations High Commissioner for Human Rights (2009) *Annual Report of the United Nations High Commissioner for Human Rights* (Geneva: United Nations).

SELF-TEST QUESTIONS

1 Why is mental health one of the very few areas of the law where treating a patient without their consent is permitted?

2 Is it possible to distinguish treatment and general care, as the MHA suggests?

3 Alice is in the early stages of dementia. She does not feed herself well, but is adamant that she wishes to remain independent. Her children are worried that she is not keeping up with normal standards of personal hygiene or nutrition. Could Alice be detained under the MHA?

Medical research

SUMMARY

This chapter will consider the legal regulation of research. It will explore what participants must know before they can give effective consent to be participants. It will examine when it is permissible to use children or those lacking capacity in research projects. The chapter will also look at what ethical issues arise in cases of medical research projects.

Introduction: background to the regulation of research

11.1 There is much medical research that does not involve any legal regulation, apart from the general laws of the land. The researcher simply mixing chemicals together or thinking abstract thoughts about ill people is subject to no particular regulation. It is where research involves doing something to people or to animals, or doing something to human material, or to data involving humans that there may be particular legal regimes.

11.2 The law on medical research is still overshadowed by the horrors of history (Foster 2001). In the name of 'medical research', appalling horrors have been carried out. Most notoriously, the Nazi regime carried out so-called research on Jews and other groups of people whom they despised. Realization of the torture that was going on in the name of research has led to a widespread acceptance that careful regulation of research is necessary to protect individuals from misuse. It is recognized that it is easy for scientific researchers to get caught up in the excitement of thinking that they have found a new cure for a terrible illness, and overlook the dangers that they are imposing on those involved in trials (Ferguson 2003).

11.3 A dramatic example of this was occurred in 2006 in a drug trial at Northwick Park Hospital in London. Six volunteers for a drug trial, most of whom were students, fell seriously ill. Their conditions were described as life-threatening and they suffered serious injuries, including the amputation of fingertips. This example shows how, even in a well-regulated system, things can go wrong. Before looking at the regulation under the current law, we need to explore the definition of 'research' a bit further.

Experimental treatment or research?

11.4 One of the difficult issues concerning medical research is where to draw the line between research and medical treatment. The significance of this distinction is that if the project is for treatment then the major issue is whether or not there is consent. However, if the project involves research then the full regulatory procedures, including approval by an ethics committee, are required. The key case is the following:

> **Simms v. Simms [2003] 1 All ER 669** JS (aged 18) and JA (aged 16) suffered from variant Creutzfeldt-Jakob Disease (v-CJD). Their parents sought declaratory relief that it was lawful for the proposed treatment to be given to them. Both JS and JA were incompetent to consent to it. The proposed treatment was new and had not been tested on humans. The treatment required surgery under general anaesthetic. The medical evidence was unanimous that in both cases the individuals would die without treatment. There was also unanimity that the effectiveness of the treatment was unknown, but that it would not be irresponsible to use it. The experts were divided on whether they themselves would be willing to use the treatment on a patient.
>
> Butler Sloss P held that it was lawful to offer the treatment. Because the two young people were incompetent to make the decision, the question was whether the proposed treatment would be in their best interests. She held that it would be. There was no responsible body of opinion which thought it irresponsible to provide the proposed treatment. In reaching this conclusion, she referred to the *Bolam* test (see Chapter 3). Although there was a 5 per cent chance of haemorrhage as a result of the procedure,

this was within the reasonable bounds of risk given the situation that the patients were in. The proposed treatment was of benefit to the patients even if there was no hope of recovery, and the hope was that the treatment would slow down deterioration or prolong life. Even though the chance of improvement was slight, it was a risk worth taking. As Butler Sloss P pointed out:

> the concept of 'benefit' to a patient suffering from v-CJD does encompass an improvement from the present state of illness, or a continuation of the existing state of illness, without deterioration for a longer period than might otherwise have occurred.

Here the condition was fatal and progressive; it was therefore reasonable to attempt experimental treatment with unknown risks and benefits. Butler Sloss P stated:

> A patient who is not able to consent to pioneering treatment ought not to be deprived of the chance in circumstances where he would have been likely to consent if he had been competent.

When considering what was in the patients' best interests, their futures with and without the treatment as well as the views of their families should be taken into account. The parents' support of the proposed treatment was said to carry 'considerable weight'.

Whether this decision is one where the patients were used as human guinea pigs or whether this was a legitimate desperate use of untried treatment will be a matter of opinion.

Declaration of Helsinki

11.5 In 1964, the World Medical Association first agreed the Declaration of Helsinki. It is regularly revised, significantly so in 2008. It plays a central role in setting the standards of medical research. The declaration includes a number of important principles:

- The need for consent for all competent participants in research.
- The rights of subjects to withdraw from the research.
- Human experimentation is to be used as a last resort where other forms of research not involving human subjects are not possible.
- There must be proportionality between the benefits of the research and the risks run by the subjects.

Paragraph 6 of the Declaration contains an overarching principle:

> In medical research involving human subjects, the well-being of the individual research subject must take precedence over all other interests.

This paragraph sets out a key principle. One cannot in the name of 'science' justify doing something that risks the well-being of the individual.

11.6 The Declaration of Helsinki is not directly enforceable as law. However, it is likely to be taken into account when deciding whether or not researchers were negligent. It is also likely to be used by research ethics committees when deciding whether to approve research projects.

General legal principles

11.7 It goes without saying that the general rules of law apply to medical research. So a researcher will owe participants a duty of care in tort and can be liable in the tort of negligence if they breach that duty. The criminal law could even become relevant if the research intentionally or recklessly caused an injury to a participant. The Human Rights Act 1998 would become relevant, and treating participants without their consent could involve breaching their rights under Article 3 or 8 of the European Convention on Human Rights (ECHR).

Research which is unlawful

11.8 As already mentioned, if the participants are harmed without their consent, then it is likely that a criminal offence will be committed. However, if there is consent, can research ever be criminal? The answer is almost certainly yes. In *R v. Brown* [1994] 1 AC 212, the House of Lords heard a case involving a group of men who were engaged in sadomasochistic practices. They inflicted on each other a variety of injuries and were charged with assaults occasioning actual bodily harm and inflicting grievous bodily harm. Their defence was based on the fact that the 'victims' had consented to the injuries being done to them. The House of Lords held that in cases involving injuries amounting to actual bodily harm or worse, the consent of the victims did not provide a defence unless the conduct fell into an 'exceptional' category of cases where the activities promoted the public good: sport, medical procedures, and ritual circumcision were some examples. Sadomasochism could not be said to be in the public good (see Padfield 2010). This case suggests that if research causes serious injuries, it will be unlawful even if there is consent, unless it might be argued that the research can be justified in the public interest. There is, therefore, some uncertainty about the point at which the harm cannot be justified.

11.9 Some research projects may not be contrary to the criminal law, but will still be rejected by a research ethics committee as being contrary to public policy. Paragraph 21 of the Helsinki Declaration states:

> Medical research involving human subjects may only be conducted if the importance of the objective outweighs the inherent risks and burdens to the research subjects.

Europe's Protocol to the Convention on Human Rights and Biomedicine, concerning Biomedical Research has a similar provision and adds:

> where the research does not have the potential to produce results of direct benefit to the health of the research participant, such research may only be undertaken if the research entails no more than acceptable risk and acceptable burden for the research participant. (Article 6(2))

These suggest that the courts will weigh up the degree of risk to participants, with the degree of benefit to the participants and the importance of the issue which the research is addressing. Causing harm to find a cure for cancer is more likely to be justified than causing harm to find a cure for wrinkles. Another factor that the international protocols mention is whether the participants suffer from the condition which the research is attempting to find a cure for.

11.10 Professional bodies have taken a strict line on the extent to which participants can be harmed in the name of research. The Royal College of Physicians suggests that in the case of healthy volunteers, only a minimal risk is acceptable. Some commentators (e.g. Jansen and Wall 2009) see this standard as too high. We allow people to engage in dangerous sports and that does not even produce a tangible benefit to society. We should certainly allow people to consent to undertake such risks in the name of medical research. As along as the research is for an important issue and there is consent and the risk is a low one, it should be permitted.

Consent

11.11 A key requirement for the legality of research is that the participant consented to treatment. The normal rules on consent, as discussed in Chapter 4, apply, but there are four particular issues which are relevant here: informed consent, duress, the right to withdraw from the research project, and the payment of participants.

Informed consent

11.12　The participants must be informed of the risks attached to the research. But how much do they need to be told? Paragraph 24 of the Declaration of Helsinki provides some guidance on the issue:

> In medical research involving competent human subjects, each potential subject must be adequately informed of the aims, methods, sources of funding, any possible conflicts of interest, institutional affiliations of the researcher, the anticipated benefits and potential risks of the study and the discomfort it may entail, and any other relevant aspects of the study. The potential subject must be informed of the right to refuse to participate in the study or to withdraw consent to participate at any time without reprisal. Special attention should be given to the specific information needs of individual potential subjects as well as to the methods used to deliver the information. After ensuring that the potential subject has understood the information, the physician or another appropriately qualified individual must then seek the potential subject's freely-given informed consent, preferably in writing. If the consent cannot be expressed in writing, the non-written consent must be formally documented and witnessed.

11.13　The British Medical Association (BMA) Guidance has provided a list of the information which should be given to research participants:

- The purpose of the research and confirmation of its ethical approval.
- Whether the participant stands to benefit directly and, if so, the difference between research and treatment.
- The meaning of relevant research terms (such as placebos).
- The nature of each procedure, and how often or for how long each may occur.
- The processes involved, such as randomization.
- The potential benefits and harms (both immediate and long term).
- Arrangements for reporting adverse events.
- The legal rights and safeguards for participants.
- Details of compensation if harm results from their participation.
- How their health data will be stored, used, and published.
- If samples of human material are donated, whether they will be used for any other research or purpose.

- Whether and how DNA will be extracted, stored, or disposed of.
- The name of the researcher they can contact with enquiries.
- If the researcher stands to benefit (for example, financially).
- The name of the doctor directly responsible for their care.
- How they can withdraw from the project.
- What information they will receive about the outcome.
- That withdrawal will not affect the quality of their health care.

11.14 The Medicines for Human Use (Clinical Trials) Regulations 2004, SI 2004/ 1031 governs research involving trials of medicine. It requires the participant to have given informed consent. Paragraph 3(1) of Part 1 of Schedule 1 explains:

> a person gives informed consent to take part in a clinical trial only if his decision:
>
> (a) is given freely after that person is informed of the nature, significance, implications and risks of the trial; and
>
> (b) either:
>
>   (i) is evidenced in writing, dated and signed, or otherwise marked, by that person so as to indicate his consent, or
>
>   (ii) if the person is unable to sign or to mark a document so as to indicate his consent, is given orally in the presence of at least one witness and recorded in writing.

The person must have met with the researcher and been informed of 'the objectives, risks and inconveniences of the trial and the conditions under which it is to be conducted'. It must also be clear to participants that they are involved in research (rather than receiving treatment).

11.15 There is surprisingly little case law on what the courts require as necessary for legal purposes. As we saw in Chapter 4, the law on what risks a doctor must disclose is somewhat unclear. The courts are likely to be influenced by the guidance in the Declaration of Helsinki and that of the BMA, set out above. These seem to suggest a higher standard for informed consent than is the case with medical treatment. Indeed, it seems that the guidance from the Declaration of Helsinki and the BMA are close to saying that the researcher must provide all the relevant information that a reasonable participant would want to know (Fox 1998).

11.16 Some of the issues which generally surround informed consent are particularly relevant here. A long document or lecture setting out all the risks of the research might be so confusing that the person cannot take all of the risks in. A shorter presentation, outlining just the key risks may be more likely to be meaningful (Pullman 2002). Perhaps the best solution is to present the patient with the major risks, and then provide them with a document or offer them further discussion in relation to the less significant risks. There is certainly a problem issue: one study looking at participants in a research project in relation to a genetic condition, indicated that they had not fully appreciated that they were involved in research, rather than treatment, and had no recollection of the consent process (Ponder et al. 2008). Perhaps this is not surprising as the very ill have plenty of things to think about.

11.17 There have been no reported cases in England involving research participants who have not been adequately informed. The following Canadian cases give some indication of what approach the English courts could adopt.

> **Halushka v. University of Saskatchewan (1965) 53 DLR (2d) 436** The defendants were a team of physicians researching anaesthesia. They were carrying out experiments with a new anaesthetic drug. Mr Halushka, a student, agreed to participate after being told that the experiment was a 'safe test' and that there was nothing that should cause him concern. He was not told of the risks of using the drugs nor of the risks inherent in the procedure. He was not informed about how the test would be carried out. Mr Halushka suffered a heart attack during the test and was unconscious for four days. He suffered long-term problems with concentration and fatigue. The Saskatchewan Court of Appeal upheld an award of $22,500. He had not been informed of the risks associated with the procedure, its probable effects, and any special or unusual risks. He was deemed to be entitled as a medical research subject to a full and frank disclosure of all the facts and risks that a reasonable person might be expected to consider before entering the test.

Duress

11.18 Where a patient is seriously ill and a new drug becomes available for their condition, a patient may feel under considerable pressure to consent to be part of a trial for it. Similarly, if a doctor is involved in researching a new drug and asks his or her patient to be involved in a trial then the patient may feel obliged to agree. The close relationship that can develop between a doctor and a patient may be such that the patient feels that they have no choice (Iltis 2005).

11.19 This issue is covered by paragraph 26 of the Declaration of Helsinki:

> When seeking informed consent for participation in a research study the physician
> should be particularly cautious if the potential subject is in a dependent relationship
> with the physician or may consent under duress. In such situations the informed
> consent should be sought by an appropriately qualified individual who is completely
> independent of this relationship.

That does not give us very clear guidance. Under the normal rule on undue influence/duress, the courts will consider the extent to which an individual feels under pressure to make a decision and the illegitimacy of the threat/request that is being made (see O'Sullivan and Hilliard 2010). A safe course of conduct may be for a doctor who is involving a patient in research to get an independent doctor to discuss the issue with the patient and confirm that they are freely consenting.

Withdrawal

11.20 It might be thought obvious that if a participant wishes to withdraw from a research project they should be free to do so at any time. This is recognized in the Declaration of Helsinki (para. 24). However, it is not a straightforward issue. As Susan Edwards and Michael McNamee (2005) note, patients who withdraw from a study can skew the results. She argues that at least the research scientist should be able to 'push' the participants to stay the course. Other commentators (e.g. Cheung 2008) are not happy with this, as the freedom of participants to withdraw should be seen as a fundamental right and researchers should not pressurize people to continue.

Payment

11.21 There is a concern that offering payments for participants means that people agree to be participants in research against their genuine wishes. A quick search on the Internet will find you a wide range of projects offering you cash to be involved in medical research, sometimes thousands of pounds. You will never get rich being a professional research participant, but you might be able to make a living wage!

11.22 There is no strict legal regulation of this issue, save that payment for organs is prohibited. The Royal College of Physicians (2007) recommends that payments should not be at a level to persuade people to volunteer 'against their better judgement'. Some participants almost become junior researchers, filling in paperwork and assessing results. In such a case, it might be thought wrong if they do not receive payment. Indeed, some commentators (e.g. Brazier 2008) are concerned that we are not paying participants enough to recognize that they are putting their health at risk. Others are concerned that payment may impact on the principle that research participants should consent in a free and voluntary way.

Research Ethics Committees (RECs)

11.23 A key role in the regulation of research is played by research ethics committees (RECs) (Beyleveld et al. 2007; McGuinness 2008). All research which is undertaken by the Department of Health or the NHS, by industries, charities, or universities must comply with the Research Governance Framework produced by the government. Only small-scale private studies will not be covered. The Framework requires the approval of a REC. Drug trials must comply with the Medicines for Human Use (Clinical Trials) Regulations 2004 and these also require the approval of a REC.

11.24 RECs, then, will need to approve virtually all research involving humans. The committee should have between seven and eighteen members. They should reflect a range of expertise and experience. There should be people on the committee who can consider the scientific, clinical, pharmacological, statistical, and methodological aspects of the research. The committee can seek advice from an expert in one of these areas, if necessary. There should be lay members (members of the public) as well as experts. There should be a mix of age, gender, and ethnic background. At least a third of the members should be independent of the NHS.

11.25 The Framework states that when RECs are deciding whether to approve the research proposal they should consider the following:

- That there are adequate arrangements to ensure the full consent of all participants or, where the participants are incompetent, that the legal requirements are met. The committee will look at the information that will be provided to the participants.
- That the legal requirements are met. For example, that the Human Tissue Act 2004 and any guidance issued by the Human Tissue Authority has been complied with.

- That the study has scientific validity. The committee will look at the conduct and design of the study. It will need to be persuaded that the research has not already been adequately done elsewhere and that the study will add something useful to the state of knowledge. Expert advice will be taken when considering these issues.

- That the study will not cause the participants undue pain or discomfort and that any pain or discomfort is in proportion to the benefits of the research.

- That the arrangements for recruitment of research participants are adequate, in particular that there is a good range of participants in terms of gender, ethnic background, age, etc.

- That the arrangements for the care and protection of research participants are adequate.

- That the participants' rights of confidentiality are adequately protected.

- That the impact of the research on the wider community has been taken into account

11.26 RECs are not expected to rule on the legality of the research. Although it would be unusual that research approved by a REC would be unlawful, as long as the researchers did what they said they were going to do.

11.27 The work of RECs is overseen by the National Patient Safety Authority. However, the committees are required to be independent. The idea behind this is that they should be free from interference from the Department of Health.

> **R v. Ethical Committee of St Mary's Hospital ex p Harriott [1988] 1 FLR 512** Ms Harriott sought *in vitro* fertilization. She had tried to adopt a child but this had been unsuccessful as she had a criminal record for offences in relation to prostitution. She saw a consultant who decided to refuse her access to IVF for the same reasons. The case was referred to the Infertility Services Ethics Committee. The committee took the view that the decision was for the medical team to take. Ms Harriott sought a judicial review of the committee's decision, claiming that the committee was obliged to investigate the issue and give her an opportunity to be heard.
>
> It was held that the committee had no duty to investigate the matter. An ethics committee was an informal body that could not be expected to give advice or investigate matters. A decision of a committee could be judicially reviewed if it was shown to be illegal or discriminatory. However, neither of those were present in this case.

Placebo

11.28 Placebos are commonly used in medical research, but they are controversial. A placebo will look like the medication which is on trial, but in fact can be a harmless substance of medically insignificant content. Typically, some participants will be given the genuine trial medication and others the placebo. This enables the researchers to compare the two groups and the effect of the medication. It means that any psychological benefits of being part of the trial group or of taking a medication are accounted for.

11.29 There is an issue of truth telling here. If participants are told that they may be taking a substance which is not the medication, then that may interfere in the assessment of the psychological effect of taking the medication. However, if participants are actively misled into believing that they will all be told that they are taking the medication, then that seems to breach the principle of truth telling. Often the issue is simply fudged with participants never being told that they are all taking the trial substance, even though that is what they may believe.

11.30 A further difficulty with placebos arises if researchers have good grounds to believe that the substance is beneficial, and the participants are all suffering from a particular condition. That will mean that a patient taking the placebo will lose out and may not be being treated justly. The problem is particularly acute if participants give up their standard medication to be part of the trial. In that case, the participant receiving the medication may actually be put in a worse position than if they had not been involved in the trial.

11.31 Placebos are discussed in the Declaration of Helsinki, Article 31:

> The benefits, risks, burdens and effectiveness of a new intervention must be tested against those of the best current proven intervention, except in the following circumstances:
>
> - The use of placebo, or no treatment, is acceptable in studies where no current proven intervention exists; or
>
> - Where for compelling and scientifically sound methodological reasons the use of placebo is necessary to determine the efficacy or safety of an intervention and the patients who receive placebo or no treatment will not be subject to any risk of serious or irreversible harm. Extreme care must be taken to avoid abuse of this option.

Research involving children

11.32 It might be thought that children should never be used in medical research. The difficulty is that certain illnesses or certain procedures are only used during childhood. If we are going to ensure that these are effective then we need to involve children in research.

11.33 It must be admitted that the law on research on children is rather uncertain. The starting point must be the normal principles of law involving children, namely that *Gillick* competent children are able to consent to treatment and those with parental responsibility can consent on their behalf. However, it would be too quick to assume that these apply to research. That is because in *Gillick*, their Lordships placed much weight on the fact that the treatment would be in the girls' best interests. And in exercising responsibility, parents, it might be thought, are required to comply with the welfare principle (Children Act 1989, s. 1), namely that they must promote their children's welfare. If the research poses a risk to children, or cannot be shown to benefit them, it might therefore not be permissible to consent.

11.34 However, it is argued that competent children and those people with parental responsibility should be permitted to consent to be involved in medical research. We allow parents to feed their children unhealthy diets or watch inappropriate television programmes. It is only at the point of significant harm that the state will intervene to protect children. It seems hard to explain why parents should not be able to involve their children in research projects approved by ethics committees. Similarly, in relation to *Gillick* competent children, it is submitted that a child should be able to undertake a worthwhile, approved research project. It teaches the child altruism and involves them in a community project. It can, therefore, be said to be in their best interests. Notably, the Helsinki Declaration also clearly envisions research to be lawful, paragraph 28 stating that

> When a potential research subject who is deemed incompetent is able to give assent to decisions about participation in research, the physician must seek that assent in addition to the consent of the legally authorized representative. The potential subject's dissent should be respected.

11.35 There are special rules that apply in the case of clinical trials involving children. Then the Medicines for Human Use (Clinical Trials) Regulations 2004 apply. These require the consent of a person with parental responsibility.

Incompetent adults

11.36 Similar issues to those discussed with children arise in relation to those adults who lack capacity. Again, there is a conflict between only involving participants in research who consent and ensuring that there is adequate research into the medical issues connected with a loss of capacity (Lewis 2002).

11.37 The Mental Capacity Act 2005, ss. 30–34 and the Medicines for Human Use (Clinical Trials) Regulations 2004 govern the area. The latter is only applicable where drugs or medicines are being trialled.

11.38 The Mental Capacity Act 2005, ss. 30–34 regulates 'intrusive' research. That is research which would be unlawful to carry out on a person with capacity, without consent. That would include research that involves the touching of the body or the administration of substances. So research that simply involved looking at a person would not count; although the Department of Health (2005) suggested that watching a person through a two-way mirror for a prolonged period of time might be regarded as intrusive (McHale 2006).

11.39 Section 30 states that intrusive research can only be carried out on a person who lacks capacity (P) if all of the following conditions are met:

(i) The research project has been approved by an 'appropriate body'. This will normally be the local REC.

(ii) The research is connected to 'an impairing condition' from which P suffers or its treatment.

(iii) There must be reasonable grounds for believing that research of comparable effectiveness cannot be carried out if the project has to be confined to, or relate only to, persons who have capacity to consent to taking part in it.

(iv) The research must either:

(*a*) have the potential to benefit P and not impose a burden on P which is disproportionate to the benefit, *or*

(*b*) be intended to provide assistance in the treatment or care of people suffering from a similar condition, as long as the risk to P from the research is negligible and does not interfere with P's freedom, action, or privacy in a significant way so as to be unduly invasive.

(v) Reasonable steps must have been taken by the researcher to identify a person who is P's carer or interested in P's welfare. The researcher must provide the carer with information about the project and ask her or him whether P should take part and what she or he thinks P's wishes and feelings would be. If the carer replies that P would not want to take part in the project then P must not take part in the project.

(vi) Research may not be carried out on P if she or he has made an effective advance decision or other statement indicating that she or he did not want to be part of the research.

(vii) Nothing may be done to P in the course of research to which P appears to object, unless it is necessary to protect P from harm.

(viii) Appropriate means must be used to maximize P's understanding of the research process and if possible enable P to be a part of the decision-making process. This might involve, for example, giving information in a simplified format.

(ix) The normal requirements which attach to research generally are satisfied.

11.40 It should be noted that these restrictions would allow research to be carried out on a person lacking capacity which is not in their best interests. This might be said to infringe the principle which otherwise is at the heart of the Mental Capacity Act 2005, namely that everything done for a person lacking capacity should promote their best interests. However, the difficulty is that if research cannot be performed on, say, those suffering from Alzheimer's disease, then an important area of medical research cannot be covered. Perhaps the better argument is that being involved in a research project is in a person's best interests, broadly conceived. It should be recalled that research cannot be done if P appears to object and that a REC will not approve the project if it poses any serious risks to participants. So the harm to those involved will be minimal and against this must be weighed up the good to them of being part of a beneficial project.

11.41 Some are concerned by the far that the legislation does not include non-intrusive research (Annas and Glantz 1986). While it might be said that simply observing a person is not harmful, it might involve a breach of their privacy and their dignity. The area needs some form of regulation. It should be recalled that any research will require the approval of a REC and it might be thought that that provides sufficient protection in an area of the research where the harm is very limited.

11.42 Before approving research involving incompetent people the REC will need to consider *inter alia*:

- Whether the outcome of the research is of potential benefit to the person or others with a similar disorder.

- The justification for including participants who may lack capacity to consent in the research and whether the research could be done solely involving those with capacity.

- The assessment of each participant's capacity as part of the consent procedure and how that will be assessed and documented.

- How the research group proposes to identify and consult an appropriate third party (such as a carer).

- Whether sufficient safeguards are in place in circumstances where it is not possible to identify a third party to represent the participant's interests.

- Whether it is clear who is responsible for identifying whether the person objects to any part of the research (whether by showing signs of resistance or otherwise) and so should be withdrawn.

11.43 The Medicines for Human Use (Clinical Trials) Regulations 2004 make special provision for clinical trials involving incompetent people. For the purpose of the Regulations, an incapable adult is 'an adult unable by virtue of physical or mental incapacity to give informed consent'. Clinical trials involving such a person are only permitted where there is the consent of a 'Personal Legal Representative', but where such a person cannot be found then the consent of a 'Professional Legal Representative' can be relied upon. A Personal Legal Representative is someone who:

1 Is not connected with the conduct of the trial.

2 Is suitable to act as the person's legal representative due to their relationship with the individual.

3 Is willing to act as a personal legal representative.

This is likely to be a close relation or friend of the individual who is willing to make decisions on their behalf. A Professional Legal Representative is someone who:

1 Is not connected with the conduct of the trial.

2 Is either (*a*) the doctor primarily responsible for the adult's medical treatment; or (*b*) a person nominated by the relevant health care provider.

11.44 Part 5 of Schedule 1 of the 2004 Regulations also contains a number of important restrictions on trials involving incompetent adults. These include the following:

- The subject has received information according to her or his capacity of understanding regarding the trial, its risks, and its benefits.

- The investigator must consider the explicit wish of a subject not to participate in the project or to withdraw from it. However, that is only required if the subject is capable of forming an opinion and assessing the information referred to in the previous paragraph.

- There are grounds for expecting that administering the medicinal product to be tested in the trial will produce a benefit to the subject outweighing the risks or produce no risk at all.

- The clinical trial is essential to validate data obtained—

  (*a*) in other clinical trials involving persons able to give informed consent, or

  (*b*) by other research methods.

- The clinical trial relates directly to a life-threatening or debilitating clinical condition from which the subject suffers.

- The clinical trial has been designed to minimize pain, discomfort, fear, and any other foreseeable risk in relation to the disease and the cognitive abilities of the patient.

- The interests of the patient always prevail over those of science and society.

It is worth emphasizing that the objection of the incompetent adult to participation is not a bar to their involvement, but should be considered by the investigator. It is hoped that it would be highly unlikely that an incompetent individual would be forced against their will to be involved.

An obligation to participate?

11.45 So far we have assumed that participants in research must consent to being involved. John Harris (2005) has queried this. He points out that the state is willing to force people to be involved in projects for the social good such as jury service, compulsory education, quarantine regulations, and (in some countries) compulsory military service. He questions whether participation in medical research might not be added to this list. Not many commentators have supported this argument. While it is unlikely that we would find a reasonable number of people to volunteer to be jurors, it seems that we are able to find enough people to volunteer for medical research. Until there is a desperate shortage, compulsion seems unnecessary.

CONCLUSION

Medical research is crucial if we are to make the advancements in medicine that we wish. Yet the desire to find cures for diseases carries dangers, too. The temptation is for researchers to cut corners in order to speed up their research or to find evidence that their new discovery is a success. That is why it is so important that there is tight and effective regulation of medical research. This chapter has summarized the attempts that the law currently makes to strike the correct balance between allowing effective research to progress, while ensuring that there is protection for research participants.

FURTHER READING

Annas, G., and Glantz, L. (1986) 'Rules for Research in Nursing Homes', *New English Journal of Medicine* 315: 1157–68.

Beyleveld, D., Townend, D., and Wright, J. (eds) (2007) *Research Ethics Committees* (Aldershot: Ashgate).

Brazier, M. (2008) 'Exploitation and Enrichment: The Paradox of Medical Experimentation', *Journal of Medical Ethics* 34: 180–3.

Cheung, P. (2008) *Public Trust in Medical Research* (Oxford: Radcliffe).

Department of Health (DoH) (2005) *Responsibilities, Liabilities and Risk Management in Clinical Trials of Medicines* (London: DoH).

Edwards, S., and McNamee, M. (2005) 'Ethical Concerns Regarding Guidelines for the Conduct of Clinical Research on Children', *Journal of Medical Ethics* 31: 351–4.

Ferguson, P. (2003) 'Legal and Ethical Aspects of Clinical Trials: The Views of Researchers', *Medical Law Review* 11: 48–66.

Ferguson, P. (2008) 'Clinical Trials and Healthy Volunteers', *Medical Law Review* 16: 23–51.

Foster, C. (2001) *The Ethics of Medical Research on Humans* (Cambridge: Cambridge University Press).

Fox, M. (1998b) 'Research Bodies: Feminist Perspectives on Clinical Research', in S. Sheldon and M. Thomson (eds), *Feminist Perspectives on Health Care Law* (London: Cavendish), pp. 214–45.

Harris, J. (2005) 'Scientific Research is a Moral Duty', *Journal of Medical Ethics* 31: 242–8.

Iltis, A. (2005) 'Timing Invitations to Participate in Clinical Research', *Journal of Medicine and Philosophy* 30: 89–106.

Jansen, L., and Wall, S. (2009) 'Paternalism and Fairness in Clinical Research', *Bioethics* 23: 172–82.

Lewis, P. (2002) 'Procedures that are against the Medical Interests of the Incompetent Person', *Oxford Journal of Legal Studies* 12: 575–618.

McGuinness, S. (2008) 'Research Ethics Committees: The Role of Ethics in a Regulatory Authority', *Journal of Medical Ethics* 34: 695–700.

McHale, J. (2006) 'Law Reform, Clinical Research and Adults without Mental Capacity', in S. McLean (ed.), *First Do No Harm* (Aldershot: Ashgate), pp. 413–32.

Morrison, D. (2005) 'A Holistic Approach to Clinical and Research Decision-Making', *Medical Law Review* 13: 45–79.

O'Sullivan, J., and Hilliard, J. (2010) *The Law of Contract* (Oxford: Oxford University Press).

Padfield, N. (2010) *Criminal Law* (Oxford: Oxford University Press).

Plomer, A. (2005) *The Law and Ethics of Medical Research* (London: Cavendish).

Pullman, D. (2002) 'Conflicting Interests, Social Justice and Proxy Consent to Research', *Journal of Medical Philosophy* 27: 523–45.

Pullman, M., Statham, H., Hallowell, N., Moon, J. A., Richards, M., and Raymond, F. L. (2008) 'Genetic Research on Rare Familial Disorders: Consent and the Blurred Boundaries between Clinical Service and Research', *Journal of Medical Ethics* 34: 690–5.

Royal College of Physicians (RCP) (2007) *Guidelines on the Practice of Ethics Committees in Medical Research with Human Participants* (London: RCP).

SELF-TEST QUESTIONS

1 As long as a participant has given effective consent to a research project, are there any reasons why the law should not permit it?

2 Is it more exploitative to pay or not to pay research participants?

3 Is it ever appropriate to involve those lacking capacity in research?

4 Does the use of placebos in medical research inevitably involve the deception of participants, and is therefore unjustified?

5 Should everyone who takes advantage of the NHS be morally required to participate in research?

6 Chi is organizing a research trial of a new drug for testicular cancer. He does not inform the participants of a 0.0001 per cent chance of infertility that might result. Ralph (one participant) suffers infertility after the trial. Chi tells the participants (truthfully) that in an earlier trial, the drug had a 56 per cent chance of success. Simon agreed to be a participant because he was suffering from testicular cancer. He gave up other medication he was on. Chi did not tell the participants that some of them would receive a placebo medication. Simon is given a placebo medication and his condition continues to deteriorate. He says that had he known that he might have been given a placebo, he would not have agreed to be a participant. Can Ralph and Simon bring successful legal actions against Chi?

Index